AGRICULTURAL BOTANY

AGRICULTURAL BOTANY

By

Dr. Shubhrata R. Mishra

Deptt. of Botany
Vikram University
Ujjain (M.P.)
(India)

DPH

DISCOVERY PUBLISHING HOUSE PVT. LTD.
NEW DELHI-110 002

Published by:
Tilak Wasan

DISCOVERY PUBLISHING HOUSE PVT. LTD.
4383/4B, Ansari Road, Darya Ganj
New Delhi-110 002 (India)
Phone : +91-11-23279245, 43596064-65
Fax : +91-11-23253475
E-mail : discoverypublishinghouse@gmail.com
sales@discoverypublishinggroup.com
parul.wasan@gmail.com
web : www.discoverypublishinggroup.com

***First Edition:* 2014**

ISBN: 978-93-5056-401-1

Agricultural Botany

Printed at:
Dynamic Printers
Delhi

Preface

However, it is equally true that the achievements of the green revolution are proving insufficient for feeding India's teeming millions. Biotechnological interventions can play a vital role by not only increasing crop productivity but also taking care of the increasing threat of biotic and abiotic stresses on crop plants. The green revolution of agriculture brought an enormous increase in food production. It not only made the world self sufficient in food but also gave the world's scientists and farmers an immense amount of self-respect.

The plant world, our world, is in constant flux. Due to human and other factors, we are seeing the possibility of extinction for many plants and animals. Plant classification aids in keeping track of our planet's endangered inhabitants. Just as importantly, we are realizing the need to understand ecological systems which preserve biodiversity. Today's scientists are exploring how genetic diversity and ecological sensitivity are necessary in solving such problems as feeding the population and fighting disease. Plant classification is vital to these endeavours.

The term *fertilization* refers to the application of plant nutrients to supplement the nutrients naturally occurring in the soil. Nutrients may be applied as commercial manufactured fertilizers, organic fertilizers and/or other soil amendments. Organic fertilizers and soil amendments are typically low in plant-available nutrient content. Adequate soil fertility is only one of the many soil-related growth factors. Fertilizers will increase desirable plant growth only if the plant is deficient in the nutrient applied and other growth factors are not also significantly limiting plant growth. Fertilization will not compensate for poor soil preparation, the lack of water, weed competition and other non-nutrient growth limiting factors! Fertilization will not enhance desired growth if the nutrients applied are not deficient.

Plant anatomy or phytotomy is the general term for the study of the internal structure of plants. While originally it included plant morphology, which is the description of the physical form and external structure of plants, since the mid-20th century the investigations of plant anatomy are considered a separate, distinct field, and plant anatomy refers to *just* the internal plant structures. Plant anatomy is now frequently investigated at the cellular level, and often involves the sectioning of tissues and microscopy.

Plants require some nutrients, such as carbon and nitrogen, in large quantities to survive. Such nutrients are termed macronutrients, where the prefix *macro*-(large) refers to the quantity needed, not the size of the nutrient particles themselves. Other nutrients, called micronutrients, are required only in trace amounts for plants to remain healthy. Such micronutrients are usually absorbed as ions dissolved in water taken from the soil, though carnivorous plants acquire some of their micronutrients from captured prey.

The book will be valuable to researchers biologists scientists and advanced students of botany agriculture pharmacy biotechnology and plant engineering.

—Author

Contents

1

Classification of Plants

INTRODUCTION

'A rose is a rose,' it has been said. And most of us know a rose when we see one, as we know the African marigolds we plant beside the potatoes and beans in our gardens, and the maples, elms, cedars, and pines that shade our backyards and line our streets. We usually call these plants by their common names. But if we wanted to know more about the cedar tree in our front yard, we would find that 'cedar' may refer to an eastern red cedar, an incense cedar, a western red cedar, an Atlantic white cedar, a Spanish cedar, a banak cedar, or the biblical cedar of Lebanon. In fact, we would find that cedars are found in three separate plant families.

Later, after discovering that our 'African' marigolds are in fact from Mexico and our 'Spanish' cedar originated in the West Indies, we would realize how misleading the common names of plants can be. The same plant can have many different common names. The European white lily has at least 245, while the marsh marigold has at least 280. Clearly, if we use only the common name of a plant, we cannot be sure of understanding very much about that plant.

It is for this reason that the scientific community prefers to use a more precise way of naming, or classification. Scientific classification, however, is more than just naming: it is a key to understanding. Botanists name a plant to give it a unique place in the biological world, as well as to clarify its relationships within that world. Classification is sometimes difficult. As modern botany has advanced, producing an increasing understanding of complex biochemical mechanisms, the criteria for the way plants are classified has undergone transformation. Even further, Nature is not fixed and plants, like us, are capable of change. Plants can vary for reasons we don't entirely understand. To be sure, plant classification is not the dull field that some might assume!

PLANTS CLASSIFIED

Science classifies living things in an orderly system through which they can be readily identified. Living things are grouped into categories of increasing size, based upon relationships within those categories. For example, all plants can be put in order from the more primitive to the more advanced. Such a ranking would look like this:

Plant Kingdom

Bryophytes: Small with leaflike, stemlike, and rootlike structures.

Disseminated by Spores: mosses, liverworts, hornworts.

Vascular Plants: Larger with true leaves, stems, and roots.

- *Seedless:* Ferns, horsetails, club mosses.
- *Seed Plants:*
    - *Gymnosperms:* Usually have cones, no flowers, seeds not enclosed in fruit: pines, spruces, firs, hemlocks, cycads, ginkgo.
    - *Angiosperms:* Have flowers, seeds enclosed in fruit
        i. *Monocotyledons:* Leaves have parallel veins, one seed leaf: grasses, orchids, lilies, palms.
        ii. *Dicotyledons:* Leaves have netted veins, two seed leaves: cherry trees, maples, coffee, daisies, etc.

This informal way of describing plant classification gives an overview of how plants are classified. Botanists use a more complex system. A botanist divides the plant kingdom into Divisions, similar to the Phyla used to divide the animal kingdom. There are twelve divisions. Referring to the above ranking, three of these divisions are Bryophytes, four are seedless plants, four are Gymnosperms, and one is Angiosperms. Each Division is further divided into Classes, which are divided into Orders, which are divided into Families, which are divided into Genera (singular, Genus), which are divided into species, which is the 'basic unit' of classification. Put somewhat simply, individuals in a species are able to breed with each other, while in broader categories individuals do not interbreed.

THE BINOMIAL SYSTEM OF CLASSIFICATION

The scientific or botanical name of a plant is the means by which we give it its unique place in the scientific and biological world. Begun by Carolus Linneaus, a Swedish botanist, in the eighteenth century, this name is binomial (has two parts), consisting of genus and species, both of which are expressed in Latin. The genus or generic name is a noun which usually names some aspect of a plant, such as Coffea, the Latinized form of the Arabic word for beverage, *kahwah*. The species or specific name is usually an adjective that describes the genus. In the case of coffee, the species is arabica, indicating that the plant was thought to originate in Arabia. The coffee plant botanical name, *Coffea arabica,* refers to only one plant and cannot be confused with any other. Its botanical name is unique to that particular plant the world over. The botanical name is often followed by a letter or letters which stand for the botanist who named that plant. The coffee plant's complete botanical name is *Coffea arabica L.,* the L. standing for Linneaus. If the original botanical name of a plant is later changed, the original classifier is still noted in parentheses. Other often used abbreviations are Sarg. for Charles Sprague Sargent, founder of Harvard University's Arnold Arboretum; Lam. for Jean Baptiste Lamarck, French evolutionist and botanist; and Audub. for John James Audubon, ornithologist, naturalist, and painter. (Interestingly, this convention of naming the discoverer is not found in the naming of animals.) Sometimes the Family name is included, which groups the genera. It can usually be distinguished by its ending—'eae.'

What The Names Mean

The genus and species names often tell something about the plant. They can describe the appearance of the plant, reflect the common name of the plant, indicate a chemical present in the plant, tell how the plant tastes or smells, or describe how the plant grows. The genus or species name can honour someone, a botanist, a person in power, someone historically prominent. The name can reflect the country or origin of a plant.

For example, *Erythroxylum* coca, the plant from which we derive cocaine, is named after erythro meaning red and xylo meaning wood, literally 'red stem.' (Coca, the species name, is the common name of the plant.) The *jaborandi* tree *Pilocarpus jaborandi* has a genus name which indicates that the alkaloid pilocarpine can be extracted from the plant. The species name *jaborandi* means 'one who makes saliva or one who spits,' referring to the use of the plant as an expectorant.

TYPES OF CLASSIFICATIONS

Classifications are orderly ways to present information and, depending upon their objectives, can be artificial, natural, or phylogenetic (phyletic), which includes phenetic and cladistic.

ARTIFICIAL AND NATURAL CLASSIFICATIONS

Classifications that use single or at most only a few characteristics to group plants usually are artificial classifications—that is, all the plants in a single group share the same characteristics, but they are not closely related to one another genetically. Popular floras (books to identify plants of a certain area) sometimes group plants using colour of their flowers, or their growth form (trees, shrubs, herbs, and so on). Although such books are useful in finding the names of taxa, they provide few clues about relationships among the taxa and hence are not predictive, which means that you can deduce nothing more about the plant other than that it exhibits the characteristics used to classify it. Natural classifications group together plants with many of the same characteristics and are highly predictive. That is, by enumerating the characteristics of a plant, one can predict the natural group to which it belongs. Taxonomic floras, for example, identify species, genera, and families by listing as many characteristics as possible concerning anatomy, morphology, cytology, ecology, biochemistry, genetics, and distribution.

PHYLOGENETIC (PHYLETIC) CLASSIFICATIONS

Phyletic classifications are natural classifications that try to identify the evolutionary history of natural groups. When botanists accepted Darwin's theory of evolution near the end of the last century, the reasons why some groups of plants looked alike became clear: They were related to one another by a common ancestry. The mission of taxonomy since Darwin has become a quest for evolutionary relationships, not just at the lower levels of the hierarchy, but at the upper levels as well.

The evolutionary history of a taxon is called its phylogeny. To establish phylogenies, decisions must be made concerning which characteristics are 'primitive' and which 'advanced'—that is, which taxon is the ancestor of the others. Early phylogenetic classifications were based primarily upon plant morphology and anatomy with great emphasis upon reproductive morphology, which is more stable and less influenced by the environment than is vegetative morphology. Today, taxonomists additionally use the techniques of biochemistry and molecular biology to add details of internal organization and mechanisms to the classifications. But phylogenies, no matter how carefully constructed, are dependent upon someone's interpretation of data, and herein lies the problem: Systematists frequently differ in their interpretations of relationships. A phylogenetic classification is a hypothesis, a scientific explanation of the data and, like any hypothesis, is subject to further testing.

Certain assumptions are necessary in phylogenetic classifications. A taxon should be monophyletic (all of the members of the taxon should be descendants of a single common ancestor). The characters or features used to identify the taxa must be homologous, which means that they must have a common origin, but not necessarily a common function. For example, all the parts of a flower—petals, sepals, stamens, and carpels—originate in the same way as leaves from primordia in meristems. Although they now have different functions in the flower (they're not photosynthetic), some sepals and petals structurally resemble leaves. Leaves and the parts of the flower are homologous structures.

Some features that look alike do not have a common origin and are said to be analogous. An example of analogous structures is the prickles on two groups of succulent desert plants, the cacti and the euphorbs. Cacti have spines that are modified leaves; euphorbs have thorns that are modified branches.

Spines and thorns look alike and are functionally similar in that both keep animals from eating the plants. Spines and thorns are analogous. This example of analogy is also an example of convergent evolution. The cactus family and the euphorb family both developed the same morphology in response to a desert environment—the cacti in North and South America, the euphorbs in Africa and Asia. The families are not related and have no recent common ancestor.

Numerical taxonomy (phenetics): Systematists have tried many ways to make phyletic classifications more subjective. When computers became readily accessible in the 1960s, numerical taxonomy or phenetics became a popular approach. In practice, measurements were made of a large number of characters of a taxon, at least 60 per plant and often 100 or more. No special importance was attributed to any one of the characters. After the measurements were complete on hundreds of individuals, the data were analysed statistically with computer programmes and cluster analysis or other methods to show purported natural groupings of plants with overall similarities. Systematists' interpretations were thought to be minimized in this fashion.

Cladistics: Cladistics is the most popular method of classifying organisms today. In contrast to phenetics, in which similarities are sought using as many characters as possible, cladists look for patterns using derived character states (that is, features that have evolved from an ancestral character group). The intent is to find groups of organisms that share a common ancestor and to diagram the relationship of the groups, called clades, in a cladogram. The branching points (nodes) separate groups that have diverged in the evolutionary past from a common ancestor. All the taxa below the node lack the character state, all those above it retain it. Homologous (inherited) characters are chosen to categorize an organism and its character states. The states are hypothesized to be either ancestral or derived (evolved), and the cladogram is a test of the hypothesis.

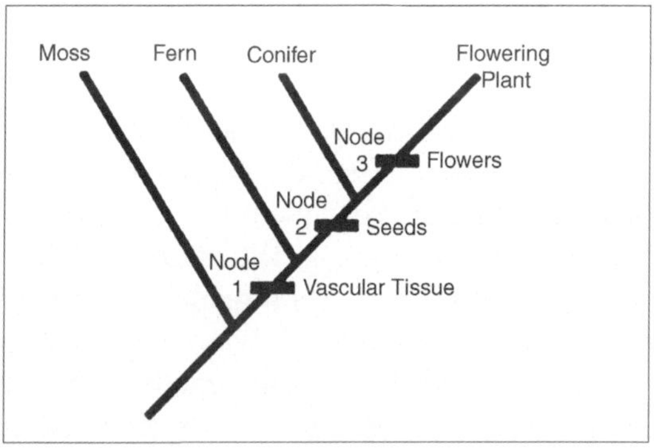

Figure 1.1

Molecular biology and phylogeny: The most promising developments in formulating a phylogeny for the entire tree of life come today from molecular biology, where new tools and techniques allow researchers to use as character states the molecular sequences of amino acids as well as those of nucleotides in nucleic acids.

The latter is the most fundamental of comparisons for, of course, the genes control the structure of life itself. The closer the similarity in sequences of molecules among groups of organisms, the closer the relationship of the groups. Widely different sequences indicate a different evolutionary history and ancestry.

CLASSIFICATION OF CROP PLANTS

Classification Based on Climate

- *Tropical:* Crops grow well in warm & hot climate, e.g. Rice, sugarcane, Jowar etc.
- *Temperate:* Crops grow well in cool climate, e.g. Wheat, Oats, Gram, Potato etc.

Classification Based on Growing Season

- *Kharif/Rainy/Monsoon Crops:* The crops grown in monsoon months from June to Oct.-Nov., Require warm, wet weather at major period of crop growth, also required short day length for flowering, e.g. Cotton, Rice, Jowar, bajara.
- *Rabi/winter/cold Seasons Crops:* Require winter season to grow well from Oct. to March month. Crops grow well in cold and dry weather. Require longer day length for flowering, e.g. Wheat, gram, sunflower etc.
- *Summer/Zaid Crops:* Crops grown in summer month from March to June. Require warm day weather for major growth period and longer ay length for flowering, e.g. Groundnuts, Watermelon, Pumpkins, Gourds.

Use/Agronomic Classification

- *Grain Crops:* May be cereals as millets cereals are the cultivated grasses grown for their edible starchy grains. The larger grain used as staple food is cereals, e.g. rice, Jowar, wheat, maize, barley, and millets are the small grained cereals which are of minor importance as food, e.g. Bajara.
- *Pulse/legume Crops:* Seeds of leguminous crops plant used as food. On splitting they produced dal which is rich in protein, e.g. green gram, black gram, soybean, pea, cowpea etc.
- *Oil seeds Crops:* Crop seeds are rich in fatty acids, are used to extract vegetable oil to meet various

requirements, e.g. Groundnut, Mustard, Sunflower, Sesamum, linseed etc.

- *Forage Crop:* It refers to vegetative matter fresh as preserved utilized as food for animals. Crop cultivated & used for fickler, hay, silage. Ex-sorghum, elephant grass, guinea grass, berseem & other pulse bajara etc.
- *Fiber Crops:* Crown for fibre yield. Fiber may be obtained from seed, e.g. Cotton, steam, jute, Mesta, sun hemp, flax.
- *Roots Crops:* Roots are the economic produce in root crop, e.g. sweet, potato, sugar beet, carrot, turnip etc.
- *Tuber Crop:* Crop whose edible portion is not a root but a short thickened underground stem, e.g. Potato, elephant, yam.
- *Sugar Crops:* The two important crops are sugarcane and sugar beet cultivated for production for sugar. Starch crops: grown for the production of starch, e.g. tapioca, potato, sweet potato.
- *Dreg Crop:* Used for preparation for medicines, e.g. tobacco, mint, pyrethrum.
- *Spices & condiments/spices Crops:* Crop plants as their products are used to flavour taste and sometime colour the fresh preserved food, e.g. ginger, garlic, chili, cumin onion, coriander, cardamom, pepper, turmeric etc.
- *Vegetables Crops:* May be leafy as fruity vegetables, e.g. Palak, mentha, Brinjal, tomato.
- *Green Manure Crop:* Grown and incorporated into soil to increase fertility of soil, e.g. sun hemp.
- *Medicinal & Aromatic Crops:* Medicinal plants includes cinchona, isabgoli, opium poppy, senna, belladonna, rauwolfra, iycorice and aromatic plants such as lemon grass, citronella grass, palmorsa, Japanese mint, peppermint, rose geranicem, jasmine, henna etc.

Classification based on Life of Crops/Duration of Crops

- *Seasonal Crops:* A crop completes its life cycle in one season-Karin, Rabi. summer, e.g. rice, Jowar, wheat etc.

- *Two Seasonal Crops:* Crops complete its life in two seasons, e.g. Cotton, turmeric, ginger.
- *Annual Crops:* Crops require one full year to complete its life in cycle, e.g. sugarcane.
- *Biennial Crops:* which grows in one year and flowers, fructifies & perishes the next year? e.g. Banana, Papaya.
- *Perennial Crops:* Crops live for several years, e.g. Fruit crops, mango, guava etc.

Classification based on Cultural Method/water

- *Rain Fed:* Crops grow only on rain water, e.g. Jowar, Bajara, Mung etc.
- *Irrigated Crops:* Crops grows with the help of irrigation water, e.g. Chili, sugarcane, Banana, papaya etc.

Classification based on Root System

- *Tap Root System:* The main root goes deep into the soil, e.g. Tur, Grape, Cotton etc.
- *Adventitious/Fiber Rooted:* The crops whose roots are fibrous shallow & spreading into the soil, e.g. Cereal crops, wheat, rice etc.

Classification based on economic importance:

- *Cash Crop:* Grown for earning money, e.g. Sugarcane, cotton.
- *Food Crops:* Grown for raising food grain for the population and & fodder for cattle, e.g. Jowar, wheat, rice etc.

Classification based on No. of Cotyledons

- Monocots or monocotyledons: Having one cotyledon in the seed, e.g. all cereals & Millets.
- Dicots or dicotyledonous: Crops having two cotyledons in the seed, e.g. all legumes & pulses.

Classification based on Photosynthesis (Reduction of CO_2/Dark Reaction)

- *C3 Plants:* Photo respiration is high in these plants C3 Plants have lower water use efficiency. The initial product of C assimilation in the three 'C' compounds. The enzyme involved in the primary carboxylation is ribulose-1,-Biophospate carboxylose, e.g. Rice, soybeans, wheat, barley cottons, potato.

- *C4 Plants:* The primary product of C fixation is four carbon compounds which may be malice acid or acerbic acid. The enzymes responsible for carboxylation are phosphoenol Pyruvic acid carboxylose which has high affinity for CO_2 and capable of assimilation CO_2 event at lower concentration, photorespiration is negligible. Photosynthetic rates are higher in C_4 than C_3 plants for the same amount of stomatal opening. These are said to be drought resistant & they are able to grow better even under moisture stress. C_4 plants translate photosynthates rapidly, e.g. Sorghum, Maize, napter grass, sesame etc.
- *Cam Plants:* (Cassulacean acid metabolism plants) the stomata open at night and large amount of CO_2 is fixed as a malice acid which is stored in vacuoles. During day stomata are closed. There is no possibility of CO2 entry. CO_2 which is stored as malice acid is broken down & released as CO_2. In these plants there is negligible transpiration. C_4 & cam plant have high water use efficiency. These are highly drought resistant, e.g. Pineapple, sisal & agave.

Classification based on Length of Photoperiod Required for Floral Initiation

Most plants are influenced by relative length of the day & night, especially for floral initiation, the effect on plant is known as photoperiodism depending on the length of photoperiod required for floral ignition, plants are classified as:

- *Short-day Plants:* Flower initiation takes plate when days are short less then ten hours, e.g. rice, Jowar, green gram, black gram etc.
- *Long day's Plants:* Require long days are more than ten hours for floral ignition, e.g. Wheat, Barley,

- *Day neutral Plants:* Photoperiod does not have much influence for phase change for these plants, e.g. Cotton, sunflower. The rate of the flowering initiation depends on how short or long is photoperiod. Shorter the days, more rapid initiation of flowering in short days plants. Longer the days more rapid are the initiation of flowering in long days plants.

PHYLOGENY

Phylogeny, the history of the evolution of a species or group, especially in reference to lines of descent and relationships among broad groups of organisms.

Fundamental to phylogeny is the proposition, universally accepted in the scientific community, that plants or animals of different species descended from common ancestors. The evidence for such relationships, however, is nearly always incomplete, for the vast majority of species that have ever lived are extinct, and relatively few of their remains have been preserved in the fossil record. Most phylogenies therefore are hypotheses and are based on indirect evidence. Different phylogenies often emerge using the same evidence. Nevertheless, there is universal agreement that the tree of life is the result of organic descent from earlier ancestors and that true phylogenies are discoverable, at least in principle.

TAXONOMIC SYSTEMS

Taxonomy, the science of classifying organisms, is based on phylogeny. Early taxonomic systems had no theoretical basis; organisms were grouped according to apparent similarity. Since the publication in 1859 of Charles Darwin's *On the Origin of Species by Means of Natural Selection*, however, taxonomy has been based on the accepted propositions of evolutionary descent and relationship.

The data and conclusions of phylogeny show clearly that the tree of life is the product of a historical process of evolution and that degrees of resemblance within and between groups correspond to degrees of relationship by descent from common ancestors. A fully developed phylogeny is essential for the devising of a taxonomy that reflects the natural relationships within the world of living things.

Evidence for Specific Phylogenies

Biologists who postulate phylogenies derive their most useful evidence from the fields of paleontology, comparative anatomy, comparative embryology, and molecular genetics. Studies of the molecular structure of genes and of the geographic distribution of flora and fauna are also useful. The fossil record is often used to determine the phylogeny of groups containing hard body parts; it is also used to date divergence times of species in phylogenies that have been constructed on the basis of molecular evidence.

Most of the data used in making phylogenetic judgments have come from comparative anatomy and from embryology, although these are rapidly being surpassed by systems constructed using molecular data. In comparing features common to different species, anatomists try to distinguish between homologies, or similarities inherited from a common ancestor, and analogies, or similarities that arise in response to similar habits and living conditions.

Biochemical investigations carried out in the latter half of the 20th century contributed valuable data to phylogenetic studies. By counting differences in the sequence of units that make up protein and deoxyribonucleic acid (DNA) molecules, researchers have devised a tool for measuring the degree to which different species have diverged since evolving from a common ancestor. Because mitochondrial DNA has very high mutation rates compared with nuclear DNA, it has been useful for establishing relationships among groups that have diverged recently. Essentially, the application of molecular genetics to systematics is similar to the use of radioisotopes in geologic dating: molecules change at different rates, with some, such as mitochondrial DNA, evolving rapidly and others, such as ribosomal RNA, evolving slowly. An important assumption then in using molecules for phylogeny reconstruction is to select the appropriate gene for the age of the taxon under study.

Phenetics Versus Cladistics

The methodology of phylogenetic work rests on two approaches: phenetics and phylogenetic systematics (cladistics). Phenetics bases classification strictly on similarities among organisms and emphasizes numerical analyses of an observed set of phenotypic characteristics. Cladistics bases classification of a group of species solely on their most recent common ancestor. Cladistics only uses shared derived characters—that is, select characteristics that infer monophyly or those that are expressed in all descendants of a common ancestor. The most direct difference between the two methods is that phenetics classifies species using as many characteristics as possible and arranges them by similarity regardless of any evolutionary relationships.

Major Evolutionary Steps

The phylogeny of life, as drawn from fossils and living species, indicates that the earliest organisms were probably the result of a long chemical evolution, in which random reactions in the primeval seas and atmosphere produced amino acids and then proteins. It is supposed that droplets containing proteins then formed membranes by binding molecules to their surface, and these membrane-bound proteins are said to have become organisms when they developed the capacity to reproduce. It is not certain whether these earliest self-reproducing organisms were proteins, nucleic acid–protein associations, or viruses. There is general agreement that they were heterotrophic organisms—*i.e.*, those that required nourishment in the form of organic matter from early seas. Later, autotrophic forms appeared, having the ability to make their own food from inorganic matter. These organisms were the earliest bacteria; they could store energy as food and release energy as needed through respiration.

Cyanobacteria (blue-green algae) are thought to have been the next evolutionary step in that they were able to use photosynthetic pigments to manufacture their own supply of food and therefore were not totally dependent on their environment for nutrients. After the cyanobacteria there appeared an extensive array of algae, molds, protozoans, plants, and animals. Three groups of algae can be dismissed with passing mention, as they arose from uncertain ancestors and have given rise to no further groups. These groups are the chrysophytes (golden algae, chiefly diatoms); the pyrrophytes (cryptomonads and dinoflagellates); and the rhodophytes. Three more groups have greater phylogenetic importance: the chlorophytes (green algae), which almost certainly gave rise to the land plants—*i.e.*, the bryophytes (mosses and liverworts) and the tracheophytes, or vascular plants (including all the higher plants); the euglenoids (unicellular, flagellate organisms), which suggest a broad connection between plants and animals at this primitive level; and the phaeophytes (brown algae), which some biologists have considered to be a probable source of the animal kingdom. Finally, the protozoans were derived from unknown, more primitive ancestors, and one or more groups of protozoans have given rise to metazoans—*i.e.*, multicellular animals.

Evolution of Land Plants

Land plants contain two major groups, bryophytes and tracheophytes, which differ in many ways but which share distinctive characteristics for adaptation to dry land. These include the housing of the plant embryo in maternal tissue. Bryophytes are descended from green algae and include mosses, liverworts, and hornworts. Only small quantities of water are needed for their reproduction, so that the sperm may travel to the eggs. The fertilized egg matures within the maternal tissue. The plant is protected from desiccation by a waxy cuticle. Bryophytes have apparently not advanced far beyond their algal predecessors and do not seem to be the evolutionary source of other groups.

All the dominant plants on Earth are included in the tracheophytes. The tracheophytes' development of large plant bodies was made possible by vascular parts that carry water and food inside these plants and by a dominant sporophyte stage with a microscopic-sized gametophyte. Tracheophytes' tissues have differentiated into leaves, stems, and roots and, in the highest plants, into seeds and flowers. In explaining the evolution of tracheophytes, it has been suggested that a mutant form of green algae developed a primitive rootlike function with which to supply itself with water and minerals. The progeny of this organism eventually developed bundles of vascular tissues, a stem and leaves, and a cuticle for protection. The early vascular plants are called psilophytes. The development of seeds arose from the retention of the embryo inside maternal tissue. Early seed ferns gave rise to the gymnosperm group, including pines, spruces, and firs. Flowering plants, known as angiosperms, probably came from the gymnosperm phase and have two subgroups: the dicotyledons and the monocotyledons.

Animal Evolution

The problem of the origin of multicellular animals (metazoans) was long dominated by German embryologist Ernst Haeckel's theory that the original metazoan ancestor was a spherical protozoan that was structurally similar to the cnidarians (*e.g.*, jellyfish, corals). Today there are two alternative explanations. The first traces metazoans back to flagellates, the presumed ancestors of flattened, ciliated animals (planulas) that eventually led to cnidarians, ctenophores, and flatworms. Another theory hypothesizes that multinucleated protozoans, dividing into subcells, were the original metazoans, which developed into simple flatworms. Fossil evidence of Ediacara fauna, dating from 630 to 542 million years ago, suggests that the earliest multicellular life originated from soft-bodied aquatic animals such as jellyfish and worms.

Lower metazoan forms developed the first symmetrical arrangement of body parts about a main axis, thus establishing the bilateral symmetry that characterizes most animals; major exceptions are the echinoderms (*e.g.*, starfish, sea cucumbers). The development of tissues into an outer ectoderm (providing protection and carrying sense apparatus), a middle mesoderm (muscle, cartilage, bone, and other supportive tissue), and an inner endoderm (serving digestion and reproduction needs) was an important phase. Another important trend was cephalization (head formation). The anterior end of the body generally holds the central nervous system, sense organs, and mouth.

Two current theories postulate the lineage of the higher metazoans. The monophyletic sequence suggests that four groups evolved from lower forms to higher: Ameria (unsegmented animals), which includes flatworms, cnidarians, ctenophores, and mollusks; Polymeria (segmented animals), which includes annelids and arthropods; Oligomeria (reduced segmentation), which includes insects and echinoderms; and Chordonia (chordates), which includes all the vertebrates. The (alternative) diphyletic theory has been proposed by many zoologists. It contends that the higher metazoans had two lines of descent, one of which led to annelids, arthropods, and mollusks and the other of which led to echinoderms and chordates. Both groups emanated from an ancient flatworm. Humans are included in the chordates. Three basic structures are shared by all chordates: a dorsal nerve tube (brain and spinal cord in vertebrates); a notochord (supporting rod under the nerve tube); and a pharynx perforated by gill slits, at least during the embryonic stage.

Applications of Phylogeny

An exciting development in phylogenetics is the application of phylogenies to various modern problems. In medicine, phylogenies have been used to trace the origins and transmission rates of infectious diseases such as AIDS, influenza, and dengue. Phylogenies developed from molecular genetics have been particularly useful in conservation biology for identifying the evolutionary distinctiveness of endangered species, parentage in captive breeding programmes, and levels of hybridization and inbreeding across species. Phylogenetic analyses have also been used as admissible evidence in criminal court cases involving the determination of purposeful viral transmission.

2

Plant Nutrition

INTRODUCTION

Plants use inorganic minerals for nutrition, whether grown in the field or in a container. Complex interactions involving weathering of rock minerals, decaying organic matter, animals, and microbes take place to form inorganic minerals in soil. Roots absorb mineral nutrients as ions in soil water. Many factors influence nutrient uptake for plants. Ions can be readily available to roots or could be 'tied up' by other elements or the soil itself. Soil too high in pH (alkaline) or too low (acid) makes minerals unavailable to plants.

FERTILITY OR NUTRITION

The term 'fertility' refers to the inherent capacity of a soil to supply nutrients to plants in adequate amounts and in suitable proportions. The term 'nutrition' refers to the interrelated steps by which a living organism assimilates food and uses it for growth and replacement of tissue. Previously, plant growth was thought of in terms of soil fertility or how much fertilizer should be added to increase soil levels of mineral elements. Most fertilizers were formulated to account for deficiencies of mineral elements in the soil. The use of soilless mixes and increased research in nutrient cultures and hydroponics as well as advances in plant tissue analysis have led to a broader understanding of plant nutrition. Plant nutrition is a term that takes into account the interrelationships of mineral elements in the soil or soilless solution as well as their role in plant growth. This interrelationship involves a complex balance of mineral elements essential and beneficial for optimum plant growth.

ESSENTIAL VERSUS BENEFICIAL

The term essential mineral element (or mineral nutrient) was proposed by Arnon and Stout. They concluded three criteria must be met for an element to be considered essential. These criteria are: 1. A plant must be unable to complete its life cycle in the absence of the mineral element. 2. The function of the element must not be replaceable by another mineral element. 3. The element must be directly involved in plant metabolism. These criteria are important guidelines for plant nutrition but exclude beneficial mineral elements. Beneficial elements are those that can compensate for toxic effects of other elements or may replace mineral nutrients in some other less specific function such as the maintenance of osmotic pressure. The omission of beneficial nutrients in commercial production could mean that plants are not being grown to their optimum genetic potential but are merely produced at a subsistence level.

Mineral Elements

There are actually 20 mineral elements necessary or beneficial for plant growth. Carbon (C), hydrogen (H), and oxygen (O) are supplied by air and water. The six macronutrients, nitrogen (N), phosphorus (P), potassium (K), calcium (Ca), magnesium (Mg), and sulfur (S) are required by plants in large amounts. The rest of the elements are required in trace amounts (micronutrients). Essential trace elements include boron (B), chlorine (Cl), copper (Cu), iron (Fe), manganese (Mn), sodium (Na), zinc (Zn), molybdenum (Mo), and nickel (Ni). Beneficial mineral elements include silicon (Si) and cobalt (Co). The beneficial elements have not been deemed essential for all plants but may be essential for some. The distinction between beneficial and essential is often difficult in the case of some trace elements. Cobalt for instance is essential for nitrogen fixation in legumes. It may also inhibit ethylene formation and extend the life of cut roses. Silicon, deposited in cell walls, has been found to improve heat and drought tolerance and increase resistance to insects and fungal infections. Silicon, acting as a beneficial element, can help compensate for toxic levels of manganese, iron, phosphorus and aluminum as well as zinc deficiency. A more holistic approach to plant nutrition would not be limited to nutrients essential to survival but would include mineral elements at levels beneficial for optimum growth. With developments in analytical chemistry and the ability to eliminate contaminants in nutrient cultures, the list of essential elements may well increase in the future.

The Mineral Elements in Plant Production

The use of soil for greenhouse production before the 1960s was common. Today a few growers still use soil in their mixes. The bulk of production is in soilless mixes. Soilless mixes must provide support, aeration, nutrient and moisture retention just as soils do, but the addition of fertilizers or nutrients are different. Many soilless mixes have calcium, magnesium, phosphorus, sulfur, nitrogen, potassium and some micronutrients incorporated as a pre-plant fertilizer. Nitrogen and potassium still must be applied to the crop during production. Difficulty in blending a homogenous mix using pre-plant fertilizers may often result in uneven crops and possible toxic or deficient levels of nutrients. Soilless mixes that require addition of micro and macronutrients applied as liquid throughout the growth of the crop, may actually give the grower more control of his crop. To achieve optimum production, the grower can adjust nutrient levels to compensate for other environmental factors during the growing season. The absorption of mineral ions is dependent on a number of factors in addition to weather conditions. These include the cation exchange capacity or CEC and the pH or relative amount of hydrogen (H^+) or hydroxyl ions (OH^-) of the growing medium, and the total alkalinity of the irrigation water.

Cec Or Cation Exchange Capacity

The Cation Exchange Capacity refers to the ability of the growing medium to hold exchangeable mineral elements within its structure. These cations include ammonium nitrogen, potassium, calcium, magnesium, iron, manganese, zinc and copper. Peat moss and mixes containing bark, sawdust and other organic materials all have some level of cation exchange capacity.

ph: What Does It Mean

The term pH refers to the alkalinity or acidity of a growing media water solution. This solution consists of mineral elements dissolved in ionic form in water. The reaction of this solution whether it is acid, neutral or alkaline will have a marked effect on the availability of mineral elements to plant roots. When there is a greater amount of hydrogen H^+ ions the solution will be acid (<7.0). If there is more hydroxyl OH- ions the solution will be alkaline (>7.0). A balance of hydrogen to hydroxyl ions yields a pH neutral soil (=7.0). The range for most crops is 5.5 to 6.2 or slightly acidic. This creates the greatest average level for availability for all essential plant nutrients. Extreme fluctuations of higher or lower pH can cause deficiency or toxicity of nutrients.

THE ELEMENTS OF COMPLETE PLANT NUTRITION

The following is a brief guideline of the role of essential and beneficial mineral nutrients that are crucial for growth. Eliminate any one of these elements, and plants will display abnormalities of growth, deficiency symptoms, or may not reproduce normally.

Macronutrients

Nitrogen is a major component of proteins, hormones, chlorophyll, vitamins and enzymes essential for plant life. Nitrogen metabolism is a major factor in stem and leaf growth (vegetative growth). Too much can delay flowering and fruiting. Deficiencies can reduce yields, cause yellowing of the leaves and stunt growth. Phosphorus is necessary for seed germination, photosynthesis, protein formation and almost all aspects of growth and metabolism in plants. It is essential for flower and fruit formation. Low pH (<4) results in phosphate being chemically locked up in organic soils. Deficiency symptoms are purple stems and leaves; maturity and growth are retarded. Yields of fruit and flowers are poor. Premature drop of fruits and flowers may often occur. Phosphorus must be applied close to the plant's roots in order for the plant to utilize it. Large applications of phosphorus without adequate levels of zinc can cause a zinc deficiency.

Potassium is necessary for formation of sugars, starches, carbohydrates, protein synthesis and cell division in roots and other parts of the plant. It helps to adjust water balance, improves stem rigidity and cold hardiness, enhances flavour and colour on fruit and vegetable crops, increases the oil content of fruits and is important for leafy crops. Deficiencies result in low yields, mottled, spotted or curled leaves, scorched or burned look to leaves.. Sulfur is a structural component of amino acids, proteins, vitamins and enzymes and is essential to produce chlorophyll. It imparts flavour to many vegetables. Deficiencies show as light green leaves. Sulfur is readily lost by leaching from soils and should be applied with a nutrient formula. Some water supplies may contain Sulfur.

Magnesium is a critical structural component of the chlorophyll molecule and is necessary for functioning of plant enzymes to produce carbohydrates, sugars and fats. It is used for fruit and nut formation and essential for germination of seeds. Deficient plants appear chlorotic, show yellowing between veins of older leaves; leaves may droop. Magnesium is leached by watering and must be supplied when feeding. It can be applied as a foliar spray to correct deficiencies.

Calcium activates enzymes, is a structural component of cell walls, influences water movement in cells and is necessary for cell growth and division. Some plants must have calcium to take up nitrogen and other minerals. Calcium is easily leached. Calcium, once deposited in plant tissue, is immobile (non-translocatable) so there must be a constant supply for growth. Deficiency causes stunting of new growth in stems, flowers and roots. Symptoms range from distorted new growth to black spots on leaves and fruit. Yellow leaf margins may also appear.

Micronutrients

Iron is necessary for many enzyme functions and as a catalyst for the synthesis of chlorophyll. It is essential for the young growing parts of plants. Deficiencies are pale leaf colour of young leaves followed by yellowing of leaves and large veins. Iron is lost by leaching and is held in the lower portions of the soil structure. Under conditions of high pH (alkaline) iron is rendered unavailable to plants. When soils are alkaline, iron may be abundant but unavailable. Applications of an acid nutrient formula containing iron chelates, held in soluble form, should correct the problem.

Manganese is involved in enzyme activity for photosynthesis, respiration, and nitrogen metabolism. Deficiency in young leaves may show a network of green veins on a light green background similar to an iron deficiency. In the advanced stages the light green parts become white, and leaves are shed. Brownish, black, or grayish spots may appear next to the veins. In neutral or alkaline soils plants often show deficiency symptoms. In highly acid soils, manganese may be available to the extent that it results in toxicity.

Boron is necessary for cell wall formation, membrane integrity, calcium uptake and may aid in the translocation of sugars. Boron affects at least 16 functions in plants. These functions include flowering, pollen germination, fruiting, cell division, water relationships and the movement of hormones. Boron must be available throughout the life of the plant. It is not translocated and is easily leached from soils. Deficiencies kill terminal buds leaving a rosette effect on the plant. Leaves are thick, curled and brittle. Fruits, tubers and roots are discoloured, cracked and flecked with brown spots.

Zinc is a component of enzymes or a functional cofactor of a large number of enzymes including auxins (plant growth hormones). It is essential to carbohydrate metabolism, protein synthesis and internodal elongation (stem growth). Deficient plants have mottled leaves with irregular chlorotic areas. Zinc deficiency leads to iron deficiency causing similar symptoms. Deficiency occurs on eroded soils and is least available at a pH range of 5.5- 7.0. Lowering the pH can render zinc more available to the point of toxicity.

Copper is concentrated in roots of plants and plays a part in nitrogen metabolism. It is a component of several enzymes and may be part of the enzyme systems that use carbohydrates and proteins. Deficiencies cause die back of the shoot tips, and terminal leaves develop brown spots. Copper is bound tightly in organic matter and may be deficient in highly organic soils. It is not readily lost from soil but may often be unavailable. Too much copper can cause toxicity. Molybdenum is a structural component of the enzyme that reduces nitrates to ammonia. Without it, the synthesis of proteins is blocked and plant growth ceases. Root nodule (nitrogen fixing) bacteria also require it. Seeds may not form completely, and nitrogen deficiency may occur if plants are lacking molybdenum. Deficiency signs are pale green leaves with rolled or cupped margins.

Chlorine is involved in osmosis (movement of water or solutes in cells), the ionic balance necessary for plants to take up mineral elements and in photosynthesis. Deficiency symptoms include wilting, stubby roots, chlorosis (yellowing) and bronzing. Odors in some plants may be decreased. Chloride, the ionic form of chlorine used by plants, is usually found in soluble forms and is lost by leaching. Some plants may show signs of toxicity if levels are too high.

Nickel has just recently won the status as an essential trace element for plants according to the Agricultural Research Service Plant, Soil and Nutrition Laboratory in Ithaca, NY. It is required for the enzyme urease to break down urea to liberate the nitrogen into a usable form for plants. Nickel is required for iron absorption. Seeds need nickel in order to germinate. Plants grown without additional nickel will gradually reach a deficient level at about the time they mature and begin reproductive growth. If nickel is deficient plants may fail to produce viable seeds. Sodium is involved in osmotic (water movement) and ionic balance in plants.

Cobalt is required for nitrogen fixation in legumes and in root nodules of nonlegumes. The demand for cobalt is much higher for nitrogen fixation than for ammonium nutrition. Deficient levels could result in nitrogen deficiency symptoms.

Silicon is found as a component of cell walls. Plants with supplies of soluble silicon produce stronger, tougher cell walls making them a mechanical barrier to piercing and sucking insects. This significantly enhances plant heat and drought tolerance. Foliar sprays of silicon have also shown benefits reducing populations of aphids on field crops. Tests have also found that silicon can be deposited by the plants at the site of infection by fungus to combat the penetration of the cell walls by the attacking fungus. Improved leaf erectness, stem strength and prevention or depression of iron and manganese toxicity have all been noted as effects from silicon. Silicon has not been determined essential for all plants but may be beneficial for many.

FERTILITY AND FERTILIZATION OF PLANT NUTRITION

The term *fertilization* refers to the application of plant nutrients to supplement the nutrients naturally occurring in the soil. Nutrients may be applied as commercial manufactured fertilizers, organic fertilizers and/or other soil amendments. Organic fertilizers and soil amendments are typically low in plant-available nutrient content. Adequate soil fertility is only one of the many soil-related growth factors. Fertilizers will increase desirable plant growth only if the plant is deficient in the nutrient applied and other growth factors are not also significantly limiting plant growth. Fertilization will not compensate for poor soil preparation, the lack of water, weed competition and other non-nutrient growth limiting factors! Fertilization will not enhance desired growth if the nutrients applied are not deficient.

From the nutritional perspective, a plant cannot tell if applied nutrients come from a manufactured fertilizer or a natural source. Plants use nutrients in ionic forms. Soil microorganisms must break down organic soil amendments, organic fertilizers and many manufactured fertilizers before the nutrients become usable by plants. From a nutritional perspective, the primary difference between manufactured and organic soil amendments/organic fertilizers is the speed at which nutrients become available for plant use. For manufactured fertilizer, their release is typically, but not always, a few days to weeks. Some are specially formulated as 'controlled release', 'slow release' or 'time release' products that release over a period of months. With natural-organic fertilizer, nutrients typically become available over a period of months or years. However, there are exceptions to this general rule. The high salt content of some manufactured fertilizers and some organic soil amendments could slow the activity of beneficial soil microorganisms.

Benefits of organic fertilizers and soil amendments include improvements in soil tilth (suitability of the soil to support plant growth). This should not be confused with 'fertilization', a distinctly different soil management objective. Organic soil amendments are typically low in nutrient content. Remember that fertility is only part of the soil's role in supporting plant growth. The organic content of the soil also directly affects plant growth due to its influence on soil tilth and the activity of beneficial soil microorganisms. Relying solely on manufactured fertilizers is not recommended as this does not support good soil tilth.

PLANT NUTRIENTS

Plants need 17 elements for normal growth. Carbon, hydrogen, and oxygen come from the air and water. Soil is the principle source of other nutrients. *Primary nutrients* (nitrogen, phosphorus, and potassium) are used in relatively large amounts by plants, and often are supplemented as fertilizers.

Secondary nutrients (calcium, magnesium, and sulfur) are also used in large amounts but are typically readily available and in adequate supply. *Micronutrients* or trace elements are needed only in small amounts. These include iron, zinc, molybdenum, manganese, boron, copper, cobalt, and chlorine.

Table 2.1 Essential Plant Nutrients.

Nutrient	Lons Absorbed by Plants
Structural Elements	
Carbon, C	CO_2
Hydrogen, H	H_2O
Oxygen, O	O_2
Primary Nutrients	
Nitrogen, N	NO^-_3, NH^+_4
Phosphorus, P	$H_2PO^-_4$, HPO^+_4
Potassium, K	K^+
Secondary Nutrients	
Calcium, Ca	Ca^{+2}
Magnesium, MG	Mg^{+2}
Sulfur, S	SO_4
Micronutrients	
Boran, B	$H_2BO^-_3$
Chlorine, Cl	Cl^-
Cobalt, Co	Co^{+2}
Copper, Cu	Cu^{+2}
Iron, Fe	Fe^{+2}, Fe^{+3}
Manganese, Mn	Mn^{+2}
Molybdenum, MO	MoO^{-2}_4
Zinc, Zn	Zn^{+2}

Roots take up nutrients primarily as *ions* dissolved in the soil's water. The ions may be positively charged (*cations*) or negatively charged (*anions*). The nutrient ion soup in the soil's water is in a constant state of flux as the variety of ions dissolve in and precipitate out of solution.

Clay particles and organic matter in the soil are negatively charged, attracting the positively charged cations (like ammonium, NH_4^+, and potassium, K^+) and making the cations resistant to leaching. Negatively charged anions (like nitrate, NO_3^-) are prone to leaching and can become a water pollution problem. Both ammonium and nitrate are important plant nitrogen sources and are commonly found in salt forms in fertilizers.

The *Cation Exchange Capacity, CEC,*is a measurement of the soil's capacity to hold cation nutrients. More precisely, it is a measurement of the capacity of the negatively charged clay and organic matter to attract and hold positively charged cations. CEC is useful in comparing the potential for different soils to hold and supply nutrients for plant growth.

NUTRITIONALLY IMPROVED AGRICULTURAL CROPS

Agricultural innovation has always involved new, science-based products and processes that have contributed reliable methods for increasing productivity and sustainability. Biotechnology has introduced a new dimension to such innovation, offering efficient and cost-effective means to produce a diverse array of novel, value-added products and tools.

The first generation of biotechnology products commercialized were crops focusing largely on input agronomic traits whose value was largely opaque to consumers. The coming generations of crop plants can be grouped into four broad areas, each presenting what, on the surface, may appear as unique challenges to regulatory oversight. The present and future focus is on continuing improvement of agronomic traits such as yield and abiotic stress resistance in addition to the biotic stress tolerance of the present generation; crop plants as biomass feedstocks for biofuels and 'biosynthetics'; value-added output traits such as improved nutrition and food functionality; and plants as production factories for therapeutics and industrial products. From a consumer perspective, the focus on value-added traits, especially improved nutrition, is of greatest interest.

Developing plants with these improved traits involves overcoming a variety of technical, regulatory, and indeed perception challenges inherent in the perceived and real challenges of complex modifications. Both traditional plant breeding and biotechnology-based techniques are needed to produce plants with the desired quality traits. Continuing improvements in molecular and genomic technologies are contributing to the acceleration of product development.

NUTRITION VERSUS FUNCTIONALITY

At a fundamental level, food is viewed as a source of nutrition to meet daily requirements at a minimum in order to survive but with an ever greater focus on the desire to thrive. In the latter instance, there is an ever-growing interest in the functionality of food. Functional foods have been defined as any modified food or food ingredient that may provide a health benefit beyond the traditional nutrients it contains. The term nutraceutical is defined as 'any substance that may be considered a food or part of a food and provides health benefits, including the prevention and treatment of disease'.

From the basic nutrition perspective, there is a clear dichotomy in demonstrated need between different regions and socioeconomic groups, the starkest being over-consumption in the developed world and undernourishment in less developed countries. Dramatic increases in the occurrence of obesity and related ailments in developed countries are in sharp contrast to the chronic malnutrition in many less developed countries. Both problems require a modified food supply, and the tools of biotechnology have a part to play. Worldwide, plant-based products comprise the vast majority of human food intake, irrespective of location or financial status. In some cultures, either by design or default, plant-based nutrition actually comprises 100% of the diet. Therefore, it is to be expected that nutritional improvement can be achieved via modifications of staple crops.

While the correlative link between food and health is still open to debate, a growing body of evidence indicates that food components can influence physiological processes at all stages of life. Functional food components are of increasing interest in the prevention and/or treatment of at least four of the leading causes of death in the United States: cancer, diabetes, cardiovascular disease, and hypertension. The U.S. National Cancer Institute estimates that one in three cancer deaths are diet related and that eight of 10 cancers have a nutrition/diet component. Inverse relationships have been observed between carotenoid-rich foods and certain cancers. Other nutrient-related correlations link dietary fat and fibre to the prevention of colon cancer, folate to the prevention of neural tube defects, calcium to the prevention of osteoporosis, psyllium to the lowering of blood lipid levels, and antioxidant nutrients to the scavenging of reactive oxidant species and protection against oxidative damage of cells that may lead to chronic disease, to list just a few. Many food components are known to influence the expression of both structural genes and transcription factors (Tfs) in humans. The large diversity of phytochemicals suggests that the potential impact of phytochemicals and functional foods on human and animal health is worth examining as targets of biotechnology efforts.

On the functionality side, there is a mirror component from the perspective of the genetic makeup of the individual doing the consuming. This field of personal response to nutrients is further divided into two thematic subsets with subtle differences. Nutrigenomics is the prospective analysis of differences among nutrients in the regulation of gene expression, while nutrigenetics is the analysis of genetic variations among individuals with respect to the interaction between diet and disease. These spheres of enquiry are designed to provide nutritional recommendations for personalized or individualized nutrition. Haplotyping studies are beginning to indicate gender-and ethnicity-specific polymorphisms that are implicated in susceptibilities to polygenic disorders such as diabetes, cardiovascular disease, and some cancers. For example, several studies have reported some evidence to suggest that the risks from high intake of well-done meat are higher in fast or presumed fast acetylator haplotypes (NAT1 and/or NAT2) or in rapid NAT2 (haplotypes) and CYP1A2 phenotypes. During cooking of muscle meat at high temperature, some amino acids may react with creatine to give heterocyclic aromatic amines. Heterocyclic aromatic amines can be activated through acetylation to reactive metabolites, which bind DNA and cause cancers. Only NAT2 fast acetylators can perform this acetylation. Studies have shown that the NAT2 fast acetylator genotype had a higher risk of developing colon cancer in people who consumed relatively large quantities of red meat. Understanding individual response is at least as complex a challenge as the task of increasing or decreasing the amount of a specific protein, fatty acid, or other component of the plant itself. It is of little use producing a plant with a supposed nutritional benefit unless that benefit actually improves the health of humans or animals.

From a health perspective, plant components of dietary interest can be broadly divided into four main categories, the first two to be enhanced and the latter two to be limited or removed: macronutrients (proteins, carbohydrates, lipids [oils], fibre); micronutrients (vitamins, minerals, functional metabolites); antinutrients (substances such as phytate that limit the bioavailability of nutrients); and allergens (intolerances and toxins).

The Technology

As noted, plants are a treasure trove of interesting and valuable compounds, since they must glean everything from the spot on earth where they are rooted and they cannot escape when threatened; therefore, they have evolved a most impressive panoply of products to thrive in ever-changing environments despite these limitations. It is estimated that plants produce up to 200,000 phytochemicals across their many and diverse members; obviously, a more truncated subset of this number is available on our food palate, with approximately 25,000 different metabolites in general plant foods. The quality of crop plants, nutritionally or otherwise, is a direct function of this metabolite content. This brings metabolomic approaches front and centre both in better understanding what has occurred during crop domestication (lost and silenced traits) and in designing new paradigms for more targeted crop improvement that are better tailored to current needs. In addition, of course, with modern techniques we have the potential to trawl the rest of that biochemical treasure trove to find and introgress traits of value that were outside the scope of previous breeding strategies.

Research to improve the nutritional quality of plants has historically been limited by a lack of basic knowledge of plant metabolism and the compounding challenge of resolving the complex interactions of thousands of metabolic pathways. Both traditional plant breeding and biotechnology techniques are needed to metabolically engineer plants with desired quality traits. Metabolic engineering is generally defined as the redirection of one or more enzymatic reactions to improve the production of existing compounds, produce new compounds, or mediate the degradation of undesirable compounds. It involves the redirection of cellular activities by the modification of the enzymatic, transport, and regulatory functions of the cell. Significant progress has been made in recent years in the molecular dissection of many plant pathways and in the use of cloned genes to engineer plant metabolism.

With the tools now being harnessed through the many 'omics' and 'informatics' fields, there is the potential to identify genes of value across species, phyla, and kingdoms. Through advances in proteomics and glycomics, we are beginning to quantify simultaneously the levels of many individual proteins and to follow posttranslational alterations that occur in pathways. Ever more sophisticated metabolomic tools and analysis systems allow the study of both primary and secondary metabolic pathways in an integrated fashion. However, the increasing sophistication of this tool also demonstrates some anomalies in relying on this approach. For example, in potato (*Solanum tuberosum*), flow injection mass spectrometry analysis of a range of genotypes revealed genotypic correlations with quality traits such as free amino acid content. Yet, matrix-assisted laser desorption/ionization chemotyping and gas chromatography-mass spectrometry profiling of tomato (*Solanum lycopersicum*) cultivars have revealed extensive differences in metabolic composition (sugars, amino acids, organic acids) despite close specific/ genotypic similarities. Likewise, with regard to metabolomic analysis on the consumer side, little is known of the extent to which changes in the nutrient content of the human diet elicit changes in metabolic profiles. Moreover, the metabolomic signal from nutrients absorbed from the diet must compete with myriad nonnutrient signals that are absorbed, metabolized, and secreted.

Although progress in dissecting metabolic pathways and our ability to manipulate gene expression in genetically modified (GM) plants has progressed apace, attempts to use these tools to engineer plant metabolism have not quite kept pace. Since the success of this approach hinges on the ability to change host metabolism, its continued development will depend critically on a far more sophisticated knowledge of plant metabolism, especially the nuances of interconnected cellular networks, than currently exists. This complex interconnectivity is regularly demonstrated. Relatively minor genomic changes (point mutations, single gene insertions) are regularly observed following metabolomic analysis, leading to significant changes in biochemical composition. Giliberto *et al.* used a genetic modification approach to study the mechanism of light influence on antioxidant content (anthocyanin, lycopene) in the tomato cv Moneymaker. However, other, what on the surface would appear to be more significant, genetic changes unexpectedly yield little phenotypic effect.

Likewise, there are unexpected outcomes, such as the fact that significant modifications made to primary Calvin cycle enzymes (Fru-1,6-bisphosphatase and phosphoribulokinase) have little effect while modifications to minor enzymes (*e.g.* aldase, which catalyzes a reversible reaction) seemingly irrelevant to pathway flux have major effects. These observations drive home the point that a thorough understanding of the individual kinetic properties of enzymes may not be informative as to their role. They also make clear that caution must be exercised when extrapolating individual enzyme kinetics to the control of flux in complex metabolic pathways. With these evolving tools, a better understanding of the global effects of metabolic engineering on metabolites, enzyme activities, and fluxes is beginning to be developed. Attempts to modify storage proteins or secondary metabolic pathways have also been more successful than have alterations of primary and intermediary metabolism. While offering great opportunities, this plasticity in metabolism complicates potential routes to the design of new, improved crop varieties. Regulatory oversight of engineered products has been designed to detect such unexpected outcomes in biotech crops, and as demonstrated by Chassy *et al.*, existing analytical and regulatory systems are adequate to address novel metabolic modifications in nutritionally improved crops.

One potential approach to counter some of the complex problems in the metabolic engineering of pathways involves the manipulation of Tfs that control networks of metabolism. For example, expression of the maize (*Zea mays*) Tfs C1 and R, which regulate the production of flavonoids in maize aleurone layers under the control of a strong promoter, resulted in a high accumulation rate of anthocyanins in Arabidopsis (*Arabidopsis thaliana*), presumably by activating the entire pathway. DellaPenna found that Tf RAP2.2 and its interacting partner SINAT2 increased carotenogenesis in Arabidopsis leaves. Expressing the Tf Dof1 induced the up-regulation of genes encoding enzymes for carbon skeleton production, a marked increase of amino acid content, and a reduction of the Glc level in transgenic Arabidopsis, and the DOF Tf AtDof1.1 (OBP2) up-regulated all steps in the glucosinolate biosynthetic pathway in Arabidopsis. Such expression experiments hold promise as an effective tool for the determination of transcriptional regulatory networks for important biochemical pathways. In summary, metabolic engineers must not only understand the fundamental physiology of the process to be affected but also the level, timing, subcellular location, and tissue or organ specificity that will be required to ensure successful trait modification. Gene expression can be modulated by numerous transcriptional and post transcriptional processes. Correctly choreographing these many variables is the factor that makes metabolic engineering in plants so challenging.

As a corollary to these techniques, there are several new technologies that can overcome the limitation of single gene transfers and facilitate the concomitant transfer of multiple components of metabolic pathways. One example is multiple transgene direct DNA transfer, which simultaneously introduces all of the components required for the expression of complex recombinant macromolecules into the plant genome, as demonstrated by Nicholson *et al.*, who successfully delivered into rice (*Oryza sativa*) plants four transgenes that represent the components of a secretory antibody.

More recently, Carlson *et al.* constructed a minichromosome vector that remains autonomous from the plant's chromosomes and stably replicates when introduced into maize cells. This work makes it possible to design minichromosomes that carry cassettes of genes, enhancing the ability to engineer plant processes such as the production of complex biochemicals.

Christou and Kohli demonstrated that gene transfer using minimal cassettes is an efficient and rapid method for the production of transgenic plants containing and stably expressing several different transgenes. Since no vector backbones are required, thus preventing the integration of potentially recombinogenic sequences, they remain stable across generations. These groups' constructions facilitate the effective manipulation of multigene pathways in plants in a single transformation step, effectively recapitulating the bacterial operon model in plants.

More recently, Christou and colleagues demonstrated this principle by engineering the entire carotenoid pathway in white maize, visually creating a latter day rainbow equivalent of Indian maize depending on the integrated transgene complement.

This system has an added advantage from a commercial perspective in that these methods circumvent problems with traditional approaches that not only limit the amount of sequences transferred but may disrupt native genes or lead to poor expression of the transgene, thus reducing both the numbers of transgenic plants that must be screened and the subsequent breeding and introgression steps required to select a suitable commercial candidate.

The agronomically improved GM crops now being grown on more than 114 million ha around the world are products of the application of these technologies to crop plants. They generally involve the relatively simple task of adding a single gene or a small number of genes to plants. These genes in the main function outside of the plant's primary metabolic processes and thus have little or no effect on the composition of the plants.

In addition to numerous success stories, some studies, as noted, even with these simpler modifications, have yielded unanticipated results. For example, the concept of gene silencing emerged from the unexpected observation that adding a chalcone synthase gene to increase colour in *Petunia* spp. resulted instead in the switching off of colour, producing white and variegated flowers. This initially unexpected observation, now termed RNA interference, is one of the principal tools applied in everything from the analysis of molecular evolution to designing targeted therapeutics. In plants, it has now been turned to advantage in the first generation, developing robust virus resistance through coat protein posttranscriptional gene silencing, and in nutritional improvement, such as switching off of expression of an allergen in soybean (*Glycine max*).

To summarize, omics-based strategies for gene and metabolite discovery, coupled with high-throughput transformation processes and automated analytical and functionality assays, have accelerated the identification of product candidates. Identifying rate-limiting steps in synthesis could provide targets for genetically engineering biochemical pathways to produce augmented amounts of compounds and new compounds. Targeted expression will be used to channel metabolic flow into new pathways, while gene-silencing tools can reduce or eliminate undesirable compounds or traits or switch off genes to increase desirable products. In addition, molecular marker-based breeding strategies have already been used to accelerate the process of introgressing trait genes into high-yielding germplasm for commercialization.

MACRONUTRIENTS

Fiber

Fiber is a group of substances chemically similar to carbohydrates, but nonruminant animals including humans poorly metabolize fibre for energy or other nutritional uses. Fiber is only found in foods derived from plants and never occurs in animal products. Fiber provides bulk in the diet, such that foods rich in fibre offer satiety without contributing significant calories. Current controversies aside, there is ample scientific evidence to show that prolonged intake of dietary fibre has various positive health benefits, especially the potential for reduced risk of colon and other types of cancer. Fiber type and quantity are undoubtedly under genetic control, although this topic has been little studied. The technology to manipulate fibre content and type by genetic engineering would be a great benefit to the health status of many individuals who refuse, for taste or other reasons, to include adequate amounts of fibre in their daily diet. For example, fibre content could be added to more preferred foods or the more common sources of dietary fibre could be altered for greater health benefits.

Nonruminant animals do not produce enzymes necessary to digest cellulose-based plant fibre. Plants low in fibre should yield more digestible and metabolizable energy and protein and less manure and methane when fed to monogastric species. Vermerris and Bout cloned a *Brown midrib* gene that encodes caffeic acid *O*-methyltransferase, a lignin-producing enzyme. They generated mutants that give rise to plants that contain significantly lower lignin in their leaves and stems, leading to softer cell walls compared with the wild type. The plant-softening mutations improve the digestibility of the food, and livestock also seem to prefer the taste. Such improved fibre digestibility in ruminants should have significant beneficial effects, because the efficiency of digestion of most high-fibre diets for ruminants is far from optimized.

Novel Lipids

Gene technology and plant breeding are combining to provide powerful means for modifying the composition of oilseeds to improve their nutritional value and provide the functional properties required for various food oil applications. Genetic modification of oilseed crops can provide an abundant, relatively inexpensive source of dietary fatty acids with wide-ranging health benefits. Production of such lipids in vegetable oil provides a convenient mechanism to deliver healthier products to consumers without the requirement for significant dietary changes. Major alterations in the proportions of individual fatty acids have been achieved in a range of oilseeds using conventional selection, induced mutation, and, more recently, posttranscriptional gene silencing. Examples of such modified oils include low-and zero-saturated fat soybean and canola oils, canola oil containing medium-chain fatty acids, high-stearic acid canola oil (for trans-fatty acid-free products), high-oleic acid (monounsaturated) soybean oil, and canola oil containing the polyunsaturated fatty acids γ-linolenic acid (GLA; 18:3 n-6) and stearidonic acid (SDA; C18:4 n-3), very-long-chain fatty acids, and ω-3 fatty acids. Many of these modified oils are being marketed, and a number of countries have a regulatory system in place for the premarket safety review of novel foods produced through conventional technology.

Medium chain fatty acids range from 6 to 10 carbons long and are only minor components of natural foods, with the exception of coconut and palm kernel oils. When medium-chain triglycerides (MCTs) are substituted for long-chain triglycerides (LCTs) in the diet, animals gain less weight, store less adipose tissue, and experience an increase in metabolic rate. Mice fed diets with MCTs have also been shown to possess increased endurance in swimming tests over that of mice fed diets with LCTs. Expression of an acyl-ACP thioesterase cDNA from *Cuphea hookeriana* in seeds of transgenic canola, an oilseed crop that normally does not accumulate any capric and caprylic acids, resulted in a dramatic increase in the levels of these two MCTs.

Edible oils rich in monounsaturated fatty acids provide improved oil stability, flavour, and nutrition for human and animal consumption. Oleic acid (18:1), a monounsaturate, can provide more stability than the polyunsaturates linoleic acid (18:2) and linolenic acid (18:3). From a health aspect, the monounsaturates are also preferred. Antisense inhibition of oleate desaturase expression in soybean resulted in oil that contained more than 80% oleic acid (23% is normal) and had a significant decrease in polyunsaturated fatty acids. High-oleic-acid soybean oil is naturally more resistant to degradation by heat and oxidation and so requires little or no postrefining processing (hydrogenation), depending on the intended vegetable oil application.

In 2009, DuPont hopes to introduce soybean oil composed of at least 80% oleic acid, linolenic acid of about 3%, and over 20% less saturated fatty acids than commodity soybean oil. Monsanto's Vistive contains less than 3% linolenic acid, compared with 8% for traditional soybeans. These result in more stable soybean oil and less need for hydrogenation and concomitant reduction in trans-fatty acids. For lower trans-fats in livestock products, Nicholas Roberts and Richard Scott at AgResearch (New Zealand) are researching an ingenious method to prevent plant-derived cis-polyunsaturated fatty acids from being transformed into saturated trans-fats in the rumen by borrowing an adaptation from plants themselves. They are engineering forage crops, such as grasses and legumes, with polyoleosin genes from sesame, which should result in triglycerides being encapsulated within self-assembling polyoleosin micelles, thus sealing them off from bacterial activity during transit though the rumen.

A key function of α-linolenic acid is as a substrate for the synthesis of longer chain ω-3 fatty acids found in fish, eicosapentaenoic acid (EPA; C20:5n-3) and docosahexaenoic acid (DHA; C22:6n-3), which play an important role in the regulation of inflammatory immune reactions and blood pressure, brain development in utero, and, in early postnatal life, the development of cognitive function. SDA (C18:4n-3), EPA, and DHA also possess anticancer properties. Research indicates that the ratio of n-3 to n-6 fatty acids may be as important to health and nutrition as the absolute amounts present in the diet or in body tissues. Current western diets tend to be relatively high in n-6 fatty acids and relatively low in n-3 fatty acids. Production of a readily available source of long-chain polyunsaturated fatty acids, specifically ω-3 fatty acids, delivered in widely consumed prepared foods could deliver much needed ω-3 fatty acids to large sectors of the population with skewed n-6:n-3 ratios. In plants, the microsomal ω-6 desaturase-catalysed pathway is the primary route of production of polyunsaturated lipids. Ursin has introduced the Δ-6 desaturase gene from a fungus (*Mortierella*), succeeding in producing ω-3 in canola. In a clinical study, James *et al.* observed that SDA was superior to α-linolenic acid as a precursor by a factor of 3.6 in producing EPA, DHA, and docosapentaenoic acid (C22:5n-3). Transgenic canola oil was obtained that contains more than 23% SDA, with an overall n-6:n-3 ratio of 0.5.

However, not all ω-6 fatty acids are created equal. GLA (C18:3n-6) is an ω-6 fatty acid with health benefits that are similar and complementary to the benefits of ω-3 fatty acids, including anti-inflammatory effects, improved skin health, and weight loss maintenance. Arcadia Biosciences has engineered GLA safflower oil, with up to 40% GLA, essentially quadrupling the levels obtained in source plants such as evening primrose and borage. Structural lipids also have positive health benefits; for example, in addition to their effect in lowering cholesterol, membrane lipid phytosterols have been found to inhibit the proliferation of cancer cells by inducing apoptosis and G1/S cell cycle arrest through the 3-hydroxy-3-methylglutaryl-CoA reductase target.

Vitamins and Minerals

Micronutrient malnutrition, the so-called hidden hunger, affects more than half of the world's population, especially women and preschool children in developing countries. Even mild levels of micronutrient malnutrition may damage cognitive development, lower disease resistance in children, and increase the incidence of childbirth mortality. The costs of these deficiencies, in terms of diminished quality of life and lives lost, are enormous. The clinical and epidemiological evidence is clear that select minerals (iron, calcium, selenium, and iodine) and a limited number of vitamins (folate, vitamins E, B6, and A) play a significant role in the maintenance of optimal health and are limiting in diets.

Using various approaches, vitamin E levels are being increased in several crops, including soybean, maize, and canola, while rice varieties are being developed with the enhanced vitamin A precursor, β-carotene, to address vitamin A deficiency that leads to macular degeneration and affects development. Ameliorating another major deficiency in less developed countries, minerals such as iron and zinc have also been addressed. Other targets include improved iron content, ferritin-rich lettuce (*Lactuca sativa*), bioavailable phosphorus, and divalent ions released from phytate, folate-enriched tomatoes, and isoflavonoids.

As with macronutrients, one way to ensure an adequate dietary intake of nutritionally beneficial phytochemicals is to adjust their levels in plant foods. Until recently, such work had been hindered by the difficulty of isolating the relevant genes (*e.g.* for vitamin biosynthesis). However, the advent of genomics during the past few years has provided new routes for such work. Using nutritional genomics, DellaPenna isolated a gene, γ-tocopherol methyltransferase, that converts the lower activity precursors to the highest activity vitamin E compound, α-tocopherol. With this technology, the vitamin E content of Arabidopsis seed oil has been increased nearly 10-fold and progress has been made to move the technology to agricultural crops such as soybean, maize, and canola. Rice is a staple that feeds nearly half the world's population, but milled rice does not contain any β-carotene or its carotenoid precursors. Integrating observations from prokaryotic systems into their work enabled researchers to clone the majority of carotenoid biosynthetic enzymes from plants during the 1990s. Taking advantage of this, Golden rice, with β-carotene expression in the endosperm, was created. The health benefits of the original

Golden rice and, especially, Golden rice II are well reviewed. A similar method was used by Monsanto to produce β-carotene in canola.

Iron is the most commonly deficient micronutrient in the human diet, and iron deficiency affects an estimated 1 to 2 billion people. Anemia, characterized by low hemoglobin, is the most widely recognized symptom of iron deficiency, but there are other serious problems, such as impaired learning ability in children, increased susceptibility to infection, and reduced work capacity. A research group employed the gene for ferritin, an iron-rich soybean storage protein, under the control of an endosperm-specific promoter. Grain from transgenic rice plants contained three times more iron than normal rice. To increase the iron content in the grain further, the researchers focused on iron transport within the plant. Researchers demonstrated endosperm-specific coexpression of recombinant soybean ferritin and *Aspergillus* phytase in maize, which resulted in significant increases in the levels of bioavailable iron. A similar result was achieved with lettuce.

Functional Metabolites

Unlike for vitamins and minerals, the primary evidence for the health-promoting roles of phytochemicals comes from epidemiological studies, and the exact chemical identities of many active compounds have yet to be determined. However, for select groups of phytochemicals, such as nonprovitamin A, carotenoids, glucosinolates, and phytoestrogens, the active compound or compounds have been identified and rigorously studied. A great irony of nature is that the body's natural metabolism involving oxygen also produces a host of toxic compounds called 'free radicals.' These compounds can harm body cells by altering molecules of protein and fat and by damaging DNA. Antioxidants counteract, or neutralize, the harmful effects of free radicals.

Epidemiologic studies have suggested a potential benefit of the carotenoid lycopene in reducing the risk of prostate cancer, particularly the more lethal forms of this cancer. Five studies support a 30% to 40% reduction in risk associated with high tomato or lycopene consumption in the processed form in conjunction with lipid consumption, although other studies with raw tomatoes were not conclusive. As a nonpolar carotenoid, lycopene is more soluble in a lipid base; in addition, carotenoid-binding proteins are broken down during processing, leading to greater bioavailability. While modifying polyamines to retard tomato ripening, Mehta *et al.* discovered an unanticipated enrichment in lycopene, with levels up by 2- to 3.5-fold compared with the conventional tomatoes. This is a substantial enrichment, exceeding that so far achieved by conventional means. This novel approach may work in other fruits and vegetables.

Stilbenes, including resveratrol (3,5,42 trihydroxystilbene), are phenolic natural products that accumulate in a wide range of plant species, including pine (*Pinus* spp.), peanut (*Arachis hypogaea*), rhubarb (*Rheum* spp.), and grape. Resveratrol inhibits platelet aggregation and eicosanoid synthesis and is thought to contribute to improved heart function and lower blood cholesterol, based on epidemiological studies. It was shown to have 'chemopreventive' activity, preventing the formation of tumors in mouse skin bioassays, and, therefore, may help reduce cancer rates in humans. More recent studies appear to demonstrate that it mimics the life-extending effect on rodents of severe caloric restriction. This diet extends the life span of rodents by 30% to 50%, and even if it is started later it has a benefit proportionate to the remaining life span. The method of action is believed to be in protecting the sirtuins, genes implicated in DNA modification and life extension. The April 2008 purchase of Sirtris by Glaxo Smith Kline demonstrates that big pharma is now showing an interest in the arena of food functionality. Resveratrol glucoside production has been achieved in alfalfa (*Medicago sativa*), wheat, kiwi (*Actinidia deliciosa*), and tomato.

Other phytochemicals of interest include the flavonoids, such as tomatoes expressing chalcone isomerase, which show increased contents of the flavanols rutin and kaempferol glycoside; glucosinolates and their related products, such as indole-3 carbinol; catechin and catechol; isoflavones, such as genistein and daidzein; anthocyanins; and some phytoalexins. A comprehensive list of phytochemicals. Although there is a growing knowledge base indicating that elevated intakes of specific phytochemicals may reduce the risk of disease, such as certain cancers, cardiovascular diseases, and chronic degenerative diseases associated with aging, further research and epidemiological studies are still required to prove definitive relationships.

ANTINUTRIENTS, ALLERGENS AND TOXINS

Plants produce many defence strategies to protect themselves from predators, and many of these, such as resveratrol and glucosinate, which are primarily pathogen-protective chemicals, also have demonstrated beneficial effects for human and animal health. Many, however, have the opposite effect. For example, phytate, a plant phosphate storage compound, is an antinutrient, as it strongly chelates iron, calcium, zinc, and other divalent mineral ions, making them unavailable for uptake. Nonruminant animals generally lack the phytase enzyme needed for digestion of phytate. Poultry and swine producers add processed phosphate to their feed rations to counter this. Excess phosphate is excreted into the environment, resulting in water pollution. When low-phytate soybean meal is utilized along with low-phytate maize for animal feeds, the phosphate excretion in swine and poultry manure is halved. A number of groups have added heat-and acid-stable phytase from *Aspergillus fumigatus* to make the phosphate and liberated ions bioavailable in several crops. To promote the reabsorption of iron, a gene for a metallothionein-like protein has also been engineered. Low-phytate maize was commercialized in the United States in 1999. Research indicates that the protein in low-phytate soybeans is also slightly more digestible than the protein in traditional soybeans. In a poultry feeding trial, better results were obtained using transgenic plant material than with the commercially produced phytase supplement. Poultry grew well on the engineered alfalfa diet without any inorganic phosphorus supplement, which shows that plants can be tailored to increase the bioavailability of this essential mineral.

Other antinutrients that are being examined as possible targets for reduction are trypsin inhibitors, lectins, and several other heat-stable components found in soybeans and other crops. Likewise, strategies are being applied to reduce or limit food allergens (albumins, globulins, etc.), malabsorption and food intolerances (gluten), and toxins (glycoalkaloids, cyanogenic glucosides, phytohemagglutinins) in crop plants and undesirable aesthetics such as caffeine. Examples include changing the levels of expression of the thioredoxin gene to reduce the intolerance effects of wheat and other cereals. Using RNA interference to silence the major allergen in soybean (p34, a member of the papain superfamily of Cys proteases) and rice, blood serum tests indicate that p34-specific IgE antibodies could not be detected after consumption of gene-silenced beans.

Biotechnology approaches can be employed to down-regulate or even eliminate the genes involved in the metabolic pathways for the production, accumulation, and/or activation of these toxins in plants. For example, the solanine content of potato has already been reduced substantially using an antisense approach, and efforts are under way to reduce the level of the other major potato glycoalkaloid, chaconine. Work has also been done to reduce cyanogenic glycosides in cassava through expression of the cassava enzyme hydroxynitrile lyase in roots. When 'disarming' plant natural defences in this way, we need to be cognizant of potentially increased susceptibility to pests and diseases, so the base germplasm should have input traits to counter this.

IMPLICATIONS FOR SAFETY ASSESSMENT

On the surface, it may appear that the greater complexity involved in modifying the nutritional content of crop plants would necessitate more rigorous oversight than the simpler modifications. However, extensive research reported previously and updated in a more recent case study analysis indicates that existing oversight systems are more than adequate. Trait modifications with the addition of one or two genes that do not act on central or intermediary metabolism produce targeted, predictable outcomes, whereas major modifications of metabolic pathways can produce unanticipated effects. Therefore, it is very encouraging that the ever-evolving and increasingly sensitive and discriminating analytical technologies have been able to detect and assess the safety of these unanticipated effects. In addition, regulatory oversight of GM products has been designed to detect such unexpected outcomes.

At a very fundamental level, a recent report on genome-wide analyses of introgression from oak (*Quercus* spp.) to fruit flies indicates that a substantial fraction of genomes are malleable. Hybridization gives rapid genomic changes, chromosomal rearrangements, genome expansion, differential expression, and gene silencing (transposable elements). In the context of this sea of malleability, reports have demonstrated that GM crops have a composition more similar to the isogenic parental strain used in their development than to other breeding cultivars of the same genus and species and in some instances even the location in which they are grown, and on occasion the latter 'terroir' effect demonstrated greater variation than breeding strategy. This effect has been observed at the proteome level for potato, tomato, and wheat. Parallel results have been observed at the metabolomic level for wheat and potato. As more metabolic modifications are introduced, we must continue to study plant metabolism and the interconnected cellular networks of plant metabolic pathways to increase the likelihood of predicting pleiotropic effects that may occur as a result of the introduced genetic modification.

THE FUTURE OF CROP BIOTECHNOLOGY

Research to improve the nutritional quality of plants has historically been limited by a lack of basic knowledge of plant metabolism and the almost insurmountable challenge of resolving complex branches of thousands of metabolic pathways. With the tools now available to us through the fields of genomics and bioinformatics, we have the potential to fish in silico for genes of value across species, phyla, and kingdoms and subsequently to study the expression and interaction of transgenes on tens of thousands of endogenous genes simultaneously. With advances in proteomics, we should also be able to simultaneously quantify the levels and interactions of many proteins or follow posttranslational alterations that occur. With these newly evolving tools, we are beginning to get a handle on the global effects of metabolic engineering on metabolites, enzyme activities, and fluxes. Right now, for essential macronutrients and micronutrients that are limiting in various regional diets, the strategies for improvement are clear and the concerns, such as pleiotropic effects and safe upper limits, are easily addressed. However, for many other health-promoting phytochemicals, clear links with health benefits remain to be demonstrated. Such links, if established, will make it possible to identify the precise compound or compounds to target and which crops to modify to achieve the greatest nutritional impact and health benefits. The achievement of this aim will be a truly interdisciplinary effort, requiring expertise and input from many disparate fields, ranging from the obvious human physiology and plant research to the less obvious 'omics' and analytic fields. With these emerging capabilities, the increase in our basic understanding of plant secondary metabolism during the coming decades will be unparalleled and will place plant researchers in the position of being able to modify the nutritional content of major and minor crops to improve many aspects of human and animal health and well-being.

NUTRITION IN PLANTS

Plants, unlike animals, do not have to obtain organic materials for their nutrition, although these form the bulk of their tissues. By trapping solar energy in photosynthetic systems, they are able to synthesize nutrients from carbon dioxide (CO_2) and water. However, plants do require inorganic salts, which they absorb from the soil surrounding their roots; these include the elements phosphorus (in the form of phosphate), chlorine (as the chloride ion), potassium, sulfur, calcium, magnesium, iron, manganese, boron, copper, and zinc. Plants also require nitrogen, in the form of nitrate (NO_3^-)

or ammonium (NH_4^+) ions. They will, in addition, take up inorganic compounds that they themselves do not need, such as iodides and cobalt and selenium salts.

The nutrients found in soil result in part from the gradual breakdown of the rocky material on the Earth's surface as a result of rain and, in some areas, freezing. Primarily composed of alumina and silica, rocks also contain smaller amounts of all the mineral elements needed by plants. Another source of soil nutrients is the decomposition of dead plants and animals and their waste products. Although a spadeful of soil may seem inert to the eye—apart from an occasional earthworm—it contains millions of microorganisms, the net effect of which is to break down organic materials, releasing simpler mineral salts. Furthermore, two groups of bacteria fix atmospheric nitrogen—that is, they are able to incorporate this relatively inert element into nitrate ions. Bacteria of the genus *Azobacter* live freely in soil, while those of the genus *Rhizobium* live sheltered in the roots of leguminous plants such as peas and beans. Cyanobacteria (blue-green algae) also can fix nitrogen and are important for growing rice in the flooded paddy fields of Southeast Asia.

In areas of intensive farming, where crops are harvested at least once a year and no animals browse the fields, human intervention in the form of fertilizers is important. A traditional form of fertilizer has been animal manure, or muck, made from the straw bedding of cattle that has been soaked in excreta and allowed to ferment for a period. Since the 1800s farmers also have used artificial fertilizers, at first using naturally occurring mixtures of chemicals such as chalk (supplying calcium), rock phosphates, and the natural manure known as guano. Commercial guano consists of the accumulated deposits of bird droppings and is valued for its high concentration of nitrates. Modern chemical fertilizers include one or more of three important elements: nitrogen, potassium, and phosphorus. Most nitrogenous fertilizers are produced by a technique in which nitrogen and hydrogen are combined at very high pressures in the presence of catalysts to form ammonia (NH_3). This can then be injected into the soil as a gas that is quickly absorbed or, more commonly, converted into solid products such as ammonium salts, urea, and nitrates, which can be used as ingredients in mixed fertilizers.

NUTRITION IN BACTERIA

These small organisms, popularly thought of only as sources of infection, are of vital importance in the overall life cycles of plants and animals. They commonly have to digest their food, as do larger organisms, and their cell walls do not allow the passage of large compounds. If the bacteria are in a liquid containing sugars, the sugars will diffuse through the bacterial wall and then typically be consolidated into larger molecules so that the concentration gradient will continue to promote inward diffusion. However, in order to utilize larger molecules such as starches and protein, bacteria have to excrete digestive enzymes (*i.e.*, catalysts) into the surrounding fluid. This is obviously an expensive function for an individual organism, because much of the secreted enzymes and also the digested products may drift away from, rather than towards, the bacterial cell. However, for a cluster of thousands or millions of bacteria acting in the same way, the process is less expensive.

Bacteria vary greatly in their nutritional requirements. Some, like plants, require a source of energy such as sugars and only inorganic nutrients. Some are aerobic, meaning that they require oxygen in order to capture energy—for example, by oxidation of sugars to carbon dioxide and water. Others are anaerobic (in some cases, actually poisoned by oxygen) and require an energy source such as a sugar that they can ferment either to lactic acid or to ethanol and carbon dioxide—obtaining less energy in the process, but enough to meet their needs.

Apparently as an adaptation to many generations of living in a nutrient-rich medium, some bacteria have lost the ability to synthesize many essential compounds. For example, many of the *Lactobacilli*, commonly found in unsterilized milk, require essentially all the water-soluble vitamins and amino acids needed by animals. Because of this, they have been used as convenient models for assaying the value of foods as sources of particular nutrients.

NUTRITION IN ANIMALS

Simple observation reveals that the animal kingdom is dependent on plants for food. Even meat-eating, or carnivorous, animals such as the lion feed on grazing animals and thus are indirectly dependent on the plant kingdom for their survival.

Herbivores

Plant cell walls are constructed mainly of cellulose, a material that the digestive enzymes of higher animals are unable to digest or disrupt. Because of this, even the nutritious contents of plant cells are not fully available for digestion. As an evolutionary response to this problem, many leaf eaters, or herbivores, have developed a pouch at the anterior end of the stomach, called the rumen, that provides a space for the bacterial fermentation of ingested leaves. In ruminant species such as cattle and sheep, fermented material, called cud, is regurgitated from the rumen so that the animal can chew it into even smaller pieces and spread the ruminal fluid throughout the mass of ingesta. Microorganisms found in the ruminal fluid ferment cellulose to acetic acid and other short-chain fatty acids, which can then be absorbed and utilized as energy sources. Protein within the cells of the leaves is also released and degraded; some is resynthesized for digestion as microbial protein in the true stomach and small intestine. Another action of ruminal bacteria is the synthesis of some water-soluble vitamins so that, under most conditions, the host animal no longer requires them to be supplied in its food.

Because conditions in the rumen are anaerobic, another effect of ruminal fermentation is that the fatty material in the food becomes hydrogenated. Many metabolic reactions in organisms involve the removal of hydrogen atoms, and if the surplus hydrogen cannot be combined with oxygen to form water, an alternative pathway is for it to be added to unsaturated fatty acids. The result is more saturated fatty acids, which, after absorption, form deposits of harder fat. Thus, beef fat (suet) is characteristically harder at room temperature than is pork or chicken fat. Butterfat, too, is relatively saturated, being kept somewhat soft at room temperature only by the inclusion of short-chain fatty acids in the glycerol esters. This lack of the essential polyunsaturated fatty acids in ruminant fats can make them less desirable as human food.

Other herbivores make efficient use of leafy foods through hindgut fermentation. In animal species generally, the main breakdown of foods by enzymes and absorption into the bloodstream occurs in the small intestine. The main function of the large intestine is then to absorb most of the water remaining so as to conserve losses when the water supply is limited. In the 'hindgut fermenters,' undigested food residues undergo bacterial fermentation in the cecum, a side pocket at the distal end of the small intestine, before moving into the large intestine. In the large intestine the short-chain fatty acids produced in the cecum are absorbed and utilized. Animals in this class include horses, zebras, elephants, rhinoceroses, koalas, and rabbits.

Hindgut fermenters are somewhat less efficient than are ruminants at digesting very high-fibre foods. However, only indigestible residues are fermented in the cecum, so that hindgut fermenters do not experience the inevitable energy loss that occurs when dietary carbohydrates are fermented in the rumen. Also, the smaller bulk of the cecum allows these animals to be more athletic and better able to escape their carnivore predators.

Carnivores

Carnivores necessarily form only a small portion of the animal kingdom, because each animal must eat a great many other animals of equivalent size in order to maintain itself over a lifetime. In addition to possessing the teeth and claws needed to kill their prey and then tear the flesh apart, carnivores have digestive enzymes that are able to break down muscle protein into amino acids, which can then diffuse through the walls of the small intestine. Therefore, carnivores have no need for any special development of the gut that allows for fermentation. Carnivores are also able to utilize animal fat. If their prey is small, they can chew and swallow bones, which serve as a source of calcium. Some carnivores, particularly cats (family *Felidae*), are obligate carnivores, meaning they cannot obtain all the nutrients that they need from the plant kingdom and bacteria. In particular, obligate carnivores lack the enzyme needed to split carotene, obtained from plants, into vitamin A. Instead, these animals obtain vitamin A from the liver of their prey. Obligate carnivores are similarly unable to synthesize some essential very-long-chain, highly unsaturated fatty acids that other animals can make from shorter fatty acids found in plants.

Omnivores

Omnivores are miscellaneous species whose teeth and digestive systems seem designed to eat a relatively concentrated diet, since they have no large sac or chamber for the fermentation of fibrous material. They are able to chew and digest meat, though they do not have an absolute requirement for it unless there is no other practical source of vitamin B_{12} (cobalamin). Humans are in this category, as are dogs, rodents, and most monkeys. All omnivores have active bacterial flora in their small cecum and large intestine and can absorb short-chain fatty acids at this point but not vitamins. Some species obtain essential vitamins by coprophagy, the eating of a proportion of their fecal pellets that contain vitamins synthesized by bacteria. Chickens, too, are omnivores. They have to swallow food without chewing it, but the food passes to an organ called the gizzard, where seeds and other foods are ground to a slurry, often with the aid of swallowed stones.

NUTRIENTS

Some precursors (*i.e.*, the substances from which other substances are formed) of cell materials can be synthesized by the cell from other materials, while others must be supplied in foods. All the inorganic materials required for growth, together with an assortment of organic compounds whose number may vary from 1 to 30 or more, depending on the organism, fall into the latter category. Although organisms are able to synthesize nonessential nutrients, such nutrients are frequently utilized directly if present in food, thereby saving the organism the need to expend the energy required to synthesize them.

Inorganic Nutrients

A number of inorganic elements (minerals) are essential for the growth of living things. Boron, for example, has been demonstrated to be required for the growth of many—perhaps all—higher plants but has not been implicated as an essential element in the nutrition of either microorganisms or animals. Trace amounts of fluorine (as fluoride) are certainly beneficial, and perhaps essential, for proper tooth formation in higher animals. Similarly, iodine (as iodide) is required in animals for formation of thyroxine, the active component of an important regulatory hormone. Silicon (as silicate) is a prominent component of the outer skeletons of diatomaceous protozoans and similar organisms and is required in them for normal growth. In higher animals the requirement for silicon is much smaller. A less obvious example of a specialized mineral requirement is provided by calcium, which is required by higher animals in comparatively large amounts because it is a major component of bone and eggshells (in birds); for other organisms, calcium is an essential nutrient but only as a trace element. Mineral elements in wide variety are present in trace amounts in almost all foodstuffs. It cannot be assumed that the nonessential mineral elements play no useful role in metabolism.

Important antagonistic relationships between certain mineral nutrients also are known. A large excess of rubidium, for example, interferes with the utilization of potassium in some lactic-acid bacteria; zinc can interfere with manganese utilization in the same organism. In animal nutrition, excessive molybdenum or zinc (both of which are essential minerals) interferes with the utilization of copper, another essential mineral, and, in higher plants, excessive zinc can lead to a disorder that is known as iron chlorosis. Proper nutrient growth media for microorganisms and plants or diets for animals, therefore, require not only that the essential mineral elements be provided in sufficient amounts but also that they be used in the proper ratios to each other.

Organic Nutrients

The organic nutrients are the necessary building blocks of various cell components that certain organisms cannot synthesize and therefore must obtain preformed. These compounds include carbohydrates, protein, and lipids. Other organic nutrients include the vitamins, which are required in small amounts, because of either the catalytic role or the regulatory role they play in metabolism.

Proteins

The main organic material in the working tissue of both plants and animals is protein, large molecules containing chains of condensed units of some 20 different amino acids. In animals, protein food is digested to free amino acids before entering the bloodstream. Plants can synthesize their own amino acids, which are required for protein production, provided they have a source of nitrate or other simple nitrogenous compounds and sulfur, needed for the synthesis of cysteine and methionine. Animals can also synthesize some amino acids from ammonium ions and carbohydrate metabolites; however, others cannot be synthesized and are therefore dietary essentials. Two amino acids, cysteine and tyrosine, can be synthesized only by metabolism of the essential amino acids methionine and phenylalanine, respectively. Bacteria living in the rumen of ruminant animals can synthesize all the amino acids commonly present in protein, and the true stomach of the ruminant will continue to receive microbial protein of reasonably good quality for digestion.

Animals need protein to grow. This requirement is roughly proportional to the growth rate and is reflected in the protein content of the milk secreted during the suckling period. For example, a piglet doubles its birth weight in 18 days, and sow's milk has protein at a level supplying 25 percent of the total energy. In contrast, humans take approximately 180 days to double their birth weight, and breast milk contains protein at a level equivalent to only about 8 percent of the total energy. Young animals fed experimental diets completely lacking one essential amino acid all exhibit an immediate cessation of growth.

Adults, too, require protein in fairly large amounts, more than would be needed to replace the small amount of protein lost by the body through urine, feces, and shed hair and skin. It is true that animal tissues are continually 'turning over' their proteins—*i.e.*, hydrolyzing and re-synthesizing them—but this does not explain the additional protein requirement, since the amino acids released are available for reuse. It appears, however, that the enzymes available to metabolize excess amino acids do not inactivate completely when the body is short of protein but instead remain at an 'idling' rate. Normally, this is not a disadvantage, since the diets of adult animals, including humans, contain more protein than is required to balance the idling losses. It also appears that, in the course of evolution, the idling rates have become roughly adjusted to the normal protein intake. Thus, adult rodents living on a range of foods—some quite low in protein—need no more than 5 percent of their energy in the form of protein. In contrast, cats, whose ancestral carnivorous diet was much higher in protein, need some 20 percent in their diet to balance minimal losses.

INTERDEPENDENCY OF NUTRITIONAL REQUIREMENTS

The effects of one mineral nutrient in reducing or increasing the requirement for another have been mentioned previously. Similar relationships occur among organic nutrients and originate for several reasons.

Competition for Sites of Absorption by the Cell

Since absorption of nutrients frequently occurs by way of active transport within cell membranes, an excess of one nutrient (A) may inhibit absorption of a second nutrient (B), if they share the same absorption pathway. In such cases, the apparent requirement for nutrient B increases; B, however, can sometimes be supplied in an alternate form that is able to enter the cell by a different route. Many examples of amino acid antagonism, in which inhibition of growth by one amino acid is counteracted by another amino acid, are best explained by this mechanism. For example, under some conditions *Lactobacillus casei* requires both D- and L-alanine, which differ from each other only in the position of the amino, or NH_2, group in the molecule, and the two forms of this amino acid share the same absorption pathway. Excess D-alanine inhibits growth of this species, but the inhibition can be alleviated either by supplying additional L-alanine or, more effectively, by supplying peptides of L-alanine. The peptides enter the cell by a pathway different from that of the two forms of alanine and, after they are in the cell, can be broken down to form L-alanine. Relationships of this type provide one explanation for the fact that peptides are frequently more effective than amino acids in promoting growth of bacteria.

Competition for Sites of Utilization within the Cell

This phenomenon is similar to that regarding competition for absorption sites, but it occurs inside the cell and only between structurally similar nutrients (*e.g.*, leucine and valine; serine and threonine).

Precursor-product Relationships

The requirement of rats and humans for the essential amino acids phenylalanine and methionine is substantially reduced if tyrosine, which is formed from phenylalanine, or cysteine, which is formed from methionine, is added to the diet. These relationships are explained by the fact that tyrosine and cysteine are synthesized in animals from phenylalanine and methionine, respectively. When the former (product) amino acids are supplied preformed, the latter (precursor) amino acids are required in smaller amounts. Several instances of the sparing of one nutrient by another because they have similar precursor-product relationships have been identified in other organisms.

Changes in Metabolic Pathways within the Cell

Rats fed diets containing large amounts of fat require substantially less thiamin (vitamin B_1) than do those fed diets high in carbohydrate. The utilization of carbohydrate as an energy source (*i.e.*, for ATP formation) is known to involve an important thiamin-dependent step, which is bypassed when fat is used as an energy source, and it is assumed that the lessened requirement for thiamin results from the change in metabolic pathways.

SYNTROPHISM

Since the nutritional requirements and metabolic activities of organisms differ, it is clear that two or more different organisms growing relatedly may produce different overall changes in the environment. A rough example is provided by a balanced aquarium, in which aquatic plants utilize light and the waste products of animals—*e.g.*, carbon dioxide, water, ammonia—to synthesize cell materials and generate oxygen, which in turn provide the materials necessary for animal growth. Such relationships are common among micro-organisms; *i.e.*, intermediate or end products of metabolism of one organism may provide essential nutrients for another. The mixed populations that result in nature provide examples of this phenomenon, which is called syntrophism; in some instances, the relationship may be so close as to constitute nutritional symbiosis, or mutualism. Several examples of this phenomenon have been found among thiamin-requiring yeasts and fungi, certain of which (group A) synthesized the thiazole component of thiamin molecule but require the pyrimidine portion preformed; for a second group (group B), the relationship is reversed. When group A and group B are grown together in a thiamin-free medium, both types of organisms survive, since each organism synthesizes the growth factor required by its partner; neither organism grows alone under these same conditions. Thus, two or more types of microorganisms frequently grow in situations in which only one species would not.

Such nutritional interrelationships may explain the fact that the nutritionally demanding lactic-acid bacteria are able to coexist with the nutritionally nondemanding coliform bacteria in the intestinal tracts of animals. It is known that the bacterial flora of the intestinal tract synthesize sufficient amounts of certain vitamins (*e.g.*, vitamin K, folic acid) so that detection of deficiency symptoms in rats requires special measures, and the role of rumen bacteria in ruminant animals (*e.g.*, cows, sheep) in rendering otherwise indigestible cellulose and other materials available to the host animal is well-known. These few examples indicate that syntrophic interrelationships are widespread in nature and may contribute substantially to the nutrition of a wide variety of species.

NUTRITIONAL EVOLUTION OF ORGANISMS

Little is known about the nutritional evolution of living organisms. Nucleic acids, proteins, carbohydrates, and fats, which are present in all living cells, are formed by specific reaction sequences from a limited number of smaller compounds, most of which are common to all living organisms and, according to current theories, were available on Earth before life arose. Since less complex metabolic organization and less energy are required to synthesize cellular proteins from preformed amino acids than from carbon dioxide and other precursors, it is assumed that the simplest early forms of life were heterotrophic organisms requiring many organic nutrients for growth and that they selected such nutrients from their surroundings. As the supply of these preformed substances was exhausted, the organisms presumably developed the capacity to synthesize these preformed substances from simpler (precursor) materials present in the environment; in some organisms, this synthesizing capacity eventually evolved to the extent that carbon from carbon dioxide could be utilized to synthesize organic compounds.

At this point, autotrophy, as it now is known, became possible; autotrophy, in fact, may have evolved as a result of the exhaustion of the supply of preformed organic materials in the environment and the consequent necessity of organisms to synthesize the requirements themselves in order to survive. Implicit in this theory is the demonstrable assumption that autotrophic cells contain the most complex biosynthetic organization found in living things and that heterotrophic cells are simpler in that certain biosynthetic pathways do not occur. After the evolution of photosynthesis, a constantly renewable source of the organic compounds necessary for heterotrophic cell growth became available. It became feasible that those organisms whose environments provided a constantly available supply of a given compound could lose, through changes in their genetic material (mutations), the ability to synthesize that compound and still survive. Entire biosynthetic pathways may have been lost in this way; as long as such mutant organisms remained in an environment that supplied the necessary compound, the simplification in cellular organization and the energy saved by using preformed cell components would have given them a competitive advantage over the more complex parents from which they were derived and permitted stabilization of the mutation within the cell type. A theory that the requirements of modern organisms for essential organic nutrients arose through the loss of synthetic abilities present in more complex parent organisms was confirmed by the discovery that artificially produced mutant offspring of microorganisms can be readily obtained and may require the presence of one or more preformed organic compounds that the parent microorganisms could synthesize.

3

The Vegetative Shoot: Stems, Leaves and Buds

SHOOT APICAL MERISTEMS

Shoot apical meristems are minute yet complex structures that are ensheathed within new developing leaves or bracts. A vegetative meristem gives rise to leaves or other organs, for example thorns, tendrils, axillary buds and internodes. Axillary buds are themselves complete shoot meristems from which branches are produced. In angiosperms, when a plant shifts from vegetative to reproductive growth some meristems undergo a transition to the reproductive state and give rise either to multiple flowers in an inflorescence, as in mango, or to a single terminal flower, for example a poppy or waterlily.

All axial growth from meristems, be they vegetative or floral, is continuous or indeterminate until topped by the formation of a flower. When this occurs, floral organ primordia arise in whorls from the shoot meristem and differentiate into the familiar sepals, petals, stamens and carpels. Sometimes, however, the indeterminate inflorescence meristem reverts back instead to a vegetative status. Think of a bottlebrush or a pineapple with a leafy axis extending beyond the flower or fruit. What determines whether a meristem is vegetative or floral? In many species, environmental signals cause the switching between vegetative and floral states and a picture is now emerging of the genes and molecular mechanisms responsible for dening structures that are generated by meristems.

Although meristems function as generic sources of cells for differentiation into organs, each type of meristem is programmed to produce only certain structures. Across all species, there is a small, nite range of these structures, yet we observe an amazingly diverse array of nal vegetative and floral morphologies. A leaf is always recognisable as a leaf but consider the vast structural differences between a pine needle, a waterlily pad and a tree fern frond. The generation and spatial patterning of plant organs are determined by early events within the vegetative meristem. This precise positioning of organs around the shoot meristem is called phyllotaxis. Later in development, a dramatic meristematic switch will give rise to a terminal inflorescence, often with an abrupt change in patterning of organs. Phyllotaxis also applies to floral structures, for example spiral patterns of scales of a pine cone or flowers of *Grevillea*, or vertical rows on a *Banksia* inflorescence. Organ spacing is a nal determinant of shoot appearance. For example, leaves forming a rosette as in *Arabidopsis* are separated by short internodes compared with longer internodes intervening between whorls of leaves of a blue gum seedling. The resulting morphologies are strikingly different.

⊠⊠⊠⊠⊠⊠⊠⊠⊠⊠⊠⊠⊠⊠⊠⊠⊠⊠⊠⊠⊠⊠

Shoot meristems are small, with a dome typically of 100–300 μm in diameter consisting of no more than a few hundred cells. In the 1970s, Williams published elegant reconstructions of shoot meristems derived from serial sections which revealed the extent of variability in the shape and dimensions of shoot apices. However, the overriding organisation is of a central dome with groups of cells partitioned off from its periphery to form either determinate organ primordia or secondary meristems (axillary buds). Some cells in between are not destined to become primordia and will instead later become the internodes of the axis. Different models have been proposed to describe the regions of shoot meristems. In a functional sense, vegetative meristems have three main components: the central zone, peripheral zone and the le meristem zone, all of which tend to disappear or become indistinct in infloresence meristems.

Table. 3.1: Different Cell Layers within the shoot Apical Meristem Contribute to Different Argans and Tissue Layers.

Cell	Layer Tissue
1.1	Epidermis of shoot organs, stem, leaves
1.2	Mesophyll cells of leaf
1.3	Vascular tissue of leaf and sterm Pith and cortex of sterm.

Superimposed on this functional zonation are usually three distinct cell layers which give rise to separate cell lineages. These cell layers, designated L1, L2 and L3, are distinguishable by their positions in the meristem and their pattern of cell divisions, and are evident in both vegetative and reproductive meristems.

Surface cells of L1 divide anticlinally while within the meristem and during sub-sequent differentiation of the organs. Not surprisingly, they form the epidermis. Within the apical dome, the plane of cell division within L2 is also purely anticlinal, but later on during organ formation divisions occur in other planes. In contrast, cells of the deepest layer, L3, divide in all planes. The two inner layers, L2 and L3, contribute cells to form the body of the plant with the proportion of cells derived from each layer varying in different organ types. Although the cell lineages produced by each layer usually contribute to distinct regions within each organ, invasion of cell derivatives of one layer into another has been observed.

Invading cells differentiate in accordance with their new position, which we interpret to mean that developmental fate of cells appears to be governed more by position than by cell lineage. However, meristematic cells may already be functionally distinct as evidenced by patterns of gene expression which reflect the layered cellular organisation.

In order to maintain the very precise organisation of vegetative meristems over long periods, or to accommodate rapid changes during flower formation, some signalling process must exist to coordinate division between the cell layers. Evidence for such signalling has been established through the development of chimeras, where genetically different cell types exist together in a single apex, yet still achieve normal developmental patterns.

Phyllotaxis and Internode Length

We previously raised the question of what determines phyllotaxis and internode length. Organs derived from the shoot meristem can arise in whorls (two or more organs simultaneously at one node), alternately (two less displaced by 180° with a single organ at each node) or in spirals (each organ displaced from the previous one by approximately 137° with a single organ at each node). These organs may be separated by very short or long internodes. Phyllotaxis patterns are usually stable, but often change abruptly with floral induction or when seedlings undergo transition to their mature morphology. In many species of *Eucalyptus*, this 'phase change' from juvenile to adult is very striking and is accompanied by a change from whorled to alternate or spiral phyllotaxis. How is the change in phyllotaxis effected? We gain some insight from experiments on chrysanthemum meristems where application of the inhibitor of polar auxin transport TIBA induced changes in inter-node length and displacement angle between leaf primordia.

The data are consistent with a change from 137° spiral (control) to alternate (50 ppm TIBA) phyllotaxis and are presumed to result from increased concentrations of auxin in the meristem resulting from inhibition of transport away from the existing primordia. Meristems are deduced to be sites of auxin synthesis. One interpretation is that each primordium acts as a eld with a dened radius of inhibition preventing other primordia from initiating too close to it. Another option is mechanical control by pressure and tension gradients within the meristem. Supporting evidence comes from experiments on cells in tissue culture in which applied pressure altered their morphogenetic patterns. At a whole-plant scale, tension and compression wood in trees are further examples of specic developmental responses to physical forces.

Determination of Shoot Meristem and Organ identity

Genes Controlling Meristem Identity

What determines whether a meristem is vegetative or reproductive has long been a vexing question. Now, by using molecular technology and studying the transition of meristems from vegetative to reproductive in species amenable to analysis of single gene mutations, for example *Arabidopsis* and *Antirrhinum,* some of the mystery is being unravelled. Considering the obvious morphological and functional differences between a vegetative shoot and an inflorescence, we can reasonably assume that a number of genes will be expressed sequentially during determination of first the inflorescence, second the flowers and finally the sets of floral organs. Identification of at least six groups of genes in *Arabidopsis* has confirmed that this is indeed so.

Three groups are involved in establishing the identity of organs of the flower. Expression of the other genes influences identity of the meristem as an indeterminate structure. Two genes, *Leafy* (*Lfy*) and *Apetala 1* (*Ap1*) in *Arabidopsis* and *floricaula* (*Flo*) and *Squamosa* (*Squa*) in *Antirrhinum,* have been shown, by *in situ* hybridisation of their RNA to thin slices of the meristem, to be expressed in bract and floral bud tissue in inflorescences. If these genes are not expressed, inflorescence development is incomplete with some primordia remaining vegetative and some becoming partially floral. These genes do not appear to be expressed in the apical dome, which is consistent with the inflorescence initially remaining indeterminate. This pattern of gene expression has been shown to depend upon the expression of a third gene, *Terminal flower* (*Tfl*) in *Arabidopsis* and *Centroradialis* (*Cen*) in *Antirrhinum*. In *tfl* or *cen* mutant plants, a terminal flower develops and prevents further growth of the inflorescence. The story is complex and incomplete. Although different names have been assigned to the genes identified for each genus studied, a common and elegant pattern of gene regulation during transition to a reproductive meristem is emerging.

Organ Determination

Table. 3.2: Determination in Primordia of the fern Osmunda. Leaf Primordia from the Youngest (P1) to those 10 Plastochrons older (P10) were Excised and cultured on agar. The younger Primordia can Develop Instead as shoot, but as Primordia grow older, Determination as leaves, not Shoots becomes more and more fixed.

	Percentage of Primordia Developing as		
Primordia	**Leaves**	**Shoots**	**Doubtful or no Growth**
P1	10	35	55
P2	10	60	30
P3	20	50	30
P4	20	55	25
P5	40	55	5
P6	60	40	0
P7	80	20	0
P8	89	5	5
P9	95	0	5
P10	100	0	0

Studies of gene regulation during the transition from vegetative to reproductive meristems have established that differential expression of suites of genes in specic regions of the meristem is responsible for the organ identity of each primordium derived from the periphery of the inflorescence or floral meristem. The determination of primordia derived from the vegetative meristem, for example as leaves, thorns or lateral axes, will also be regulated through gene expression, but the identity of the genes involved is unknown. However, information about the timing of determination of leaves has been obtained by excising primordia from the shoot meristem and culturing them on agar. Data for fern primordia indicate that young primordia (P1–6) remain undetermined and can differentiate into either leaves or shoots (lateral axes), but as primordia grow older, determination as leaves becomes more fixed. In fern meristems, time between appearance of successive primordia may be several days, so determination appears to be a surprisingly protracted process. However, similar experiments on angio-sperm shoot meristems (*e.g.* tobacco) demonstrate that determination occurs much earlier, at P1–2. Clearly, much remains to be discovered about the timing of these processes and of the nature of communication between cells that allows coordinated formation of organs.

Genes that Define Primordium Identity

Whorl Number

Activity		1	2	3	4
	A				
	B				
	C				

Wild Type

Whorl Identity	1	2	3	4
Speal	A			
Petal		A + B		
Stamen			B + C	
Carpel				C

'B Function' Mutant (e.g. Apetala 3):

Whorl Identity	1	2	3	4
Sepal	A			
Sepal		A		
Carpel			C	
Carpel				C

Several Homologous Homoeotic gens have been Discovered in Arabidopsis and Antirrhimum. More than one gens is involved with at Least the A and B Functions.

Gene Type	Arabidopsis Mutants	Antirrhinum Mutant Equivalents
A	Apctala 1*, Apctala 2	Squamosa*, –
B	Apctala3*, Pistillata*	Deficiens*, Globosa*
C	Agamous*	Plena*

*Gene with Homology to MADS box Class.

Figure 3.1: A Model of how three Gene Activities (A, B, C) in Successive Whorls of Floral Primordia can Specify Organ Identity. Each Gene Class is Expressed in Two Adjacent Whorls. This Model was Originally Developed from Studies on Homoeotic Mutants of *Arabidopsis* and *Antirrhinum*; Similar Mutants have Subsequently been Found in many other Species such as Maize, Tomato and Tobacco.

Since the late 1980s we have seen major advances in our understanding of the molecular genetics of control of flower development, and this includes several mutants with altered organ identity in *Arabidopsis* and snapdragon (*Antirrhinum*). These mutants are termed homoeotic because normal organs may develop in abnormal positions. The simplest transformations are (1) sepals to carpels and petals to stamens, (2) petals to sepals and stamens to carpels, and (3) stamens to petals and carpels to sepals.

On this basis, it appears that wild-type floral development depends on the activities of three gene classes (A, B and C) with each function being active in two adjacent whorls. This means that A is active in sepal and petal whorls, B is active in petals and stamens, and C is active in stamens and carpels. Activity of A alone leads to sepals, activity of A and B together lead to petals, B and C together lead to stamens, and activity of C alone leads to carpels. Activity of A is also involved earlier, during meristem identity determination before any organ determination has occurred. More than one gene is involved with each of the three functions so we have yet to comprehend fully aspects of this model, such as gene hierarchy and overlap of functions.

VEGETATIVE REPRODUCTION

Vegetative reproduction (vegetative propagation, vegetative multiplication, vegetative cloning) is a form of asexual reproduction in plants. It is a process by which new individuals arise without production of seeds or spores. It can occur naturally or be induced by horticulturists.

Although most plants normally reproduce sexually, many have the ability for vegetative propagation, or can be vegetatively propagated if small pieces are subjected to chemical (hormonal) treatments. This is because meristematic cells capable of cellular differentiation are present in many plant tissues. Horticulturalists are interested in understanding how meristematic cells can be induced to reproduce an entire plant.

Success rates and difficulty of propagation vary greatly. For example willow and coleus can be propagated merely by inserting a stem in water or moist soil. On the other hand, monocotyledons, unlike dicotyledons, typically lack a vascular cambium and therefore are harder to propagate.

TYPES

In a wide sense, methods of vegetative propagation include cutting, vegetative apomixis, layering, division, budding, grafting and tissue culture. Cutting is the most common artificial vegetative propagation method, where pieces of the 'parent' plant are removed and placed in a suitable environment so that they can grow into a whole new plant, the 'clone', which is genetically identical to the parent. Cutting exploits the ability of plants to grow adventitious roots (*i.e.* root material that can generate from a location other than the existing or primary root system, as in from a leaf or cut stem) under certain conditions.

Vegetative propagation is usually considered a cloning method. However, there are several cases where vegetatively propagated plants are not genetically identical. Root cuttings of thornless blackberries will revert to thorny type because the adventitious shoot develops from a cell that is genetically thorny. Thornless blackberry is a chimera, with the epidermal layers genetically thornless but the tissue beneath it genetically thorny. Similarly, leaf cutting propagation of certain chimeral variegated plants, such as snake plant (*Sansevieria trifasciata*), will produce mainly nonvariegated plants. Grafting is often not a complete cloning method because sexual seedlings are used as rootstocks. In that case only the top of the plant is clonal. In some crops, particularly apples, the rootstocks are vegetatively propagated so the entire graft can be clonal if the scion and rootstock are both clones.

Apomixis (including apospory and diplospory) is a type of reproduction that does not involve fertilisation. In flowering plants, unfertilized seeds are involved, or plantlets that grow instead of flowers. Hawkweed (*Hieracium*), dandelion (*Taraxacum*), some citrus (*Citrus*) and Kentucky blue grass (*Poa pratensis*) all use this form of asexual reproduction. Bulbils are sometimes formed instead of the flowers of garlic. These cases would not be vegetative reproduction because normally reproductive parts were involved. They would be considered asexual reproduction however. Vegetative reproduction involves only vegetative structures, *i.e.* roots, stems or leaves.

In spore-bearing plants, apospory is the asexual development of 2n gametophytes from sporophytes without undergoing meiosis or spore formation.

VEGETATIVE STRUCTURES

Virtually all types of shoots and roots are capable of vegetative propagation, including stems, basal shoots, tubers, rhizomes, stolons, corms, bulbs, and buds. In a few species (such as *Kalanchoë*), leaves are involved in vegetative reproduction.

- The rhizome is a modified underground stem serving as an organ of vegetative reproduction, *e.g.* *Polypodium* (polypody), Iris, Couch Grass and Nettles.
- Prostrate aerial stems, called runners or stolons are important vegetative reproduction organs in some species, such as the strawberry, numerous grasses, and some ferns.
- Adventitious buds form on roots near the ground surface, on damaged stems (as on the stumps of cut trees), or on old roots. These develop into above-ground stems and leaves.
- A form of budding called suckering is the reproduction or regeneration of a plant by shoots that arise from an existing root system. Species that characteristically produce suckers include Elm (*Ulmus*), Dandelion (*Taraxacum*), and members of the Rose Family (*Rosa*).
- Another type of a vegetative reproduction is the production of bulbs. Plants like onion (*Allium cepa*), hyacinth (*Hyacinth*), narcissus (*Narcissus*) and tulips (*Tulipa*) reproduce by forming bulbs.
- Other plants like potatoes (*Solanum tuberosum*) and dahlia (*Dahlia*) reproduce by a method similar to bulbs: they produce tubers.

- Gladioli and crocuses (*Crocus*) reproduce by forming a bulb-like structure called a corm.
- Some orchids reproduce by the growth of keikis from the stem or cane of the parent plant.

NATURAL VEGETATIVE PROPAGATION

Natural vegetative reproduction is mostly a process found in herbaceous and woody perennial plants, and typically involves structural modifications of the stem, although any horizontal, underground part of a plant (whether stem, leaf, or root) can contribute to vegetative reproduction of a plant. Most plant species that survive and significantly expand by vegetative reproduction would be perennial almost by definition, since specialized organs of vegetative reproduction, like seeds of annuals, serve to survive seasonally harsh conditions. A plant that persists in a location through vegetative reproduction of individuals over a long period of time constitutes a clonal colony.

In a sense, this process is not one of 'reproduction' but one of survival and expansion of biomass of the individual. When an individual organism increases in size via cell multiplication and remains intact, the process is called 'vegetative growth'. However, in vegetative reproduction, the new plants that result are new individuals in almost every respect except genetic. Of considerable interest is how this process appears to reset the aging clock.

Artificial Vegetative Propagation

It is very common practice to vegetatively propagate cultivars that have desirable characteristics. Man-made methods of vegetative reproduction are usually enhancements of natural processes, but range from rooting cuttings to grafting and artificial propagation by laboratory tissue culture. In horticulture, a 'cutting' is a piece that has been cut off from a mother plant and then caused to grow into a whole plant. Often this involves a piece of stem that is treated with rooting liquid or powder containing hormones. In some species root cuttings can produce shoot growth. When the cutting has become a self-sufficient plant, it is genetically identical to the mother plant. A related form of regeneration is that of grafting. A stem piece or a single bud (the scion) is joined onto the stem of a plant that has roots (the rootstock), or a stem piece can be joined to a root piece. A popular use of grafting is to produce fruit trees, sometimes with more than one variety of the same fruit species growing from the same stem. Rootstocks for fruit trees are either seedlings or propagated by layering.

Cultivated Plants Propagated by Vegetative Methods

A number of commonly cultivated plants are usually propagated by vegetative means rather than by seeds.

This is a listing of such plants:

- African violets—leaf cuttings.
- Apple—grafting.
- Avocado—grafting.
- Banana—sucker removal blackberries (*Rubus occidentalis*)—stem cuttings.
- Peach—grafting.
- Canna—division.
- Cannabis—stem cuttings.
- Citrus (lemon, orange, grapefruit, Tangerine)—grafting.
- Date—sucker removal.
- Fig—stem cuttings.
- Grapes—stem cuttings, grafting.
- Hops—stem cuttings
- Manioc (cassava)—stem cuttings.
- Maple—stem cuttings, grafting.
- Nut crops (walnut, pecan)—grafting.
- Pineapple—stem cuttings.
- Pear—grafting.
- Plum—stem cuttings.
- Poplar—stem cuttings.
- Potato—stem (tuber) cuttings.
- Garden strawberry—runners (stolons).
- Sugar cane—stem cuttings
- Tea—stem cuttings.

- Vanilla—stem cuttings.
- Verbena—stem cuttings.
- Willow—stem cuttings.

VEGETATIVE PROPAGATION

Regeneration of new plants from the vegetative parts of the parent plant is called vegetative propagation or vegetative reproduction. Vegetative propagation is done with the help of vegetative parts such as roots, stem or leaves. These parts may also be variously modified for vegetative propagation.

Natural vegetative propagation is of different types based on the vegetative organ involved.

VEGETATIVE PROPAGATION BY ROOTS

Roots of some plants develop new plants either by directly producing shoots or producing buds. Shoots are produced by roots of woody plants like Dalbergia, Murraya etc. Adventitious buds are formed on the roots of plants like sweet potato, dahlia, asparagus, tapioca, etc. These buds detach from the root and develop into new plants.

VEGETATIVE PROPAGATION BY STEM

Root Tubers of Dahlia

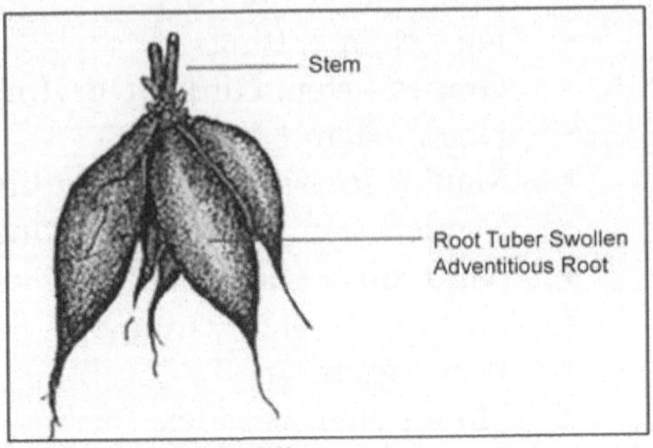

Root Tubers of Dahlia

Stem has nodes and internodes. The nodes develop leaves. In the axils of the leaves buds develop called the axillary buds. They develop into new plants on detachment from the parent plant or even when the stem portion remains attached. There are different types of stems for vegetative propagation. They are:

Subaerial Stems

The branches that arise from the stem which is very close to the surface of the ground break off from the parent plant and develop new plants.

These branches are classified as follows:

Runners-For example, strawberry, grass, etc.

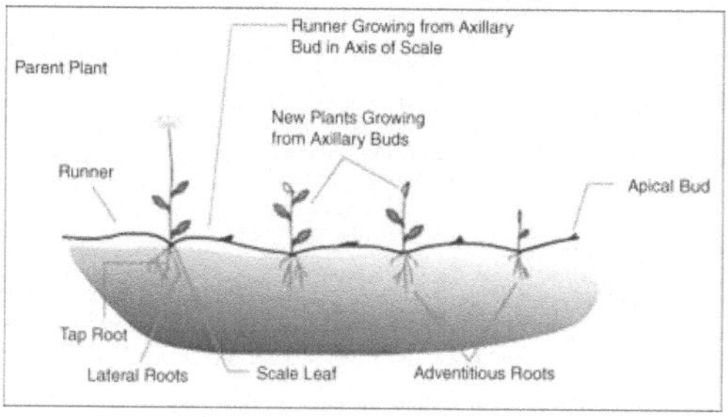

Strawberry Runner

Suckers - For example, mint, Chrysanthemum

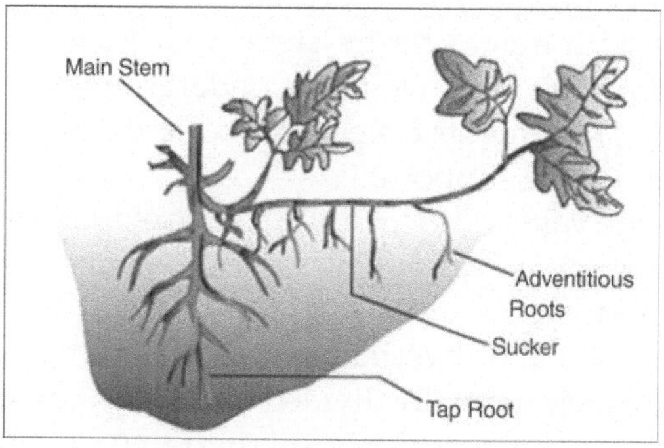

Vegetative Propagation by a Sucker of Chrysanthemum

Stolon-For example, gooseberry, jasmine, etc.

Offset-For example, Eichhornia (water hyacinth), Pistia, etc.

STEMS

The stem is a part of the plant that holds up other structures such as the leaves and flowers. This is important as the leaves need to be held up to the sun to get its light for photosynthesis and the flowers need to be held up to be available for pollination.

Stems also carry water and minerals up from the roots to the leaves to help with photosynthesis and take food back down to be stored and distributed to the plant as it has need. The tubes in the stem that take the water and minerals up into the plant are the xylem and the tubes that carry the food back down are called the phloem.

Stems can be of several sorts, herbaceous and woody. The herbaceous stems are green and fairly bendable. The woody stems as their name implies, are covered by bark. The herbaceous stem has more pith for its size. The cambium which causes woody stems to get bigger in width is not as active in the herbaceous stems.

Most herbaceous plants are annuals or planted yearly. The herbaceous stem has little notches where leaves develop. Woody stems have scars where twigs and fruit have dropped off and little openings for transpiration.

There are different sorts of aerial stems or stems that are upright. They include tendrils, runners and thorns. Succulents are plants with bigger fleshy stems that help plants retain water in dry areas. Some stems are underground such as bulbs and tubers. There are also stems that cannot hold themselves up, but need to be supported.

Stems are valuable to man as a source of food and its wood is used for many products. The sap from many stems is used for resins and latexes.

A stem is one of two main structural axes of a vascular plant. The stem is normally divided into nodes and internodes, the nodes hold buds which grow into one or more leaves, inflorescence (flowers), conifer cones, roots, other stems etc. The internodes distance one node from another. The term shoots is often confused with stems; shoots generally refer to new fresh plant growth and does include stems but also to other structures like leaves or flowers.

The other main structural axis of plants is the root. In most plants stems are located above the soil surface but some plants have underground stems. A stem develops buds and shoots and usually grows above the ground. Inside the stem, materials move up and down the tissues of the transport system.

Stems have four main functions which are:

- Support for and the elevation of leaves, flowers and fruits. The stems keep the leaves in the light and provide a place for the plant to keep its flowers and fruits.
- Transport of fluids between the roots and the shoots in the xylem and phloem.
- Storage of nutrients.
- The production of new living tissue. The normal life span of plant cells is one to three years. Stems have cells called meristems that annually generate new living tissue.

Specialized Terms for Stems

Stems are often specialized for storage, asexual reproduction, protection or photosynthesis, including the following:

- Acaulescent—used to describe stems in plants that appear to be stemless. Actually these stems are just extremely short, the leaves appearing to rise directly out of the ground, *e.g.* some *Viola* species.
- Arborescent—tree like with woody stems normally with a single trunk.
- Bud—an embryonic shoot with immature stem tip.
- Bulb—a short vertical underground stem with fleshy storage leaves attached, *e.g.* onion, daffodil, tulip. Bulbs often function in reproduction by splitting to form new bulbs or producing small new bulbs termed bulblets. Bulbs are a combination of stem and leaves so may better be considered as leaves because the leaves make up the greater part.
- Caespitose—when stems grow in a tangled mass or clump or in low growing mats.
- Cladode (including phylloclade)—a flattened stem that appears more-or-less leaf like and is specialized for photosynthesis, *e.g.* cactus pads.
- Climbing—stems that cling or wrap around other plants or structures.

- Corm—a short enlarged underground, storage stem, *e.g.* taro, crocus, gladiolus.
- Decumbent—stems that lie flat on the ground and turn upwards at the ends.
- Fruticose—stems that grow shrublike with woody like habit.
- Herbaceous—non woody, they die at the end of the growing season.
- Prickle—a sharpened extension of the stem's outer layers, *e.g.* roses.
- Pseudostem—a false stem made of the rolled bases of leaves, which may be 2 or 3 m tall as in banana
- Rhizome—-a horizontal underground stem that functions mainly in reproduction but also in storage, *e.g.* most ferns, iris
- Runner (plant part)—a type of stolon, horizontally growing on top of the ground and rooting at the nodes, aids in reproduction. *e.g.* garden strawberry, *Chlorophytum comosum.*
- Scape—a stem that holds flowers that comes out of the ground and has no normal leaves. Hosta, Lily, Iris, Garlic.
- Stolon—a horizontal stem that produces rooted plantlets at its nodes and ends, forming near the surface of the ground.
- Thorn—a modified stem with a sharpened point.
- Tree—a woody stem that is longer than 5 metres with a main trunk.
- Tuber—a swollen, underground storage stem adapted for storage and reproduction, *e.g.* potato.
- Woody—hard textured stems with secondary xylem.

STEM STRUCTURE

Stem usually consist of three tissues, dermal tissue, ground tissue and vascular tissue. The dermal tissue covers the outer surface of the stem and usually functions to waterproof, protect and control gas exchange. The ground tissue usually consists mainly of parenchyma cells and fills in around the vascular tissue. It sometimes functions in photosynthesis. Vascular tissue provides long distance transport and structural support. Most or all ground tissue may be lost in woody stems. The dermal tissue of aquatic plants stems may lack the waterproofing found in aerial stems. The arrangement of the vascular tissues varies widely among plant species.

Dicot Stems

Dicot stem with primary growth have pith in the centre, with vascular bundles forming a distinct ring visible when the stem is viewed in cross section. The outside of the stem is covered with an epidermis, which is covered by a waterproof cuticle. The epidermis also may contain stomata for gas exchange and multicellular stem hairs. A cortex consisting of Hypodermis (collenchyma cells) and Endodermis (starch containing cells) is present above the pericycle and vascular bundles.

Woody dicots and many nonwoody dicots have secondary growth originating from their lateral or secondary meristems: the vascular cambium and the cork cambium or phellogen. The vascular cambium forms between the xylem and phloem in the vascular bundles and connects to form a continuous cylinder. The vascular cambium cells divide to produce secondary xylem to the inside and secondary phloem to the outside. As the stem increases in diameter due to production of secondary xylem and secondary phloem, the cortex and epidermis are eventually destroyed. Before the cortex is destroyed, a cork cambium develops there. The cork cambium divides to produce waterproof cork cells externally and sometimes phelloderm cells internally. Those three tissues form the periderm, which replaces the epidermis in function. Areas of loosely packed cells in the periderm that function in gas exchange are called lenticels.

Secondary xylem is commercially important as wood. The seasonal variation in growth from the vascular cambium is what creates yearly tree rings in temperate climates. Tree rings are the basis of dendrochronology, which dates wooden objects and associated artifacts. Dendroclimatology is the use of tree rings as a record of past climates. The aerial stem of an adult tree is called a trunk. The dead, usually darker inner wood of a large diameter trunk is termed the heartwood and is the result of tylosis. The outer, living wood is termed the sapwood.

Monocot Stems

Stems of Two *Roystonea regia* Palms Showing Characteristic Bulge, Leaf Scars and Fibrous Roots, Kolkata, India

Vascular bundles are present throughout the monocot stem, although concentrated towards the outside. This differs from the dicot stem that has a ring of vascular bundles and often none in the centre. The shoot apex in monocot stems is more elongated. Leaf sheathes grow up around it, protecting it. This is true to some extent of almost all monocots. Monocots rarely produce secondary growth and are therefore seldom woody, with Palms and Bamboo being notable exceptions. However, many monocot stems increase in diameter via anomalous secondary growth.

Gymnosperm Stems

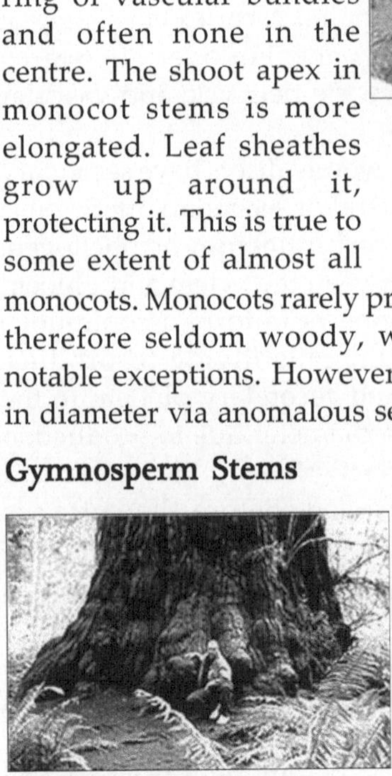

The Trunk of this Redwood Tree is its Stem.

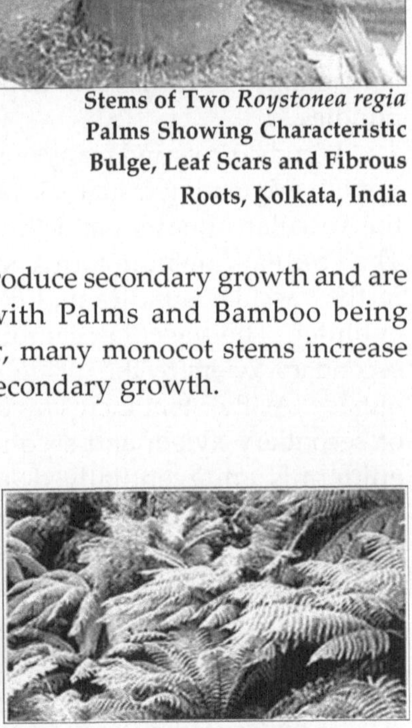

Tasmanian tree fern

All gymnosperms are woody plants. Their stems are similar in structure to woody dicots except that most gymnosperms produce only tracheids in their xylem, not the vessels found in dicots. Gymnosperm wood also often contains resin ducts. Woody dicots are called hardwoods, *e.g.* oak, maple and walnut. In contrast, softwoods are gymnosperms, such as pine, spruce and fir.

Fern Stems

Most ferns have rhizomes with no vertical stem. The exception is tree ferns, with vertical stems up to about 20 meters. The stem anatomy of ferns is more complicated than that of dicots because fern stems often have one or more leaf gaps in cross section. A leaf gap is where the vascular tissue branches off to a frond. In cross section, the vascular tissue does not form a complete cylinder where a leaf gap occurs. Fern stems may have solenosteles or dictyosteles or variations of them. Many fern stems have phloem tissue on both sides of the xylem in cross-section..

RELATION TO XENOBIOTICS

Foreign chemicals such as air pollutants, herbicides and pesticides can damage stem structures. In the case of herbicides many chemicals act by surficial effects, and other agents cause damage through uptake of the chemical herbicide, which is typically a complex organic chemical.

ECONOMIC IMPORTANCE

There are thousands of species whose stems have economic uses. Stems provide a few major staple crops such as potato and taro. Sugarcane stems are a major source of sugar. Maple sugar is obtained from trunks of maple trees. Vegetables from stems are asparagus, bamboo shoots, cactus pads or nopalitos, kohlrabi, and water chestnut. The spice, cinnamon is bark from a tree trunk. Cellulose from tree trunks is a food additive in bread, grated Parmesan cheese, and other processed foods. Gum arabic is an important food additive obtained from the trunks of *Acacia senegal* trees. Chicle, the main ingredient in chewing gum, is obtained from trunks of the chicle tree.

Medicines obtained from stems include quinine from the bark of cinchona trees, camphor distilled from wood of a tree in the same genus that provides cinnamon, and the muscle relaxant curare from the bark of tropical vines. Wood is used in thousands of ways, *e.g.* buildings, furniture, boats, airplanes, wagons, car parts, musical instruments, sports equipment, railroad ties, utility poles, fence posts, pilings, toothpicks, matches, plywood, coffins, shingles, barrel staves, toys, tool handles, picture frames, veneer, charcoal and firewood.

Wood pulp is widely used to make paper, paperboard, cellulose sponges, cellophane and some important plastics and textiles, such as cellulose acetate and rayon. Bamboo stems also have hundreds of uses, including paper, buildings, furniture, boats, musical instruments, fishing poles, water pipes, plant stakes, and scaffolding. Trunks of palm trees and tree ferns are often used for building. Reed stems are also important building materials in some areas. Tannins used for tanning leather are obtained from the wood of certain trees, such as quebracho. Cork is obtained from the bark of the cork oak. Rubber is obtained from the trunks of *Hevea brasiliensis*. Rattan, used for furniture and baskets, is made from the stems of tropical vining palms.

Bast fibres for textiles and rope are obtained from stems include flax, hemp, jute and ramie. The earliest paper was obtained from the stems of papyrus by the ancient Egyptians.

Amber is fossilized sap from tree trunks; it is used for jewellery and may contain ancient animals. Resins from conifer wood are used to produce turpentine and rosin. Tree bark is often used as a mulch and in growing media for container plants. It also can become the natural habitat of lichens.

Some ornamental plants are grown mainly for their attractive stems, e.g.:

- White bark of paper birch.
- Twisted branches of corkscrew willow and Harry Lauder's walking stick (*Corylus avellana* 'Contorta').
- Red, peeling bark of paperbark maple.

LEAVES

The leaf is a part of the plant that is charge of making food for the plant. This food making process is called photosynthesis.

Parts of the Leaf

The leaf consists of the following parts:

Petiole : A thin stalk that connects the blad of the leaf to the plant's stem. These veins are called

Blade : A thin, flat part of the leaf that extends off the end of the petiole. It is green as it contains cholorophyll which is necessary in making the plant's food..

The blade contains veins which help bring in the water necessary for photosynthesis and to transport food out to all parts of the plant. The xylem is responsible for water transportation and the phloem for food.

The blade also has several layers. The top layer is covered with a waterproof coat called the cuticle. Both the upper and lower layer contain paired cells called guard cells. These guard cells manage the stomata, little openings in the leaf that allow for the taking in of carbon dioxide and the emission of oxygen during photosynthesis. Water vapour is also emitted in a process called transpiration.

In between the top and bottom layers of the blade are cells that are full of chlorophyll that is essential for the plant to make its food during photosynthesis.

Leaves come in a variety of shapes, sizes, colour, and textures. Leaves can be grouped as simple with one blade or compound with many leaflets. The edges of leaves can be smooth, have jagged edges referred to as toothed or scalloped edges referred to as lobed edges. Leaves can also be divided into how their veins are arranged. The leaves of plants referred to as monocots have leaves that run parallel to each other off one central vein. Those that are referred to as dicots have leaves with veins that branch out two different ways. Pinnate have one main vein called the midrib, and smaller branching veins. Palmates have several large veins branching from the leaf base into the blade.

Some leaves have special features such as spines and bud scales to protect them. Some are climbing (tendrils). Others catch insects. Some store water. These are called succulents or store food such as bulb scales.

INTERACTIONS WITH OTHER ORGANISMS

Leaf Damaged by Insects with Chewing Mouthparts, Probably Weevils or Katydids.

Dew on a Leaf.

Although not as nutritious as other organs such as fruit, leaves provide a food source for many organisms. Animals that eat leaves are known as folivores. The leaf is a vital source of energy production for the plant, and plants have evolved protection against folivores such as tannins, chemicals which hinder the digestion of proteins and have an unpleasant taste.

Some animals have cryptic adaptations by which they use leaves in avoiding predators. For example, the caterpillars of some leaf-roller moths will create a small home in the leaf by folding it over themselves. Some sawflies similarly roll the leaves of their food plants into tubes. Females of the Attelabidae, so-called leaf-rolling weevils, lay their eggs into leaves that they then roll up as means of protection. Some sawflies Other herbivores and their prey mimic the appearance of the leaf. Reptiles such as some chameleons, and insects such as some katydids, also mimic the oscillating movements of leaves in the wind, moving from side to side or back and forth while evading a possible threat.

BUD

In botany, a bud is an undeveloped or embryonic shoot and normally occurs in the axil of a leaf or at the tip of the stem. Once formed, a bud may remain for some time in a dormant condition, or it may form a shoot immediately. Buds may be specialized to develop flowers or short shoots, or may have the potential for general shoot development. The term bud is also used in zoology, where it refers to an outgrowth from the body which can develop into a new individual.

Bud of *Ficus Carica.*

Flower Buds have not yet Bloomed into a Full-size Flower.

The buds of many woody plants, especially in temperate or cold climates, are protected by a covering of modified leaves called *scales* which tightly enclose the more delicate parts of the bud. Many bud scales are covered by a gummy substance which serves as added protection. When the bud develops, the scales may enlarge somewhat but usually just drop off, leaving on the surface of the growing stem a series of horizontally-elongated scars. By means of these scars one can determine the age of any young branch, since each year's growth ends in the formation of a bud, the formation of which produces an additional group of bud scale scars. Continued growth of the branch causes these scars to be obliterated after a few years so that the total age of older branches cannot be determined by this means.

In many plants scales are not formed over the bud, which is then called a naked bud. The minute underdeveloped leaves in such buds are often excessively hairy. Naked buds are found in some shrubs, like some species of the Sumac and Viburnums (*Viburnum alnifolium* and *V. lantana*) and in herbaceous plants. In many of the latter, buds are even more reduced, often consisting of undifferentiated masses of cells in the axils of leaves. A terminal bud occurs on the end of a stem and lateral buds are found on the side. A head of cabbage is an exceptionally large terminal bud, while Brussels sprouts are large lateral buds.

Since buds are formed in the axils of leaves, their distribution on the stem is the same as that of leaves. There are alternate, opposite, and whorled buds, as well as the terminal bud at the tip of the stem. In many plants buds appear in unexpected places: these are known as adventitious buds.

Often it is possible to find a bud in a remarkable series of gradations of bud scales. In the buckeye, for example, one may see a complete gradation from the small brown outer scale through larger scales which on unfolding become somewhat green to the inner scales of the bud, which are remarkably leaf-like. Such a series suggests that the scales of the bud are in truth leaves, modified to protect the more delicate parts of the plant during unfavourable periods.

TYPES OF BUDS

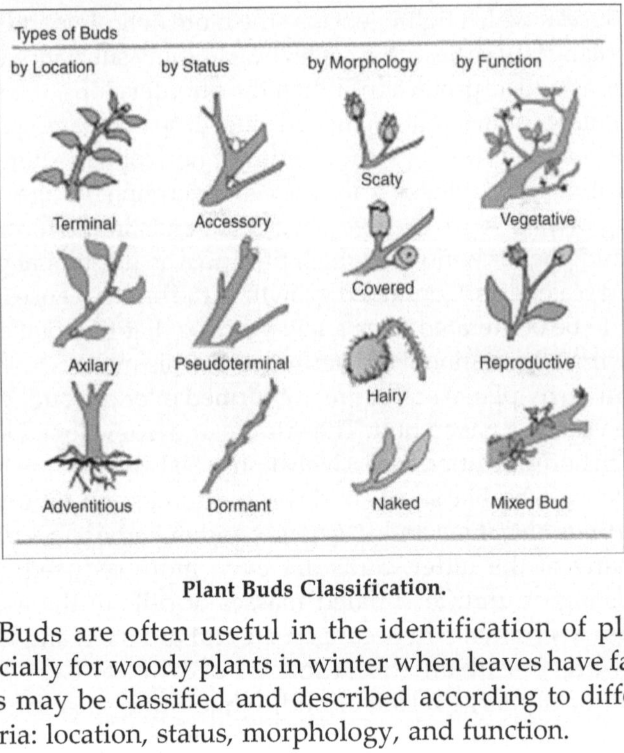

Plant Buds Classification.

Buds are often useful in the identification of plants, especially for woody plants in winter when leaves have fallen. Buds may be classified and described according to different criteria: location, status, morphology, and function.

Botanists commonly use the following terms:

- *For location:*
  - Terminal, when located at the tip of a stem (apical is equivalent but rather reserved for the one at the top of the plant);
  - Axillary, when located in the axil of a leaf (lateral is the equivalent but some adventitious buds may be lateral too);
  - Adventitious, when occurring elsewhere, for example on trunk or on roots (some adventitious buds may be former axillary ones reduced and hidden under the bark, other adventitious buds are completely new formed ones).
- *For status:*
  - Accessory, for secondary buds formed besides a principal bud (axillary or terminal);
  - Resting, for buds that form at the end of a growth season, which will lie dormant until onset of the next growth season;
  - Dormant or latent, for buds whose growth has been delayed for a rather long time. The term is usable as a synonym of *resting,* but is rather employed for buds waiting undeveloped for years, for example epicormic buds;
  - Pseudoterminal, for an axillary bud taking over the function of a terminal bud (characteristic of species whose growth is sympodial: terminal bud dies and is replaced by the closer axillary bud, for examples beech, persimmon, *Platanus* have sympodial growth).
- *For morphology:*
  - Scaly or covered, when scales (which are in fact transformed and reduced leaves) cover and protect the embryonic parts;
  - Naked, when not covered by scales;
  - Hairy, when also protected by hairs (it may apply either to scaly or to naked buds).

- *For function:*
  - Vegetative, if only containing vegetative pieces: embryonic shoot with leaves (a leaf bud is the same);
  - Reproductive, if containing embryonic flower(s) (a flower bud is the same);
  - Mixed, if containing both embryonic leaves and flowers.

Within Zoology

The term bud (as in budding) is used by analogy within zoology as well, where it refers to an outgrowth from the body which develops into a new individual. It is a form of asexual reproduction limited to animals or plants of relatively simple structure. In this process a portion of the wall of the parent cell softens and pushes out. The protuberance thus formed enlarges rapidly while at this time the nucleus of the parent cell divides. One of the resulting nuclei passes into the bud, and then the bud is cut off from its parent cell and the process is repeated. Often the daughter cell will begin to bud before it becomes separated from the parent, so that whole colonies of adhering cells may be formed. Eventually cross walls cut off the bud from the original cell.

4

Seeds and Fruits Dispersal

Seed and fruit, respectively, the characteristic reproductive body of both angiosperms (flowering plants) and gymnosperms (conifers, cycads, and ginkgos) and the ovary that encloses it. Essentially, a seed consists of a miniature undeveloped plant (the embryo), which, alone or in the company of stored food for its early development after germination, is surrounded by a protective coat (the testa). Frequently small in size and making negligible demands upon their environment, seeds are eminently suited to perform a wide variety of functions the relationships of which are not always obvious: multiplication, perennation (surviving seasons of stress such as winter), dormancy (a state of arrested development), and dispersal. Pollination and the 'seed habit' are considered the most important factors responsible for the overwhelming evolutionary success of the flowering plants, which number more than 300,000 species.

The superiority of dispersal by means of seeds over the more primitive method involving single-celled spores, lies mainly in two factors: the stored reserve of nutrient material that gives the new generation an excellent growing start and the seed's multicellular structure. The latter factor provides ample opportunity for the development of adaptations for dispersal, such as plumes for wind dispersal, barbs, and others.

Economically, seeds and the fruits that contain them are important primarily because they are sources of a variety of foods—for example, the cereal grains, such as wheat, rice, and corn (maize); the seeds of beans, peas, peanuts, soybeans, almonds, sunflowers, hazelnuts, walnuts, pecans, and Brazil nuts; and the fruits of date palm, olive, banana, avocado, apple, and orange.

Many fruits, especially those in the citrus family—limes, lemons, oranges, grapefruits—are rich in vitamin C (ascorbic acid); unpolished cereal grains are rich in vitamin B_1 (thiamine); and wheat germ in vitamin E. Other useful products provided by seeds and fruits are abundant. Oils for cooking, margarine production, painting, and lubrication are available from the seeds of flax, rape, cotton, soybean, poppy, castor bean, coconut, sesame, safflower, sunflower, the cereal grains of maize, and the fruits of olive and oil palm. Essential oils are obtained from such sources as juniper 'berries,' used in gin manufacture. Waxes such as those from bayberries (wax myrtles) and vegetable ivory from the hard fruits of a South American palm species (*Phytelephas macrocarpa*) are important products. Stimulants are obtained from such sources as the seeds of coffee, kola, guarana, and cocoa; and drugs, such as morphine, come from opium-poppy fruits. Spices—from mustard and nutmeg seeds; from the aril ('mace') covering the nutmeg seed; from fruits of anise, cumins, caraway, dill, vanilla, black pepper, red or chili pepper, allspice, and others—form a large group of economic products. Dyes (Persian berries, butternut brown, sap green) and ornaments (Job's tears from the grass *Coix*, used for curtains; *Abrus*, *Adenanthera*, and *Rhynchosia* seeds for necklaces; others for rosaries) are also provided by seeds and fruits.

SEEDS

Seeds are normally surrounded by a tough shell (*Testa*) that develops from the integument (or several integuments) and that protects a largely developed embryo and its nutriments. The embryo is thus preserved from loss of water and bad weather. The nutriments are in a special nourishing tissue, the endosperm or in the perisperm (developed from tissue of the nucellus as with pepper). They have either to be made useable and to be used during germination or they are already stored in the cotyledons (beans, peas, almonds).

Monocotyledons have normally only one cotyledon, dicots have two and gymnosperms several. With many species, the seeds are unable to germinate immediately after falling off the plant (dormancy). This dormancy can be overcome by a period of cold weather (vernalisation) so that the seeds do not germinate before the beginning of the next period of vegetation.

The number of seeds that is produced by a single plant in the course of its life varies enormously. Some species like the coconut palm produce only few but very well provided descendants while others produce up to several million seeds that are inevitably provided rather badly. Numerous devices support the dispersal of the descendants since only a suitable habitat enables the seed to develop into a viable plant. If the dispersal is achieved only through devices that the plant itself produces, it is spoken of self-dispersal or autochory. If extern factors such as wind, water, animals, etc. are involved, then the mode of dispersal is called allochor. Only rarely the seeds are spread on their own, usually the whole seed-containing fruit is scattered. Among the autochor modes of dispersal is flinging and spurting of seeds.

Dispersal by wind (anemochory) is widespread among plants. The units for dispersal are necessarily either very small and light and / or equipped with specially formed devices for flying or floating. Those devices are, for example, air-filled cavities in the seeds of orchids, seeds that are completely covered with hairs like cotton, pappus-bearing seeds (composite flowers) and units that are equipped with all different kinds of wings. Dispersal by water (hydrochory) is much less common. Seeds that are spread by water have often an outer layer that cannot be moistened or they are hairy in order to trap air bubbles. Some big fruits that are spread by ocean currents like the coconut are surrounded by a loosely structured, airy layer.

Zoochory, *i.e.* the dispersal of fruits with the aid of animals has already been met when talking about berries, drupes, and multiple fruits. If seeds are eaten and excreted again, this is called endozoochoric dispersal. Contrasting is epizoochoric dispersal where the seeds or fruits stick to the animal or its fur either by slimy secretings or by variably shaped barbs. A speciality in the dispersal through animals is that through ants (myrmecochory). Such seeds or fruits bear attachments, the elaiosomes that contain lures and nutriments. Myrmecochory is common with plants that live at the forest soil like violets (*Viola*). The given examples show that zoochory offers a variety of possible mechanisms for the dispersal of seeds. But this variety is far beyond that of the architectural design of flowers. This is due to the fact that specialization and adaptation to seed or fruit dispersing animals is far less advanced than the specialisation of pollination.

FRUITS

Fructification is a feature of angiosperms during which the seeds are encapsulated by the ovary. Gymnosperms develop seeds that lie naked on the carpels. A fruit is the state that the flower turns to during the ripening of the seeds. Perianth and stamens have usually withered and fallen off. During fructification, the gynoecium is largely rearranged, the ovary extends strongly, the stigma shrivels and the style normally degenerates or falls off but it, too, may develop further, if it serves to enlarge the fruit.

In the simplest case, the seeds are set free from the ovary after ripening by opening of the fruit (dehiscent fruits). But very often, both fruits and seeds form an integrated part of the dispersal unit (nondehiscent fruit). If this happens, the tissue of the ovary is strongly differentiated. The pericarp is the part of a fruit that is formed by the ripening of the ovary wall. It is organized into three layers: the skin (exocarp), the often fleshy middle (mesocarp), and the membranous or stony inner layer (endocarp). These layers may become skin-like and leathery, fleshy or stringy (sclerotic) during fructification. The fruits produce gadgets for the protection and the dispersal of the seeds. Additionally, other parts of the flower may contribute to the formation of the fruit, like the flower axis (strawberry) or the calyx. Depending on the organization of the gynoecium, single fruits or multiple fruits develop. Single fruits spring either from a monomer (coenocarp) gynoecium or from single carpels of an apocarp gynoecium while multiple fruits develop from flowers with a choricarp gynoecium. If the fruit opens up to free ripe seeds, it is a dehiscent fruit where the pericarp is always dry. Contrasting are indehiscent fruits where the seed is spread together with the fruit or parts of the fruit.

THE DIFFERENT DEHISCENT AND INDEHISCENT FRUIT TYPES

Follicle: It is regarded as the most primitive type of fruit and is common in the ranunculaceen family. The fruit is composed of a single carpel. Opening occurs usually at the ventral suture as with the fruits of larkspur (*Delphinium*). In rare cases, it does take place at the dorsal suture (*Magnolia*, for example).

Pulses: This is the type of fruit that occurs with leguminoses. Contrary to the follicles, both ventral and dorsal suture open at the same time. Both parts of the carpel wind normally up like a screw. The process may occur like an explosion so that the seed is hurled away with full force (autochory, see beneath).

Pods: Are typical for cruciferous plants (Cruciferae, Brassicaceae). A pod stems from a paracarp ovary. It includes only two carpels and is divided by a central septum. When ripening, two flaps fall off while the septum and the placentas (replum) stay. The seeds may stick to them for a while.

Capsules: Are a very widespread type of fruit. They develop from a coenocarp gynoecium, the pericarp is dry. The opening of the fruit can take place in multiple ways by longitudinal tears, pores or by raising of the lid. Indehiscent fruits do not scatter their seeds. It is distinguished between berries, drupes, and nuts depending on the composition of the pericarp.

The pericarp of berries becomes fleshy and juicy in all its parts and is often coloured. A berry like, for example, a tomato contains many seeds. The endocarp of drupes differentiates into a stone that encapsulates usually only one seed. The outer layers of the fruit (mesocarp and exocarp) are, just like with berries, fleshy. Well-known examples are cherries, plums, peaches, olives, and walnut. Berries and drupes have adapted to endozoochory, *i.e.* they are eaten by animals (birds, mammals) along with the seeds. The seed (sometimes together with the stony endocarp) is excreted without being digested and is thereby scattered. The whole pericarp of nuts becomes hard and develops a thick wall which includes as a rule only one seed (hazelnut, acorn).

The caryopsis of sweet grass belongs to the nuts. Its seed is surrounded by a rather thin shell that is fused with the outer layer of the fruit. Other nut types are the achenes of composite flowers (Compositae, Asteraceae) where the calyx has been rearranged into a pappus (a structure for flying). An especially interesting case is the coconut (*Cocos nucifera*) where the outer layer is fibrous so that the fruit is able to swim due to the enclosed air.

Multiple fruits develop from flowers with an apocarp (choricarp) gynoecium. The single fruit may have a dry outer layer (single-seeded nuts or follicles with only few seeds) or the outer layer may be fleshy just like that of a drupe. Several fruits are usually combined to a unit by an axial structure that is either a central axial cone (strawberry, blackberry) or an axial cupule (rose hip, apple). With some species, the numerous fruits that develop from the inflorescences stay together as a functional unit (*syconium*). Well-known examples are mulberry (*Morus*) and fig (*Ficus*).

FRUITS WITH HIGHLY SPECIALIZED DEVICES THAT SERVE THEIR DISTRIBUTION

- Distribution by wind. Flat, very light, small and dry pods with a relatively large surface and just one or two seeds per fruit (*Lunaria annua*, Brassicaceae)
- 'Bodenroller' (winged fruits rolling along the ground): three-dimensionally built, dry and very light fruits that are easily blown away in dry habitats (*Pterodiscus ungamicus*, Pedaliaceae)
- Distribution by wind, burdocks and 'Bodenroller' (winged fruits rolling along the ground), a triple

strategy. Flat, dry involucre with a large surface but rather heavy. It can therefore only travel short distances by wind alone. The spiky centre serves epizoochoric distribution by animals; the arrangement of the wing-like gadgets allows an additional drifting at the floor (*Pterocarpus angolensis*, Fabaceae).

- *Trample Burs:* lignified fruit shell with spikes and barbs that stick to the softer parts of mammals' hoofs and are dispersed this way (*Harpagophytum procumbens*, Pedaliaceae).
- *Distribution by Burdocks:* Dry fruits with barbs at their surfaces that stick to the fur of mammals. Relatively strong structure of the fruit that falls apart by and by so that the seeds are very effectively lost at different places (*Xanthium riparium*, Compositae)
- *Trample Bur:* Dry and very compactly built fruit with a 'drawing pin-principle'. This fruit is only dispersed by the hoofs of mammals, it cannot adhere to their fur (*Dicerocaryum senecioides*, Pedaliaceae)
- And one more trample bur: this one can also stick to animals' furs. The fruits are, too, able to cling one to another. The respective animal may be hurt by the spikes (*Harpagophytum procumbens*, Pedaliaceae)

Trample Bur: Dry and very compactly built fruit with a 'drawing pin-principle'.

This fruit is only dispersed by the hoofs of mammals, it cannot adhere to their fur (*Dicerocaryum senecioides*, Pedaliaceae) distribution by wind. Flat, very light, small and dry pods with a relatively large surface and just one to three seeds per fruit (*Lunaria annua*, Honesty, Silver Dollar, Pennyflower-Brassicaceae).

Distribution by Burdocks: Dry fruits with barbs at their surfaces that stick to the fur of mammals. Relatively strong structure of the fruit that falls apart by and by so that the seeds are very effectively lost at different places (*Xanthium riparium*, Compositae)

THE NATURE OF SEEDS AND FRUITS

SEEDS

Angiosperm Seeds

In the typical flowering plant, or angiosperm, seeds are formed from bodies called ovules contained in the ovary, or basal part of the female plant structure, the pistil. The mature ovule contains in its central part a region called the nucellus that in turn contains an embryo sac with eight nuclei, each with one set of chromosomes (*i.e.*, they are haploid nuclei). The two nuclei near the centre are referred to as polar nuclei; the egg cell, or oosphere, is situated near the micropylar ('open') end of the ovule.

With very few exceptions (*e.g.*, the dandelion), development of the ovule into a seed is dependent upon fertilization, which in turn follows pollination. Pollen grains that land on the receptive upper surface (stigma) of the pistil will germinate, if they are of the same species, and produce pollen tubes, each of which grows down within the style (the upper part of the pistil) towards an ovule. The pollen tube has three haploid nuclei, one of them, the so-called vegetative, or tube, nucleus seems to direct the operations of the growing structure. The other two, the generative nuclei, can be thought of as nonmotile sperm cells. After reaching an ovule and breaking out of the pollen tube tip, one generative nucleus unites with the egg cell to form a diploid zygote (*i.e.*, a fertilized egg with two complete sets of chromosomes, one from each parent). The zygote undergoes a limited number of divisions and gives rise to an embryo. The other generative nucleus fuses with the two polar nuclei to produce a triploid (three sets of chromosomes) nucleus, which divides repeatedly before cell-wall formation occurs. This process gives rise to the triploid endosperm, a nutrient tissue that contains a variety of storage materials—such as starch, sugars, fats, proteins, hemicelluloses, and phytate (a phosphate reserve).

The events just described constitute what is called the double-fertilization process, one of the characteristic features of all flowering plants. In the orchids and in some other plants with minute seeds that contain no reserve materials, endosperm formation is completely suppressed. In other cases it is greatly reduced, but the reserve materials are present elsewhere—*e.g.*, in the cotyledons, or seed leaves, of the embryo, as in beans, lettuce, and peanuts, or in a tissue derived from the nucellus, the perisperm, as in coffee. Other seeds, such as those of beets, contain both perisperm and endosperm. The seed coat, or testa, is derived from the one or two protective integuments of the ovule. The ovary, in the simplest case, develops into a fruit. In many plants, such as grasses and lettuce, the outer integument and ovary wall are completely fused, so seed and fruit form one entity; thus seeds and fruits can logically be described together as 'dispersal units,' or diaspores. More often, however, the seeds are discrete units attached to the placenta on the inside of the fruit wall through a stalk, or funiculus.

The hilum of a liberated seed is a small scar marking its former place of attachment. The short ridge (raphe) that sometimes leads away from the hilum is formed by the fusion of seed stalk and testa. In many seeds, the micropyle of the ovule also persists as a small opening in the seed coat. The embryo, variously located in the seed, may be very small (as in buttercups) or may fill the seed almost completely (as in roses and plants of the mustard family). It consists of a root part, or radicle, a prospective shoot (plumule or epicotyl), one or more cotyledons (one or two in flowering plants, several in *Pinus*), and a hypocotyl, which is a region that connects radicle and plumule. A classification of seeds can be based on size and position of the embryo and on the proportion of embryo to storage tissue; the possession of either one or two cotyledons is considered crucial in recognizing two main groups of flowering plants, the Monocotyledones and Dicotyledones.

Seedlings, arising from embryos in the process of germination, are classified as epigeal (cotyledons above ground, usually green and capable of photosynthesis) and hypogeal (cotyledons below ground). Particularly in the monocots, special absorbing organs may develop that mobilize the reserve materials and withdraw them from the endosperm; *e.g.*, in grasses, the cotyledon has been modified into an enzyme-secreting scutellum ('shield') between embryo and endosperm.

Gymnosperm Seeds

In gymnosperms (plants with 'naked seeds'—conifers, cycads, ginkgos), the ovules are not enclosed in an ovary but lie exposed on leaflike structures, the megasporophylls. A long time span separates pollination and fertilization, and the ovules begin to develop into seeds long before fertilization has been accomplished; in some cases, in fact, fertilization does not occur until the ovules ('seeds') have been shed from the tree. In the European pine *Pinus sylvestris,* for example, the female cones (essentially collections of megasporophylls) begin to develop in winter and are ready to receive pollen from the male cones in spring. During the first growing season, the pollen tube grows slowly through the nucellus, while within the ovule the megaspore nucleus, through a series of divisions, gives rise to a collection of some 2,000 nuclei, which are then individually enclosed by walls to form a structure called the female gametophyte or prothallus. At the micropylar end of the ovule, several archegonia (bottle-shaped female organs) develop, each containing an oosphere ('egg'). The pollen tube ultimately penetrates the neck of one of the archegonia. Not until the second growing season, however, does the nucleus of one of the male cells in the tube unite with the oosphere nucleus. Although more than one archegonium may be fertilized, only one gives rise to a viable embryo. During the latter's development, part of the prothallus is broken down and used. The remainder, referred to as 'endosperm,' surrounds the embryo; it is mobilized later, during germination of the seed, a process that occurs without delay when the seeds are liberated from the female cone during the third year after their initiation.

SEED DISPERSAL SYNDROME

A seed dispersal syndrome is a mutualistic plant-animal interaction. Seed dispersal syndromes are morphological characters of seeds correlated to particular seed dispersal agents. Dispersal is the event by which individuals move from the site of their parents to establish in a new area. A seed disperser is the vector by which a seed moves from its parent to the resting place where the individual will establish, for instance an animal. Similar to the term syndrome, a diaspore is a morphological functional unit of a seed for dispersal purposes.

Characteristics for seed dispersal syndromes are commonly fruit colour, mass, and persistence. These syndrome characteristics are often associated with the fruit that carries the seeds. Fruits are packages for seeds, composed of nutritious tissues to feed animals. However, fruit pulp is not commonly used as a seed dispersal syndrome because pulp nutritional value does not enhance seed dispersal success. Animals interact with these fruits because they are a common food source for them. Although, not all seed dispersal syndromes have fruits because not all seeds are dispersed by animals. Suitable biological and environmental conditions of dispersal syndromes are needed for seed dispersal and invasion success such as temperature and moisture. Seed dispersal syndromes are parallel to pollination syndromes, which are defined as floral characteristics that attract organisms as pollinators. They are considered parallels because they are both plant-animal interactions, which increase the reproductive success of a plant. However, seed dispersal syndromes are more common in gymnosperms, while pollination syndromes are found in angiosperms. Seeds disperse to increase the reproductive success of the plant. The farther away a seed is from a parent, the better its chances of survival and germination. Therefore a plant should select certain traits to increase dispersal by a vector (*i.e.* bird) to increase the reproductive success of the plant.

EVOLUTION

Seeds have evolved traits to reward animals to enhance their dispersal abilities. Differing foraging behaviours of animals can lead to selection of dispersal traits and spatial variation such as increase in seed size for mammal dispersal, which can limit seed production. Seed production is limited by some seed syndromes because of their cost to the plant. Therefore, seed dispersal syndromes will evolve in a plant when the trait benefit outweighs the cost. The seed dispersers themselves play an essential role in syndrome evolution. For example, birds put strong selection pressure on seeds for colour of fruits because of their enhanced vision. Illustrations of such colour evolution include green colour being produced because its photosynthesis abilities are less costly while red colour emerges as a byproduct for protection from arthropods.

For visible characteristic differences to develop between dispersers and non-dispersers a few conditions need to be met 1. Specialization must increase dispersal success whether morphological, physiological or behavioural 2. Energy investment for dispersal will be taken from energy investment of other traits 3. Dispersal traits will benefit the dispersers over non-dispersers. Phenotypic (visible characteristics) differences in non-dispersers and dispersers can be caused by external factors, kin competition, intraspecific competition and habitat quality.

History

In 1930, Ridley wrote an important book called The dispersal of plants throughout the world, which goes into detail about each form of dispersal; dispersal by wind, water, animals, birds, reptiles and fish, adhesion, and people. He details the morphology and traits for each dispersal method, which are later described as seed dispersal syndromes. This began the idea of seed trait selection being associated with a form of seed dispersal.

Then in 1969 van der Pijl identified seed dispersal syndromes based on each mechanism of seed dispersal in his book Principles of Dispersal in Higher Plants. He is the pinnacle of seed dispersal syndromes and is cited by many scientists who study seed dispersal syndromes. He describes the morphology of interactions between fruits and flowers, and classifies dispersal in invertebrates, fish, reptiles, birds, mammals, ants, wind, water and the plant itself. Janson in 1983 continued the study on seed dispersal syndromes and classified seed dispersal syndromes of fruit by size, colour and husk or no husks in species of Peruvian tropical forest. He went in depth about the interaction between plants that have adapted to seed dispersal by birds and mammals. Researchers added more factors to the study of seed dispersal syndromes and looked at differing fleshy fruits and their correlation to moisture and differing ecological factors. They looked at bird-dispersal and mammal-dispersal and how the fruits differed in dispersal syndromes such as colour and size. These scientists began the theory and ideas behind seed dispersal syndromes that are crucial to the evolution of reproduction in plants.

SEED DISPERSAL BY ANIMALS: BEHAVIOUR MATTERS

Plants, being stationary, require a mobile mode for seed dispersal. Modes for seed dispersal include self-projectile mechanisms, wind, water, and animals. Dispersal by animals falls into the category of plant-animal interactions, a subject of interest because of the reciprocal adaptations that can be observed. These reciprocal adaptations lead to coevolution, or change in organisms as a result of their interactions with each other.

ANIMALS AS DISPERSAL AGENTS

Plants that depend on animals for dispersal have seeds that are adapted to travelling on the outside or the inside of the animal. Seeds with burrs or hooks can attach to an animal's fur. For seeds that are transported internally, plants provide an attractive fruit pulp reward in return for the ride. The process of internal seed dispersal begins with the plant producing fruits. Next, an animal is attracted to these fruits based on their characteristics (such as odour), and begins to feed. After these fruit-eating animals (also known as frugivores) ingest fruit, they process them in their digestive tracts, and then regurgitate seeds or deposit seeds in their feces.

Behaviour, both innate and learned, is involved in every step of the dispersal process. First, the stimulus of being hungry makes the animal begin searching for food. While in this state of searching, the animal is receptive to stimuli (*e.g.*, colour, odour) that may signal the presence of food items. If the fruit encountered has an acceptable taste, the animal will probably choose to eat it. Where seeds are deposited depends on how long the animal stays at the plant feeding, and where the animal goes afterwards.

Not all animals that eat fruit are appropriate dispersers. The effectiveness of an animal as a seed dispersal agent depends on how many seeds it disperses, and how it treats these seeds. Animals that visit a plant for fruit more frequently may be more reliable than those animals that eat fruit more rarely. Some fruit-eating animals are considered seed 'predators' if they kill seeds by digesting the seed along with the fruit pulp. On the other hand, seeds can sprout better after passing through the digestive tract of certain frugivores. In addition to enhancing sprouting, an effective dispersal agent deposits seeds in appropriate habitats for their survival to reproductive adulthood. The survival of a seed greatly depends on where it lands. Seeds that move farther away from other seeds have greater success because they can better escape resource competition, interbreeding with parents, and post-dispersal mortality. Because not all animals that eat fruit are equally good at dispersing seeds, plants should change fruit characteristics to discourage frugivores that are seed predators, and encourage frugivores that are effective dispersers.

Fruit Characteristics and Forager Choice

Fruit characteristics (or fruit traits) that foragers use to choose fruit as food items include toxin content, fruit appearance, and nutrient content. Together, the presentation of these traits is called the fruiting display. Foragers learn to recognize these traits as cues to trigger selection or avoidance of certain fruits as food items. The reliability of the behavioural response depends on the consequences of eating the fruit selected. Animals will prefer fruits that fulfil nutritional requirements, but avoid those that are toxic. Reciprocal change (coevolution) between plants and frugivores can occur when behaviours of foragers select fruit traits that in turn select for foraging behaviour.

Toxins: Some fruits contain toxins to deter seed pathogens or predators. Animals can learn which fruits are toxic, and thus learn to avoid them. Toxins can also limit the amount of time a more toxin-tolerant frugivore spends feeding at the plant. Because animals are limited to the amount of toxins they can handle over a period of time, a forager must stop eating a food item when maximum toxin load is reached. The foraging animal may then leave to find an alternative source of food or to seek antidotes. By forcing an animal to leave early, the plant may be able to ensure that its seeds will be deposited far enough away to avoid inbreeding, competition, and pathogens.

Fruit Appearance: Although toxin content limits ingestion of fruit, appearance can both limit and encourage it. Fruit appearance provides salient cues for recognition of fruit as a food source. Pigments such as carotenoids, flavonoids, and betalains give fruits their colours, and volatile compounds provide odors. In general, bird-dispersed fruit are red or black, and mammal-dispersed fruit have distinctive odors. The morphology (size and shape) of a fruit may also influence forager choice. Animals are limited to food items small enough to fit in their mouths and throats, especially birds and reptiles that tend to swallow fruits whole. In addition, birds may also consider the bulkiness of seeds when choosing fruit. Not only does seed bulk take up space in the digestive tract, it also may need to be jettisoned before flight.

Nutrient Content: Finally, fruit nutrients may be important in influencing forager choice. For most temperate fruits, energy in the form of sugars is the most abundant nutrient. Other vitamins and minerals may also be influential. For example, rose hips are known to be high in vitamin C. Nutrients may be more indirect in effect than appearance. Fruit appearance provides the cue for fruit choice, but nutrients provide the positive feedback that maintains an animal's preference for the fruit.

By understanding what influences an animal's decision to choose fruit, we can attempt to predict whether or not a plant's fruiting display will lead to successful dispersal. The fruiting display must balance maximizing gains from attracting effective dispersers while minimizing losses from also attracting ineffective dispersers. Thus, we can determine the effectiveness of a fruiting display by the number of seeds successfully dispersed per effort for the entire fruit crop. Effort can be determined by identifying the factor that influences an animal's decision to choose the fruit. For example, if the animal selects fruit on the basis of energy content, then effort is the amount of kilojoules of energy of the entire fruit crop. Effectiveness is then measured in units of numbers of seeds dispersed successfully relative to the amount of energy of the fruit crop.

In conclusion, foraging behaviour is an important component of the plant-seed disperser interaction. Foraging behaviour determines how fruits are chosen, and where the seeds are deposited. Toxin content, fruit appearance, and nutrient content may influence how fruits are selected and where seeds are deposited. By examining the behavioural components of the seed dispersal process, we can better understand how coevolution between plants and their dispersers may take place.

DISPERSAL BY ANIMALS

Snails disperse the small seeds of a very few plant species (*e.g., Adoxa*). Earthworms are more important as seed dispersers. Many intact fruits and seeds can serve as fish bait, those of *Sonneratia*, for example, for the catfish *Arius maculatus*. Certain Amazon River fishes react positively to the audible 'explosions' of the ripe fruits of *Eperua rubiginosa*. Fossil evidence indicates that saurochory is very ancient. The giant Galapagos tortoise is important for the dispersal of local cacti and tomatoes. The name alligator apple for *Annona palustris* refers to its method of dispersal, an example of saurochory. Many birds and mammals, ranging in size from mice and kangaroo rats to elephants, eat and disperse seeds and fruits. In the tropics, chiropterochory (dispersal by large bats such as flying foxes, *Pteropus*) is particularly important. Fruits adapted to these animals are relatively large and drab in colour, with large seeds and a striking (often rank) odour. Such fruits are accessible to bats because of the pagoda-like structure of the tree canopy, fruit placement on the main trunk, or suspension from long stalks that hang free of the foliage. Examples include mangoes, guavas, breadfruit, carob, and several fig species. In South Africa, a desert melon (*Cucumis humifructus*) participates in a symbiotic relationship with aardvarks—the animals eat the fruit for its water content and bury their own dung, which contains the seeds, near their burrows. Furry terrestrial mammals are the agents most frequently involved in epizoochory, the inadvertent carrying by animals of dispersal units. Burrlike seeds and fruits, or those diaspores provided with spines, hooks, claws, bristles, barbs, grapples, and prickles, are genuine hitchhikers, clinging tenaciously to their carriers. Their functional shape is achieved in various ways—in cleavers, or goose grass (*Galium aparine*), and enchanter's nightshade (*Circaea lutetiana*), the hooks are part of the fruit itself; in common agrimony (*Agrimonia eupatoria*), the fruit is covered by a persistent calyx (the sepals, parts of the flower, which remain attached beyond the usual period) equipped with hooks; in wood avens (*Geum urbanum*), the persistent styles have hooked tips. Other examples are bur marigolds, or beggar's-ticks (*Bidens* species); buffalo burr (*Solanum rostratum*); burdock (*Arctium*); *Acaena;* and many *Medicago* species. The last-named, with dispersal units highly resistant to damage from hot water and certain chemicals (dyes), have achieved wide global distribution through the wool trade. A somewhat different principle is employed by the so-called trample burrs, said to lodge themselves between the hooves of large grazing mammals. Examples are mule grab (*Proboscidea*) and the African grapple plant (*Harpagophytum*). In water burrs, such as those of the water nut *Trapa,* the spines should probably be considered as anchoring devices.

DISPERSAL BY BIRDS

Birds, being preening animals, rarely carry burrlike diaspores on their bodies. They do, however, transport the very sticky (viscid) fruits of *Pisonia*, a tropical tree of the four-o'clock family, to distant Pacific islands in this way. Small diaspores, such as those of sedges and certain grasses, may also be carried in the mud sticking to waterfowl and terrestrial birds.

Synzoochory, deliberate carrying of diaspores by animals, is practiced when birds carry diaspores in their beaks. The European mistle thrush, *Turdus viscivorus*, deposits the viscid seeds of mistletoe (*Viscum album*) on potential host plants when, after a meal of the berries, it whets its bill on branches or simply regurgitates the seeds. The North American (*Phoradendron*) and Australian mistletoes (*Ameyema*) are dispersed by various birds, and the comparable tropical species of the plant family Loranthaceae by flowerpeckers (of the bird family Dicaeidae), which have a highly specialized gizzard that allows seeds to pass through but retains insects. Plants may also profit from the forgetfulness and sloppy habits of certain nut-eating birds that cache part of their food but neglect to recover everything, or drop units on their way to the hiding place. Best known in this respect are the nutcrackers (*Nucifraga*), which feed largely on the 'nuts' of beech, oak, walnut, chestnut, and hazel; the jays (*Garrulus*), which hide hazelnuts and acorns; the nuthatches; and the California woodpecker (*Balanosphyra*), which may embed literally thousands of acorns, almonds, and pecan nuts in bark fissures or holes of trees. Secondarily, rodents may aid in dispersal by stealing the embedded diaspores and burying them. In Germany an average jay may transport about 4,600 acorns per season, over distances of up to 4 km (2.5 miles). Woodpeckers, nutcrackers, and squirrels are responsible for a similar dispersal of *Pinus cembra* in the Alps near the tree line.

Most ornithochores (plants with bird-dispersed seeds) have conspicuous diaspores attractive to such fruit-eating birds as thrushes, pigeons, barbets (members of the bird family Capitonidae), toucans, and hornbills (family Bucerotidae), all of which either excrete or regurgitate the hard part undamaged. Such diaspores have a fleshy, sweet, or oil-containing edible part; a striking colour (often red or orange); no pronounced smell; a protection against being eaten prematurely in the form of acids and tannins that are present only in the green fruit; a protection of the seed against digestion—bitterness, hardness, or the presence of poisonous compounds; permanent attachment; and, finally, absence of a hard outer cover. In contrast to bat-dispersed diaspores, they occupy no special position on the plant. Examples are rose hips, plums, dogwood fruits, barberry, red currant, mulberry, nutmeg fruits, figs, blackberries, and others. The natural and abundant occurrence of *Euonymus* (cardinal's hat), which is a largely tropical genus, in temperate Europe and Asia, can be understood only in connection with the activities of birds. Birds also contributed substantially to the repopulation with plants of the island Krakatoa after the catastrophic eruption of 1883. Birds have made *Lantana* (originally American) a pest in Indonesia and Australia; the same is true of wild plums (*Prunus serotina*) in parts of Europe, *Rubus* species in Brazil and New Zealand, and olives (*Olea europaea*) in Australia.

Mimicry—the protection-affording imitation of a dangerous or toxic species by an edible, harmless one—is shown in reverse by certain bird-dispersed 'coral seeds' such as those of many species in the genera *Abrus, Ormosia, Rhynchosia, Adenanthera,* and *Erythrina*. Hard and often shiny red or black and red, many such seeds deceptively suggest the presence of a fleshy red aril and thus invite the attention of hungry birds.

DISPERSAL BY ANTS

Mediterranean and North American harvester ants (*Messor, Atta, Tetramorium,* and *Pheidole*) are essentially destructive, storing and fermenting many seeds and eating them completely. Other ants (*Lasius, Myrmica,* and *Formica* species) eat the fleshy, edible appendage (the fat body or elaiosome) of certain specialized seeds, which they disperse. Most myrmecochorous plants (species of violet, primrose, hepatica, cyclamen, anemone, corydalis, *Trillium,* and bloodroot) belong to the herbaceous spring flora of northern forests. Tree poppy (*Dendromecon*), however, is found in the dry California chaparral; *Melica* and *Centaurea* species, in arid Mediterranean regions. The so-called ant epiphytes of the tropics (*i.e.*, species of *Hoya, Dischidia, Aeschynanthus,* and *Myrmecodia*—plants that live in 'ant gardens' on trees or offer the ants shelter in their own body cavities) constitute a special group of myrmecochores that provide oil in seed hairs. The ancestral forms of these hairs must have served in wind dispersal. The primary ant attractant of myrmecochorous seeds is not necessarily oil; instead, an unsaturated, somewhat volatile fatty acid is suspected in some cases. The myrmecochorous plant as a whole may also have specific adaptations; for example, cyclamen brings fruits and seeds within reach of ants by conspicuous coiling (shortening) of the flower stalk as soon as flowering is over.

SEEDS & FRUITS DISPERSED BY WIND

Like an endless army of parachutists released from an airplane, seeds and fruits travel the wind currents and gentle breezes of the earth, possibly colonizing a distant mountain slope or fertile valley. Literally hundreds of species in many plant families have adopted this remarkable method of dispersal, including a variety of ubiquitous plants that we recognize as 'weeds.' The answer to why some weedy composites (such as the European dandelion) have worldwide distributions is truly 'blowing in the wind' (to quote from the Peter, Paul and Mary song). Some of the ingenious adaptations for this method of wind dispersal include seeds that resemble parachutes, helicopters and gliders. In fact, one species reportedly inspired the design of some early aircraft. An astronomer friend of Mr. Wolffia once observed a strange formation of flying objects through his telescope. He was focusing on a squadron of tiny parachute seeds high above his house. And the entire plant body of wolffia (the world's smallest flowering plant) may be transported by powerful cyclonic storms. In the southeastern United States there are records of wolffia plant bodies less than one millimetre long being carried by a tornado, and they have even been reported in the water of melted hailstones.

AN INTRODUCTION TO THE BOTANY OF SEEDS

Seeds provide the vital genetic link and dispersal agent between successive generations of plants. Angiosperm seeds are produced and packaged in botanical structures called fruits which develop from the 'female' pistils of flowers. Immature seeds (called ovules) each contain a minute, single-celled egg enclosed within a 7-celled embryo sac. The haploid (1n) egg is fertilized by a haploid (1n) sperm resulting in a diploid (2n) zygote that divides by mitosis into a minute, multicellular embryo within the developing seed. A second sperm unites with 2 haploid polar nuclei inside a binucleate cell called the endosperm mother cell which divides into a mass of nutritive tissue inside the seed. In most seeds the embryo is embedded in this endosperm tissue which provides sustenance to the embryo during germination. In exalbuminous seeds (found in many plants such as the legumes), the endosperm tissue is already absorbed by the time you examine a mature seed within the pod, and the 2 white fleshy halves in the seed are really the cotyledons (components of the embryo). The 2 sperm involved in the double fertilization process originated within the pollen tube that penetrated the embryo sac. The pollen grain (and pollen tube) come from the 'male' organs (called anthers) on the same plant or different parental plants in a remarkable process known as pollination. Pollination is also accomplished by the wind (or water), and it may also involve insects in some of nature's most fascinating relationships between a plant and an animal. This is especially true of the amazing fig trees and their symbiotic wasps.

One of the important functions of seeds and fruits is dispersal; a mechanism to establish the embryo-bearing seeds in a suitable place away from their parental plants. There are 3 main mechanisms for seed and fruit dispersal: (1) Hitchhiking on animals, (2) Drifting in ocean or fresh water, and (3) Floating in the wind.

Wind-dispersed seeds & fruits in different plant families:

Helicopters: A. Box Elder (Acer negundo, Aceraceae); C. Big-Leaf Maple (Acer macrophyllum, Aceraceae); E: Evergreen

Ash (Fraxinus uhdei, Oleaceae); F. Tipu Tree (Tipuana tipu, Fabaceae).

Flutterer/Spinners: B. Empress Tree (Paulownia tomentosa, Scrophulariaceae); D. Tree Of Heaven (Ailanthus altissima, Simaroubaceae); G. Jacaranda (Jacaranda mimosifolia, Bignoniaceae).

Note: The tree of heaven seed (D) actually spins along its longitudinal axis like a rolling pin.

Gliders

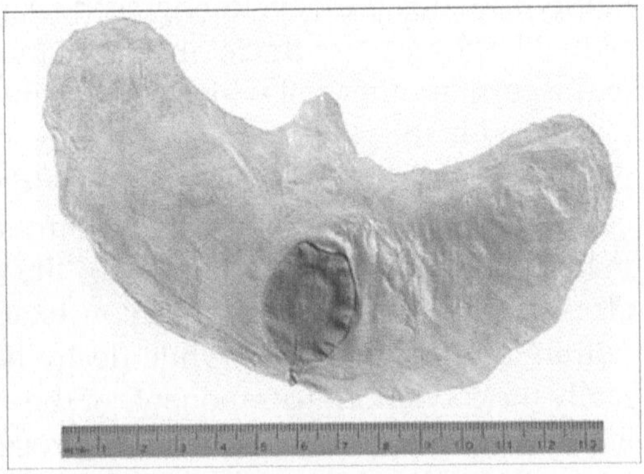

The Remarkable Winged Seed of the Tropical Asian Climbing Gourd Alsomitra Macrocarpa.

Gliders include seeds with 2 lateral wings that resemble the wings of an airplane. They become airborne when released from their fruit and sail through the air like a true glider. One of the best examples of this method is Alsomitra macrocarpa, a tropical vine in the Gourd Family (Cucurbitaceae) native to the Sunda Islands of the Malay Archipelago. Football-sized gourds hang from the vine high in the forest canopy, each packed with hundreds of winged seeds. The seeds have two papery, membranous wings, with combined wingspans of up to 5 inches (13 cm). They reportedly inspired the wing design of some early aircraft, gliders and kites. Although the seeds vary in shape, some of the most symmetrical ones superficially resemble the shape of the 'flying wing' aircraft or a modern Stealth Bomber. According to Peter Loewer, the aerodynamic seeds spiral downward in 20 foot (6 meter) circles, although a gust of wind would probably carry them much farther away.

Parachutes

Parachutes include seeds or achenes (one-seeded fruits) with an elevated, umbrella-like crown of intricately-branched hairs at the top, often produced in globose heads or puff-like clusters.

The slightest gust of wind catches the elaborate crown of plumose hairs, raising and propelling the seed into the air like a parachute. This is the classic mechanism of dispersal for the Eurasian dandelion (*Taraxacum officinale*) and includes numerous weedy and native members of the Sunflower Family (Asteraceae).

A giant Eurasian version of the dandelion called salsify or goat's beard (*Tragopogon dubius*), is one of the most successful wind-travellers in North America. Its seeds have literally blown across mountain ranges, colonizing vast fields of open land in the western United States. Three weedy species of salsify (*T. dubius*, *T. pratensis* and *T. porrifolius*) have been introduced into the western United States, 2 with yellow dandelion-type flowers and one with purple flowers. The latter, purple-flowered species (*T. porrifolius*) has a large, edible tap root with a flavour resembling oysters, hence the name 'oyster plant.'

In some parachutes, the crown of silky hairs arises directly from the top of the seed (not on an umbrella-like stalk). Again, the Sunflower Family (world's largest plant family with about 24,000 described species) contains many weedy representatives with this type of parachute seed. One of the most troublesome weeds of farm land in the western United States is wild or thistle artichoke (*Cynara carduncculus*). The large seed head of this weedy composite releases hundreds of parachute seeds which fly through the air and invade vast areas of grazing land with spiny, perennial bushes that literally take over.

The large leaf stalks (resembling giant celery stalks) are edible and are sold under the name of 'cardoon.' Populations of wild artichoke often contain so much variation between spiny and non-spiny plants, that some experts believe that they belong to one variable species. In fact, some botanists believe that the cultivated artichoke (*C. scolymus*) may be a cultivated variety of the wild *C. carduncculus*. Incidentally, the delicious artichoke is really a cooked flower head in which the outer bracts (phyllaries) and central basal portion (receptacle) are dipped in butter and eaten.

Another plant family which has evolved this parachute method of seed dispersal is the Milkweed Family (Asclepiadaceae). Hundreds of parachute seeds (each with a tuft of silky hairs) are produced within large, inflated pods called follicles. So abundant are the silky hairs, that they were actually collected and used as a substitute for kapok during World War II. Kapok comes from masses of silky hairs that line the seed capsules of the kapok tree (*Ceiba pentandra*), an enormous rain forest tree of Central and South America. Kapok is used primarily as a waterproof filler for mattresses, pillows, upholstery, softballs, and especially for life preservers. The floss silk tree (*Chorisia speciosa*), another member of the Bombax Family (Bombaceae) also produces large seed capsules lined with masses of silky hairs. This tree with its distinctive thorny trunk and showy pink flowers is commonly planted in southern California. The seeds of kapok and floss silk trees are embedded in these silky masses which aid in their dispersal by wind.

The Dogbane Family (Apocynaceae) also includes members with seed pods (follicles) and parachute seeds similar to those of milkweeds. One of the best examples is Nerium oleander, a drought-resistant, Mediterranean shrub planted throughout southern California. The foliage contains a powerful cardiac glycoside that can permanently relax the heart muscle.

Helicopters (Whirlybirds)

Helicopters (also called Whirlybirds) include seeds or one-seeded fruits (samaras) with a rigid or membranous wing at one end. The wing typically has a slight pitch (like a propeller or fan blade), causing the seed to spin as it

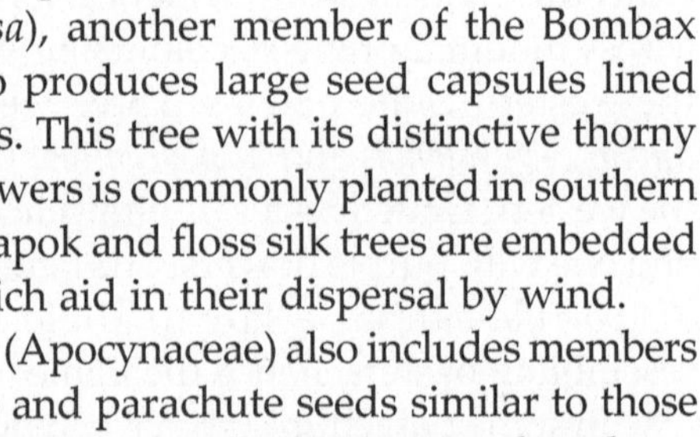

The South American Tipu Tree (Tipuana tipu) has one of the most Unusual Legumes in the World.

falls. Depending on the wind velocity and distance above the ground, helicopter seeds can be carried considerable distances away from the parent plant. The spinning action is similar to auto-rotation in helicopters, when a helicopter 'slowly' descends after a power loss.

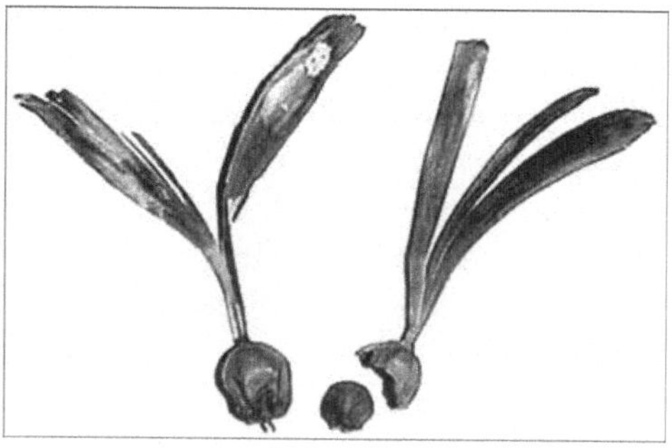

An Interesting One-seeded Winged Fruit that Spins as it Falls through the Air.

Numerous species of flowering trees and shrubs in many diverse and unrelated plant families have evolved this ingenious method of seed dispersal, good examples of convergent evolution. Representative examples of helicopter seeds and one-seeded fruits (called samaras) include the Maple Family (Aceraceae): Maples and box elder (Acer); Olive Family (Oleaceae): Ash (Fraxinus); Legume Family (Fabaceae): Tipu tree (Tipuana tipu); and the Protea Family (Proteaceae): Banksia and Hakea.

Note: This genus of tropical trees, shrubs and lianas is often placed in the hernandia family (Hernandiaceae). The unusual fruit shown above was collected and photographed at Ho'omaluhia Botanical Garden on the windward side of Oahu in the Hawaiian Islands. Identification provided by Ricarda Riina, Botany Department, University of Wisconsin.

Spinning fruits (seeds) from Thailand: A. *Diptocarpus alatus* (Diptocarpaceae). B. *Diptocarpus obtusifolius*. C. *Gluta* (Melanorrhoea) usitata (Anacardiaceae). The latter species is also called the Burmese lacquer tree and is well-known as a source of lacquer. The resin is chemically similar to the Japanese lacquer tree. Like the Japanese lacquer tree and poison oak, the resin canals also contain urushiol, a mixture of toxic phenolic compounds that cause a cell-mediated immune response in some people. Identifications courtesy of Dr. Tomiki Sando, Thailand.

Although they are classified as gymnosperms with naked seeds arising from woody cones rather than flowers, the Pine Family (Pinaceae) contains many genera with winged seeds, including Pinus (Pine), Abies (fir), Picea (spruce), Tsuga (hemlock), and many additional genera. When shed from cones high on upper branches, they fly over slopes and across deep canyons. The natural reforestation of conifers following fire is proof of the flying ability of seeds from nearby forested slopes.

Maples have a double or twin samara composed of 2 winged one-seeded fruits (double samara) joined together at their bases. When they break apart, each winged fruit flies like a typical helicopter seed. Although the Legume Family (Fabaceae) is the third largest plant family with over 18,000 described species, the vast majority of legumes do not have winged seeds or fruits. The South American tipu tree (Tipuana tipu) is a notable exception, with beautiful yellow blossoms that give rise to pendant, samara-like legumes, each with a large wing on the lower end. The dried, winged legumes spin so neatly in the air that they could be marketed as a child's toy.

The remarkable Protea Family (Proteaceae) of Australia contains some truly amazing genera with winged seeds, including Banksia and Hakea. Although they are flowering plants, banksias produce a dense flower cluster (inflorescence) that gives rise to a cone-like structure containing many woody carpels. Each carpel bears 2 winged seeds and the entire cone-like structure superficially resembles a pine cone. In fact, some banksias release their seeds following fire and even resprout from subterranean lignotubers like chaparral shrubs.

Flutterer/Spinners

The native range of hopseed bush (Dodonea viscosa), a member of the Soapberry Family (Sapindaceae), extends from Arizona to South America. It is also commonly cultivated in southern California. The papery, winged fruits flutter and spin in the air, and may be carried short distances by the wind.

The jacaranda tree (*Jacaranda mimosifolia*) of north-western Argentina. Like many other members of the Bignonia Family

(Bignoniaceae), the papery, winged seeds flutter and spin as they are carried by the wind.

Although their mode of dispersal is similar to single-winged helicopter seeds, the flutterer/spinners include seeds with a papery wing around the entire seed or at each end. When released from their seed capsules they flutter or spin through the air. Whether they spin or merely flutter depends on the size, shape and pitch of the wings, and the wind velocity. This method of wind dispersal is found in numerous species of flowering plants in many different plant families. Some examples of flutterer/spinner seeds include the Quassia Family (Simaroubaceae): Tree of heaven (*Ailanthus altissima*); Figwort Family (Scrophulariaceae): Empress tree (*Paulownia tomentosa*); Bignonia Family (Bignoniaceae): Jacaranda (*Jacaranda mimosifolia*), catalpa (*Catalpa speciosa*), desert willow (*Chilopsis linearis*), yellow bells (*Tecoma stans*), bower vine (*Pandorea jasminoides*), violet trumpet vine (*Clytostoma callistegioides*), and the fabulous trumpet trees (*Tabebuia serratifolia* and *T. ipe*); Elm Family (Ulmaceae): American and Chinese elms (*Ulmus americana* and *U. parvifolia*); Soapberry Family (Sapindaceae): Hop seed (*Dodonea viscosa*); and the Goosefoot Family (*Chenopodiaceae*): Four-wing saltbush (*Atriplex canescens*).

Any discussion of flutterer/spinners would not be complete without mentioning the quipo tree (*Cavanillesia platanifolia*), a massive rain forest tree in the bombax family (Bombacaeae) native to Panama. The enormous winged fruits of the quipo tree flutter through the air, carpeting the ground beneath the huge canopy of this striking tropical tree.

Some of the most beautiful flowering trees of the New World tropics belong to the Bignonia Family (Bignoniaceae). They typically produce long, slender (cigar-shaped) seed capsules containing masses of flat seeds with papery wings at each end. The lovely yellow bells (*Tecoma stans*) is native to Mexico and the Caribbean region, and is the official flower of the U.S. Virgin Islands. Some of the South American trumpet trees, including the pink-flowered *Tabebuia avellanedae* (listed as *T. ipe* in some references) and the yellow-flowered *Tabebuia* serratifolia, are also called ironwoods or axe-breakers (quebrachos) because of their dense, hard wood. The latter species is called 'pau d'arco' and its wood actually sinks in water, with a specific gravity of 1.20. In South America, trumpet trees drop their leaves during the dry season and produce a profusion of pink or yellow blossoms. The crowns of these huge timber trees resemble gigantic floral bouquets in the midst of the forest. As with so many tropical species, some of the trumpet trees inhabit rain forest areas that are seriously threatened by slash and burn agriculture, large plantations of exportable products, and the general annihilation of the South American rain forests.

Other South American species of Tabebuia are also referred to as pau d'arco, including the pink-flowered *T. impetiginosa* and *T. avellanedae*. According to The New York Botanical Garden Encyclopedia of Horticulture Volume 10, 1982, *T. avellanedae* is a synonym for *T. impetiginosa*, and *T. ipe* ' is so closely similar to *T. impetiginosa* that it can scarcely be more than a variety of that species.' These attractive pink-flowered species are commonly used as landscape trees in temperate regions.

The powdered inner bark of these pink-flowered species of pau d'arco is sold as a popular herbal remedy that reportedly stimulates the immune system. According to a book by Kenneth Jones, this valuable herb has been proven successful in the treatment of certain cancers, allergies associated with the Candida yeast syndrome, and in disorders involving a weakened immune system.

SPECIFIC GRAVITY

Probably the best way to appreciate the relative hardness of different woods is the concept of 'specific gravity,' a numerical scale based on 1.0 for pure water. Without getting too mathematical, the specific gravity of a substance can easily be calculated by dividing its density (in grams per cubic centimeter) by the density of pure water (one gram per cubic centimeter).

The brilliant Greek mathematician and inventor Archimedes discovered over 2,100 years ago that a body in water is buoyed up by a force equal to weight of the water displaced. Archimedes reportedly came upon this discovery in his bathtub, and ran out into the street without his clothing shouting 'Eureka, I have found it.' Since one gram of pure water occupies a volume of one cubic centimetre, anything having a specific gravity greater than 1.0 will sink in pure water.

The principles of buoyancy and specific gravity are utilized in many ways, from scuba diving and chemistry to the hardness of dry, seasoned wood. Some of the heaviest hardwood trees and shrubs of the United States have specific gravities between 0.80 and 0.95; including shagbark hickory (*Carya ovata*), persimmon (*Diospyros virginiana*) and ironwood (*Ostrya virginiana*) of the eastern states, and canyon live oak (*Quercus chrysolepis*), Engelmann oak (*Q. engelmannii*), hollyleaf cherry (*Prunus ilicifolia*) and Santa Cruz Island ironwood (*Lyonothamnus floribundus* ssp. *asplenifolius*) of southern California. Although some of these trees are called ironwoods, their dense, dry wood will still float in water. Since the pure cell wall material (lignin and cellulose) of wood has a density of about 1.5 grams per cubic centimetre, even the world's heaviest hardwoods generally have specific gravities less than 1.5 due to tiny pores (lumens) within the cell walls. True ironwoods include trees and shrubs with dry, seasoned woods that actually sink in water, with specific gravities greater than 1.0. They include lignum vitae (*Guaicum officinale*, 1.37); quebracho (*Schinopsis balansae*, 1.28); pau d'arco (*Tabebuia serratifolia*, 1.20); knob-thorn (*Acacia pallens*, 1.19); desert ironwood (*Olneya tesota*, 1.15); and ebony (*Diospyros ebenum*, 1.12). To appreciate the weight of these hardwoods, compare them with tropical American balsa (*Ochroma pyramidale*), one of the softest and lightest woods with a specific gravity of only 0.17.

Cottony Seeds and Fruits

Cottony seeds and fruits include seeds and minute seed capsules with a tuft (coma) of cottony hairs at one end, or seeds embedded in a cottony mass. Some of the examples in this group are very similar in function to parachute seeds, but probably are not carried as far by the wind. Many plant families have this type of wind dispersal, including the Willow Family (Salicaceae): Willows (Salix) and Cottonwoods (Populus); Cattail Family (Typhaceae): Cattails (Typha); Evening Primrose Family (Onagraceae): Willow-Herb (Epilobium) and *California fuchsia* (Zauschneria); Bombax Family (Bombaceae): Kapok tree (*Ceiba pentandra*) and floss silk tree (*Chorisia speciosa*); and the Sycamore Family (Platanaceae): Sycamore (Platanus).

In the California sycamore (*Platanus racemosa*), a common riparian (streamside) tree throughout the state, the one-seeded fruits (achenes or nutlets) are produced in dense, globose heads. The spherical heads hang from branches like little balls. Individual achenes have a tuft of hairs at the base which probably helps in their wind dispersal. Seeds of the South American kapok tree (*Ceiba pentandra*) and floss silk tree (*Chorisia speciosa*) are embedded in dense masses of silky hairs inside large woody capsules. This undoubtedly helps to disperse the seeds when seed-bearing masses of hair are carried by the wind. In tropical regions of the New World, the kapok grows into an enormous rain forest tree with a massive buttressed trunk. Kapok hairs are coated with a highly water-resistant, waxy cutin layer. The empty lumen (cavity) inside each hair is larger the cotton hairs; hence, the hairs are lighter. Unlike cotton hairs, kapok is difficult to spin and is not made into textiles. It is used primarily as a waterproof filler for mattresses, pillows, upholstery, softballs, and especially for life preservers. A kapok-filled life jacket can support 30 times its own weight in water.

One fuzzy brown cattail spike may contain a million tiny seeds. Each seed has a tuft of silky white hairs and is small enough to pass through the 'eye' of an ordinary sewing needle. They are shed in clouds of white fluff and float through the air like miniature parachutes. A cattail marsh covering one acre may produce a trillion seeds, more than 200 times the number of people in the world. The fluffy seeds have been used for waterproof insulation and the buoyant filling of life jackets. In addition, each plant produces billions of wind-borne pollen grains; in fact, so much pollen that it was used as flour by North American Indians and made into bread. Cottonwoods and willows also produce masses of seeds, each with a tuft of soft, white hairs. Since they are dioecious, with pollen-bearing male and seed-bearing female trees in the population, only female trees produce the actual cotton. During late spring and summer in the western United States, the cottony fluff from cottonwoods resembles newly fallen snow. Because the wind-blown fluff can be quite messy in cultivated parks and gardens, male trees are generally planted. The discriminatory label of 'cottonless cottonwood' refers to a male tree.

Tumbleweed (Russian Thistle)

The common tumbleweed or Russian thistle is a rounded, bushy annual introduced into the western United States from the plains of southeastern Russia and western Siberia in the late 1800s. The name 'thistle' comes from the stiff, sharp-pointed, awl-shaped leaves. Although it is depicted in songs of the old west, this species is a naturalized weed in North America. It is listed in most older references as Salsola kali or *S. pestifer*; however, researchers lists it as *S. tragus*. Russian thistle belongs to the goosefoot family (Chenopodiaceae), along with many weedy species and some valuable vegetables, including beets (*Beta vulgaris*), goosefoot (*Chenopodium album*) and spinach (*Spinacia oleracea*).

Tumbleweed is a prolific seeder and rapid seed germination and seedling establishment occurs after only a brief and limited rainy season. A single plant may produce 20,000 to 50,000 seeds within numerous small fruits, each surrounded by a circular, papery border. Mature plants readily break off at the ground level and are pushed along by strong gusts of wind.

As they roll along hillsides and valleys, the seeds are scartered across the landscape. Tumbleweeds often pile up in wind rows along fences and buildings. This is a troublesome weed in agricultural areas because it literally covers the farm land with bushy, prickly shrubs.

One interesting use for this plant in arid regions of the American southwest is for a 'snowman' at Christmas time.

Three proportionally sized tumbleweeds are used to make the head, thorax and main body of a 'snowman.' Another suggested use is to compress tumbleweeds into logs and use them for firewood.

Miscellaneous

Squirrel-Tail Grass (*Elymus elymoides*), formerly named Sitanion hystrix is an attractive grass native to the mountains and plains of the western United States. Seed-bearing sections (spikelets) of the flower spike (containing one-seeded fruits called grains and very long awns) are carried short distances by the wind. Although not as efficient fliers, the long awns function like the parachute bristles (pappus) of composites.

This miscellaneous category of wind-blown seeds and fruits includes plants that really don't fit the above 5 categories. The Grass Family (Poaceae) includes a number of species with plumose flower stalks that fragment into seed-bearing spikelets that blow into the wind. Some of these species have become troublesome weeds in southern California, including the South African fountain grass (*Pennisetum setaceum*). Although this tufted perennial makes an attractive, drought-resistant landscaping plant along walkways and roads, it is becoming a widespread weed in disturbed areas of San Diego County. Another species, called squirrel-tail grass (*Elymus elymoides*), resembles a weedy introduced grass, but it is actually a native perennial of dry, rocky mountains and open land in the western United States.

To appreciate its airborne seeds, you really must see this grass during a strong gust of wind on the eastern slopes of the Sierra Nevada during late summer. Mountain mahogany (*Cercocarpus minutiflorus*), a native shrub in the chaparral of southern California, produces a rather unique wind-blown fruit. The one-seeded fruit (achene) has a persistent, feathery style that glistens in the sunlight. Although they usually don't travel very far, the achenes are blown into the air by strong gusts of wind during the dry, fire season of late summer and fall. This species is not related to the West Indian mahogany (*Swietenia mahagoni*) or the Honduran mahogany (*S.*

macrophylla), members of the true Mahogany Family (Meliaceae). Mountain mahogany actually belongs to the Rose Family (Rosaceae) and produces very hard wood that sinks in water when dry. In fact, the wood of a montane species (*C. ledifolius*), has a specific gravity of 1.12, as heavy and dense as ebony (*Diospyros ebenum*).

DISPERSAL BY WATER

Many marine, beach, pond, and swamp plants have waterborne seeds, which are buoyant by being enclosed in corky fruits or air-containing fruits or both; examples of these plants include water plantain, yellow flag, sea kale, sea rocket, sea beet, and all species of Rhizophoraceae, a family of mangrove plants. Sea dispersal of the coconut palm has been well proved; the fibrous mesocarp of the fruit, a giant drupe, provides buoyancy. Once the nuts are ashore, the mesocarp also aids in the above ground germination process by collecting rainwater; in addition, the endosperm has in its 'milk' a provision for seedling establishment on beaches without much fresh water. A sea rocket species with seeds highly resistant to seawater is gaining a foothold on volcanic Surtsey Island, south of Iceland. Purple loosestrife, monkey flower, *Aster tripolium*, and *Juncus* species (rushes) are often transported by water in the seedling stage. Rainwash down mountain slopes may be important in tropical forests. A 'splashcup mechanism,' common in fungi for spore dispersal, is suggested by the open fruit capsule with exposed small seeds in the pearlwort (*Sagina*) and mitrewort (*Mitella*). Hygrochasy, the opening of fruits in moist weather, is displayed by species of *Mesembryanthemum*, *Sedum*, and other plants of dry environments.

5

Plant Cells and Tissues

PLANT CELLS

Most cells are not visible with the naked eye. However, with microscopes of various types, plant cells can be readily viewed and studied. In young parts of plant and fruits, cell shapes are generally round, while in older sections, the cells are somewhat boxlike with up to 14 sides as they become packed together.

A plant cell is bounded by a cell wall and the living portion of the cell is within the walls and is divided into two portions: the nucleus, or central control centre; and the cytoplasm, a fluid in which membrane bound organelles are found. Between the primary cell walls of adjacent plant cells, lies a pectic middle lamella. There can be a secondary cell wall which would be located just to the inside of the primary wall. Both walls consist mainly of cellulose, but the secondary cell wall may contain lignin and other substances. The outer boundary of the protoplasm (cytoplasm and nucleus) is a sandwich-like, flexible plasma membrane. This membrane regulates what enters and leaves the plant cell. Plant cell organelles include: endoplasmic reticulum, with and without ribosomes attached; Golgi bodies, mitochondria, and plastids. Plastids are chloroplasts, chromoplasts or leucoplasts—depending on the colour and likewise the function. Chloroplasts are of specific interest to those studying plants. A plant cell also, obviously, contains a nucleus which is bounded by a nuclear envelope with pores. The pores in the nuclear envelope allow for movement of substances in and out of the nucleus. Within the nucleus is a number of chromosomes. The number present is specific to the organism and it will be later noted how sex cells contain one-half the number of chromosomes, and restore chromosome number upon fertilization. All of these organelles and the nucleus are suspended in the cytoplasm. The cytoplasm has movements that are referred to as cytoplasmic streaming or cyclosis.

The particular function of the other organelles contained in plant cells can be reviewed below:

- The nucleus is in the centre of most cells. Some cells contain multiple nuclei, such as skeletal muscle, while some do not have any, such as red blood cells. The nucleus is the largest membrane-bound organelle. Specifically, it is responsible for storing and transmitting genetic information. The nucleus is surrounded by a selective nuclear envelope. The nuclear envelope is composed of two membranes joined at regular intervals to form circular openings called nuclear pores. The pores allow RNA molecules and proteins modulating DNA expression to move through the pores and into the cytosol. The selection process is controlled by an energy-dependent process that alters the diameter of the pores in response to signals. Inside the nucleus, DNA and proteins associate to form a network of threads called chromatin. The chromatin becomes vital at the time of cell division as it becomes tightly condensed thus forming the rodlike chromosomes with the enmeshed DNA. Inside the nucleus is a filamentous region called the nucleolus. This serves as a site where the RNA and protein components of ribosomes are assembled. The nucleolus is not membrane bound, but rather just a region.
- Ribosomes are the sites where protein molecules are synthesized from amino acids. They are composed of proteins and RNA. Some ribosomes are found bound to granular endoplasmic reticulum, while others are free in the cytoplasm. The proteins

synthesized on ribosomes bound to granular endoplasmic reticulum are transferred from the lumen (open space inside endoplasmic reticulum) to the golgi apparatus for secretion outside the cell or distribution to other organelles. The proteins that are synthesized of free ribosomes are released into the cytosol.

- The endoplasmic reticulum (ER) is collectively a network of membranes enclosing a singular continuous space. As mentioned earlier, granular endoplasmic reticulum is associated with ribosomes (giving the exterior surface a rough, or granular appearance). Sometimes granular endoplasmic reticulum is referred to as rough ER. The granular ER is involved in packaging proteins for the golgi apparatus. The agranular, or smooth, ER lacks ribosomes and is the site of lipid synthesis. In addition, the agranular ER stores and releases calcium ions (Ca^{2+}).
- The golgi apparatus is a membranous sac that serves to modify and sort proteins into secretory/transport vesicles. The vesicles are then delivered to other cell organelles and the plasma membrane. Most cells have at least one golgi apparatus, although some may have multiple. The apparatus is usually located near the nucleus.
- Endosomes are membrane-bound tubular and vesicular structures located between the plasma membrane and the golgi apparatus. They serve to sort and direct vesicular traffic by pinching off vesicles or fusing with them.
- Mitochondria are some of the most important structures in the cell. They are they site of various chemical processes involved in the synthesis of energy packets called ATP (adenosine triphosphate). Each mitochondrion is surrounded by two membranes. The outer membrane is smooth, while the inner one is folded into tubule structures called

cristae. Mitochondria are unique in that they contain small amounts of DNA containing the genes for the synthesis of some mitochondrial proteins. The DNA is inherited solely from the mother. Cells with greater activity have more mitochondria, while those that are less active have less need for energy producing mitochondria.

- Lysosomes are bound by a single membrane and contain highly acidic fluid. The fluid acts as digesting enzymes for breaking down bacteria and cell debris. They play an important from in the cells of the immune system.
- Peroxisomes are also bound by a single membrane. They consume oxygen and work to drive reactions that remove hydrogen from various molecules in the form of hydrogen peroxide. They are important in maintaining the chemical balances within the cell.
- The cytoskeleton is a filamentous network of proteins that are associated with the processes that maintain and change cell shape and produce cell movements in animal and bacteria cells. In plants, it is responsible for maintaining structures within the plant cell, rather then whole cell movement. The cytoskeleton also forms tracks along which cell organelles move propelled by contractile proteins attached to their various surfaces. Like a little highway infrastructure inside the cell. Three types of filaments make up the cytoskeleton.
  - Microfilaments are the thinnest and most abundant of the cytoskeleton proteins. They are composed of actin, a contractile protein, and can be assembled and disassembled quickly according to the needs of the cell or organelle structure.
  - Intermediate filaments are slightly larger in diameter and are found most extensively in regions of cells that are going to be subjected to stress. Once these filaments are assembled they are not capable of rapid disassembly.

  - Microtubules are hollow tubes composed of a protein called tubulin. They are the thickest and most rigid of the filaments. Microtubules are present in the axons and long dendrite projections of nerve cells. They are capable of rapid assembly and disassembly according to need. Microtubules are structured around a cell region called the centrosome, which surrounds two centrioles composed of 9 sets of fused microtubules. These are important in cell division when the centrosome generates the microtubluar spindle fibres necessary for chromosome separation.
- Chloroplasts It is necessary to note a bit about the form of chloroplasts, as you will encounter them throughout this tutorial. Inside a chloroplast is a matrix called the stroma. Enzymes are found in the stroma as well as grana—stacks of coin-shaped discs, called thylakoids. It is within the thylakoids that photosynthesis takes place. Note that chloroplasts, like mitochondria contain their own DNA. They do rely on proteins from the nucleus, and are considered semi-autonomous organelles.
- Vacuoles Plant cells are also notorious for having huge vacuoles. Up to 90% of the volume of a mature cell may be taken up by a single large vacuole or several vacuoles. The vacuole is bound by a special membrane, called the tonoplast, and contains cell sap—which is composed of dissolved substances and may include pigments.

CELL CYCLE

The cell cycle contains the process in which cells are either dividing or in between divisions. Cells that are not actively dividing are said to be in interphase, which has three distinct periods of intense activity that precedes the division of the nucleus, or mitosis. The division of the rest of the cell occurs as an end result of mitosis and this process occurs in regions of active cell division, called meristems. Meristems will be looked at in the plant tissue tutorial.

Mitosis is a process within the cell cycle that is divided into four phases which we will sum up here:

- Prophase—the chromosomes and their usual two-stranded nature becomes apparent, the nuclear envelope breaks down.
- Metaphase—the chromosomes become aligned at the equator of the cell. A spindle composed of spindle fibres is developed and some attach to the chromosomes at their centromere.
- Anaphase—the sister chromatids of each chromosome, that is now called the daughter chromosomes, separate lengthwise and each group of daughter chromosomes migrates to the opposite ends of the cell.
- Telophase—the groups of daughter chromosomes are grouped within a developing nuclear envelope which makes them separate nuclei. A wall forms between the two sets of daughter chromosomes thus creating two daughter cells.

In plants, as the cell wall is developing, droplets or vesicles of pectin merge forming a cell plate that eventually will become the middle lamella of the new cell wall.

PLANT CELLS COMPARED WITH ANIMAL CELLS

Animal cells do not have a cell wall. Instead of a cell wall, the plasma membrane (usually called cell membrane when discussing animal cells) is the outer boundary of animal cells. Animal tissues therefore require either external or internal support from some kind of skeleton. Frameworks of rigid cellulose fibrils thicken and strengthen the cell walls of higher plants. Plasmodesmata that connect the protoplasts of higher plant cells do not have a counterpart in the animal cell model. During telophase of mitosis, a cell plate is formed as the plant cell begins its division. In animal cells, the cell pinches in the centre to form two cells; no cell plate is laid down. Centrioles are generally not found in higher plant cells, while they are found in animal cells. Animal cells do not have plastids, which are common in plant cells (chloroplasts). Both cell types have vacuoles, however, in animal cells vacuoles are very tiny or absent, while in plant cells vacuoles are generally quite large.

PLANT TISSUES

Plants are composed of three major organ groups: roots, stems and leaves. As we know from other areas of biology, these organs are comprised of tissues working together for a common goal (function). In turn, tissues are made of a number of cells which are made of elements and atoms on the most fundamental level. We will look at the various types of plant tissue and their place and purpose within a plant. It is important to realize that there may be slight variations and modifications to the basic tissue types in special plants.

Plant tissues are characterized and classified according to their structure and function. The organs that they form will be organized into patterns within a plant which will aid in further classifying the plant. A good example of this is the three basic tissue patterns found in roots and stems which serve to delineate between woody dicot, herbaceous dicot and monocot plants. We will look at these classifications later on in the tutorial.

MERISTEMATIC TISSUES

Tissues where cells are constantly dividing are called meristems or meristematic tissues. These regions produce new cells. These new cells are generally small, six-sided boxlike structures with a number of tiny vacuoles and a large nucleus, by comparison. Sometimes there are no vacuoles at all. As the cells mature the vacuoles will grow to many different shapes and sizes, depending on the needs of the cell. It is possible that the vacuole may fill 95% or more of the cell's total volume.

There are three types of meristems:

- Apical Meristems
- Lateral Meristems
- Intercalary Meristems.

Apical meristems are located at or near the tips of roots and shoots. As new cells form in the meristems, the roots and shoots will increase in length. This vertical growth is also known as primary growth. A good example would be the growth of a tree in height. Each apical meristem will produce embryo leaves and buds as well as three types of primary meristems: protoderm, ground meristems, and procambium. These primary meristems will produce the cells that will form the primary tissues. Lateral meristems account for secondary growth in plants. Secondary growth is generally horizontal growth. A good example would be the growth of a tree trunk in girth. There are two types of lateral meristems to be aware of in the study of plants.

The vascular cambium, the first type of lateral meristem, is sometimes just called the cambium. The cambium is a thin, branching cylinder that, except for the tips where the apical meristems are located, runs the length of the roots and stems of most perennial plants and many herbaceous annuals. The cambium is responsible for the production of cells and tissues that increase the thickness, or girth, of the plant. The cork cambium, the second type of lateral meristem, is much like the vascular cambium in that it is also a thin cylinder that runs the length of roots and stems. The difference is that it is only found in woody plants, as it will produce the outer bark.

Both the vascular cambium and the cork cambium, if present, will begin to produce cells and tissues only after the primary tissues produced by the apical meristems have begun to mature. Intercalary meristems are found in grasses and related plants that do not have a vascular cambium or a cork cambium, as they do not increase in girth. These plants do have apical meristems and in areas of leaf attachment, called nodes, they have the third type of meristematic tissue. This meristem will also actively produce new cells and is responsibly for increases in length. The intercalary meristem is responsible for the regrowth of cut grass.

There are other tissues in plants that do not actively produce new cells. These tissues are called nonmeristematic tissues.

Nonmeristematic tissues are made of cells that are produced by the meristems and are formed to various shapes and sizes depending on their intended function in the plant. Sometimes the tissues are composed of the same type of cells throughout, or sometimes they are mixed.

SIMPLE TISSUES

There are three basic types, named for the type of cell that makes up their composition.

- Parenchyma cells form parenchyma tissue. Parenchyma cells are the most abundant of cell types and are found in almost all major parts of higher plants. These cells are basically sphere shaped when they are first made. However, these cells have thin walls, which flatten at the points of contact when many cells are packed together. Generally, they have many sides with the majority having 14 sides. These cells have large vacuoles and may contain various secretions including starch, oils, tannins, and crystals. Some parenchyma cells have many chloroplasts and form the tissues found in leaves. This type of tissue is called chlorenchyma. The chief function of this type of tissue is photosynthesis, while parenchyma tissues without chloroplasts are generally used for food or water storage. Additionally, some groups of cells are loosely packed together with connected air spaces, such as in water lilies, this tissue is called aerenchyma tissue. These type of cells can also develop irregular extensions of the inner wall which increases overall surface area of the plasma membrane and facilitates transferring of dissolved substances between adjacent cells. Parenchyma cells can divide if they are mature, and this is vital in repairing damage to plant tissues. Parenchyma cells and tissues comprise most of the edible portions of fruit.
- Collenchyma cells form collenchyma tissue. These cells have a living protoplasm, like parenchyma cells,

and may also stay alive for a long period of time. Their main distinguishing difference from parenchyma cells is the increased thickness of their walls. In cross section, the walls looks uneven. Collenchyma cells are found just beneath the epidermis and generally they are elongated and their walls are pliable in addition to being strong. As a plant grows these cells and the tissues they form, provide flexible support for organs such as leaves and flower parts. Good examples of collenchyma plant cells are the 'strings' from celery that get stuck in our teeth.

- Sclerenchyma cells form sclerenchyma tissue. These cells have thick, tough secondary walls that are imbedded with lignin. At maturity, most sclerenchyma cells are dead and function in structure and support.

Sclerenchyma cells can occur in two forms:

- Sclereids are sclerenchyma cells that are randomly distributed throughout other tissues. Sometimes they are grouped within other tissues in specific zones or regions. They are generally as long as they are wide. An example, would be the gritty texture in some types of pears. The grittiness is due to groups of sclereid cells. Sclereids are sometimes called stone cells.
- Fibers are sometimes found in association with a wide variety of tissues in roots, stems, leaves and fruits. Usually fibre cells are much longer than they are wide and have a very tiny cavity in the centre of the cell. Currently, fibres from over 40 different plant families are used in the manufacture of textiles, ropes, string and canvas goods to name a few.

SECRETORY CELLS AND TISSUES

As a result of cellular processes, substances that are left to accumulate within the cell can sometimes damage the protoplasm. Thus it is essential that these materials are either isolated from the protoplasm in which they originate, or be moved outside the plant body. Although most of these substances are waste products, some substances are vital to normal plant functions. Examples: oils in citrus, pine resin, latex, opium, nectar, perfumes and plant hormones. Generally, secretory cells are derived from parenchyma cells and may function on their own or as a tissue. They sometimes have great commercial value.

COMPLEX TISSUES

Tissues composed of more than one cell type are generically referred to as complex tissues. Xylem and phloem are the two most important complex tissues in a plant, as their primary functions include the transport of water, ions and soluble food substances throughout the plant. While some complex tissues are produced by apical meristems, most in woody plants are produced by the vascular cambium and is often referenced as vascular tissue. Other complex tissues include the epidermis and the periderm. The epidermis consists primarily of parenchyma-like cells and forms a protective covering for all plant organs. The epidermis includes specialized cells that allow for the movement of water and gases in and out of the plant, secretory glands, various hairs, cells in which crystals are accumulated and isolated, and other cells that increase absorption in the roots. The periderm is mostly cork cells and therefore forms the outer bark of woody plants. It is considered to be a complex tissue because of the pockets of parenchyma cells scattered throughout.

XYLEM

Xylem is an important plant tissue as it is part of the 'plumbing' of a plant. Think of bundles of pipes running along the main axis of stems and roots. It carries water and dissolved substances throughout and consists of a combination of parenchyma cells, fibres, vessels, tracheids and ray cells. Long tubes made up of individual cells are the vessels, while vessel members are open at each end. Internally, there may be bars of wall material extending across the open space. These cells are joined end to end to form long tubes. Vessel members and tracheids are dead at maturity. Tracheids have thick secondary cell walls and are tapered at the ends. They do not have end openings such as the vessels. The tracheids ends overlap with each other, with pairs of pits present. The pit pairs allow water to pass from cell to cell. While most conduction in the xylem is up and down, there is some side-to-side or lateral conduction via rays. Rays are horizontal rows of long-living parenchyma cells that arise out of the vascular cambium. In trees, and other woody plants, ray will radiate out from the centre of stems and roots and in cross-section will look like the spokes of a wheel.

PHLOEM

Phloem is an equally important plant tissue as it also is part of the 'plumbing' of a plant. Primarily, phloem carries dissolved food substances throughout the plant. This conduction system is composed of sieve-tube member and companion cells, that are without secondary walls. The parent cells of the vascular cambium produce both xylem and phloem. This usually also includes fibres, parenchyma and ray cells. Sieve tubes are formed from sieve-tube members laid end to end. The end walls, unlike vessel members in xylem, do not have openings. The end walls, however, are full of small pores where cytoplasm extends from cell to cell. These porous connections are called sieve plates. In spite of the fact that their cytoplasm is actively involved in the conduction of food materials, sieve-tube members do not have nuclei at maturity. It is the companion cells that are nestled between sieve-tube members that function in some manner bringing about the conduction of food. Sieve-tube members that are alive contain a polymer called callose. Callose stays in solution as long at the cell contents are under pressure. As a repair mechanism, if an insect injures a cell and the pressure drops, the callose will precipitate. However, the callose and a phloem protein will be moved through the nearest sieve plate where they will for a plug. This prevents further leakage of sieve tube contents and the injury is not necessarily fatal to overall plant turgor pressure.

EPIDERMIS

The epidermis is also a complex plant tissue, and an interesting one at that. Officially, the epidermis is the outermost layer of cells on all plant organs (roots, stems, leaves). The epidermis is in direct contact with the environment and therefore is subject to environmental conditions and constraints. Generally, the epidermis is one cell layer thick, however there are exceptions such as tropical plants where the layer may be several cells thick and thus acts as a sponge. Cutin, a fatty substance secreted by most epidermal cells, forms a waxy protective layer called the cuticle. The thickness of the cuticle is one of the main determiners of how much water is lost by evaporation. Additionally, at no extra charge, the cuticle provides some resistance to bacteria and other disease organisms. Some plants, such as the wax palm, produce enough cuticle to have commercial value: carnauba wax. Other wax products are used as polishes, candles and even phonographic records. Epidermal cells are important for increasing absorptive surface area in root hairs. Root hairs are essentially tubular extensions of the main root body composed entirely of epidermal cells. Leaves are not left out. They have many small pores called stomata that are surrounded by pairs of specialized epidermal cells called guard cells. Guard cells are unique epidermal cells because they are of a different shape and contain chloroplasts. There are other modified epidermal cells that may be glands or hairs that repel insects or reduce water loss.

PERIDERM

In woody plants, when the cork cambium begins to produce new tissues to increase the girth of the stem or root the epidermis is sloughed off and replaced by a periderm. The periderm is made of semi-rectangular and boxlike cork cells. This will be the outermost layer of bark. These cells are dead at maturity. However, before the cells die, the protoplasm secretes a fatty substance called suberin into the cell walls.

Suberin makes the cork cells waterproof and aids in protecting tissues beneath the bark. There are parts of the cork cambium that produce pockets of loosely packed cork cells. These cork cells do not have suberin imbedded in their cell walls. These loose areas are extended through the surface of the periderm and are called lenticels. Lenticels function in gas exchange between the air and the stem interior. At the bottom of the deep fissures in tree bark are the lenticels.

ROOTS

Upon seed germination, the embryo root, called the radicle, grows and develops into the first root. The radicle may thicken into a taproot with many branching roots, or it may develop into many adventitious roots. The direct opposite of a taproot system is a fibrous root system. This develops out of the many adventitious roots. In diameter, the roots in a fibrous system are very fine. There are many mature plants that have a combination system, which means there is a main taproot with many branching fibrous roots attached. Root hairs, or extensions of the epidermis as explained in the plant tissue tutorial, significantly increase the contact surface area of the root system. This allows for more exchange with the surrounding soil.

In general, most dicot plants (peas, carrots), or two seed-leaf plants, have taproot systems while monocot plants (corn, grasses), or one seed-leaf plants, have fibrous root systems.

Root Structure

Historically, developing roots have been categorized into four zones of development. These are not strict zones, but rather regions of cells that gradually develop into those of the next region. The zones vary widely as far as extent and levels of development.

Regions of root development:

- Root cap.
- Region of cell division.
- Region of elongation.
- Region of maturation.

Root Cap

In some plants the root cap is quite large and obvious, while in others it is nearly impossible to find. The root cap is made of parenchyma cells that form a thimble shape, as a covering for the tip of each root. The cap serves several functions. The main function being protection as the delicate root tip pushes through soil particles. In the outer cells of the root cap, the golgi bodies secrete a slimy substance that lodges in the walls and eventually pass to the outside. As the cells slough off, replaced from the inside, they form a slimy lubricant that aids root tip movement through the soil. In addition, to aiding movement, the slime is a supportive medium for beneficial bacteria.

The root cap serves in an additional capacity in determining root growth direction. As the root cap has a life span of about one week, it can serve for some interesting experiments. Whether the cap sloughs off or is cut off, the root will grow in random directions, as opposed to downward, until a new root cap is formed. This lends support to the notion that the root cap functions in the perception of gravity. On the sides of the root cap amyloplasts, or plastids containing starch grains, collect facing the direction of gravitational force. In documented experiments, when the root is tipped horizontally from it's vertical growing position, the amyloplasts will reshift themselves to the 'bottom' of the cells in which they are found. In a short time or 30 minutes to a few hours the root will resume growing downward. While the exact nature of this gravitational response, or gravitropism, is not fully known, there is some evidence that the calcium ions found in amyloplasts does influence the distribution of growth hormones in plant cells.

THE REGION OF CELL DIVISION

The region of cell division is the next zone in from the root cap. The root cap arises from the cells in this zone. This inverted cup-shaped region is composed of an apical meristem at it's edges. The cells divide every 12 to 36 hours at the tip of the meristem, while the ones at the base of the meristem may divide once every 200 to 500 hours. Interestingly enough, the divisions are rhythmic and peak usually twice a day around noon and midnight. In the interim the cells are not usually dividing. Most of the cells in this region are cube shaped with fairly large nuclei and few, if any, small vacuoles. As in stems as well, the apical meristem in the roots will subdivide and give rise to three meristematic areas: the protoderm, which gives rise to the epidermis; just to the inside of the protoderm, the ground meristem, which produces parenchyma cells of the cortex; and the solid looking cylinder in the centre of the root, the procambium, which produces primary xylem and phloem. The central pith tissue is found in many monocots, such as grasses, but is generally not seen in mature dicot plants due to compression by the vascular cylinder.

The Region of Elongation

This region is merged with the upper (towards the soil surface), region of the root apical meristem. It is in this region that the cells become several times their original length, and somewhat wider. The tiny vacuoles in each cell will merge and become one or two large vacuoles. In their final state, the enlarged vacuoles will account for up to 90% or more of the cellular volume. As only the root cap and apical meristem are actually moving through the soil, no further increase in cell size occurs above the region of elongation. While the elongated portions of the root generally remain stationary for the rest of their life, if a cambium is present there may be secondary growth and an increase in root girth.

The Region of Maturation

The region of maturation is sometimes also called the region of differentiation or root-hair zone. In this region, cells mature into the various types of primary tissues. Recall that root hairs are extensions of the epidermis that serve to increase surface area and aid in absorption of water and soil nutrients. If the region of maturation is examined carefully, it would be noted that the cuticle is very thin on the root hairs and epidermal cells of roots. It is understood that any significant amount of fatty substance would interfere with the ability to absorb water, as fats are hydrophobic—or water repelling. A root in cross-section would have an epidermis, cortex, endodermis, xylem, phloem and a pericycle. The cortex is tissue at the immediate inside of the epidermis that functions in storing food. Generally, the cortex is many cells thick and similar to the cortex of stems, with the exception of the presence of a root endodermis at the inner boundary. In stems, an endodermis is quite rare, while in roots only three species of plants are known to lack a root endodermis. The endodermis is a cylinder formed by a single layer of tightly arranged cells. The primary walls of these cells contain suberin. The waterproof suberin forms bands, called Casparian strips, around the cell walls perpendicular to the root's surface. The barrier that is formed forces all water and dissolved substances entering and leaving the central tissue core to pass through the plasma membrane or their plasmodesmata. This entire structure serves to regulate the types of minerals absorbed and transported by the root to the stems.

Next to the inside of the endodermis is a cylinder of parenchyma cells called the pericycle. The pericycle is generally one cell wide, however, it can extend for several cells depending on the plant. It is a vital tissue, as the pericycle is the point of origin for the lateral branch roots, and if it is a dicot, part of the vascular cambium. The cells in the pericycle retain their ability to divide even after they have matured. Primary xylem, which contains water conducting cells, forms at the core of the root and may or may not have observable 'branches' which extend like an 'x' to the pericycle. Primary phloem, which contains the food conducting cells, fills in the spaces between the branches of xylem. Any branch roots will usually arise in the pericycle opposite the xylem branches.

Most plants produce a fibrous root system, a taproot system, or most commonly a combination of both. However, some plants have roots with modifications that allow specific functions in addition to the absorption of water and minerals in solution.

Food-Storage Roots

In certain plants the roots, or part of the root system, is enlarged in order to store large quantities of starch and other carbohydrates. Sweet potatoes and yams, for example, have extra cambial cells that develop in the xylem portion of branch roots. The cambial cells produce numerous parenchyma cells that cause the organs to swell. Starches are then stored in the swollen areas of the root. Carrots, beets and turnips have storage organs that are actually a combination of root and stem. Approximately, the top two centimeters of a carrot are actually derived from the stem. Although, you likely will not be able to see the origin of the cells just by looking at a carrot.

Water-Storage Roots

Plants that grow in particularly arid regions are known for growing structures used to retain water. Some plants in the Pumpkin Family produce huge water storing roots. The plant will then use the stored water in times or seasons of low precipitation. Some cultures will harvest the water storing root and use them for drinking water. Plants storing up to 159 pounds (72 kilograms) of water in a single major root have been found and documented.

To propagate means to produce more of oneself. Propagative root structures are a way for a plant to produce more of itself. Adventitious buds are buds that appear in unusual places. Many plants will produce these buds along the roots that grow near the surface of the ground. Suckers, or aerial stems with rootlets, will develop from these adventitious buds. The 'new' plant can be separated from the original plant and can grow independently. Some plants will produce propagative roots up to 30 feet or more away from the parent plant. This can be a nuisance for some people, while others may enjoy the propagative qualities of their cherry tree, strawberries or horseradish plants.

Pneumatophores

Pneumatophores are spongy roots that develop in most plants that grow in water. Swamps, marshes and coastal areas are good places to find plants with pneumatophores. These specialized roots account for the fact that water, even after having air bubbled through it, has less than one thirtieth of the amount of free oxygen that is found in air. Plants growing in water may require additional methods of obtaining oxygen for respiration. Pneumatophores fill that need by rising above the water surface and facilitating gas exchange.

There are many different kinds of aerial roots produced by a wide variety of plants. Orchids produce velamen roots, corn plants have prop roots, ivies have adventitious roots and vanilla orchids even have photosynthetic roots that can manufacture food. Banyan trees have aerial roots that grow down from the tree branches until they touch find the soil. In a nutshell, aerial roots are roots that are not covered by soil hence out in the air. They can facilitate climbing and various types of support as demonstrated by ivies and creeper plants.

Contractile roots are roots that pull the plant deeper into the soil. Lily bulbs are a good example, as each bulb is pulled a little further into the soil as additional contractile roots are developed each year. When a region of stable temperature is reached, the contractile roots quit pulling. Dandelions also have contractile roots, and their presence is noticeable because the lower leaves may look like they are coming right out of the ground. In reality, the roots are pulling the stem downward. The actual mechanism of contraction involves the thickening and constriction of parenchyma cells. This causes the components of xylem to spiral into a corkscrew shape. The portion of the root that contracts may lose up to two-thirds of its length within weeks.

Tropical trees may have large buttress roots at the base of the trunk. These roots add stability to the tree and give an angular look to the lower visible portion of the trunk. Some plants, such as dodders, broomrapes and pinedrops do not have chlorophyll. They will parasitize other plants and utilize their chlorophyll and food making abilities. The parasitic mechanism involves rootlike projections called haustoria (singular haustorium). These projections develop along stems that are in contact with the host. They will penetrate the outer tissues of the host plant, and will tap into the water and food conducting tissues (xylem and phloem). Other plants with chlorphyll, such as mistletoes, will also form haustoria in order to obtain water and dissolved minerals from host plants. They are capable of producing their own food, and thus are considered to be partially parasitic.

Mycorrhizae

Mycorrhizae are fungal roots found in many plants. These fungal associations are important for both the plant and for the fungal and are therefore considered to be mutualistic. Essentially, the fungus will have a greater capacity for absorbing phosphorus than root hairs alone. The fungus will also grow and increase the absorption of water and other nutrients. In return, the plant provides sugars and amino acids vital to the survival of the fungus. Plants with mycorrhizae generally have less root hairs than those without. Nearly all woody trees and shrubs found in forests have fungal associations in their root systems. However, it has been demonstrated that mycorrhizae are particularly susceptible to acid rain. This may have a direct impact on forest health and maintenance.

Root Nodules

It is important to note that root nodules are not root knots, which are root swellings in response to worm invasions. Root nodules are beneficial bacterial colonies that are visible as small swellings in the root system. The bacteria aid the plant in fixing, or converting, atmospheric nitrogen in to a form that the plant can use. Root nodules are found extensively throughout the legume family. A nodule develops when a substance leaked into the soil by plant roots stimulates Rhizobium bacteria to produce another substance that coused root hairs to bend sharply. The bacterium may attach in the crook of the bend and then 'invade' the cell with a tubular infection thread. This thread does not penetrate the cell wall and plasma membrane. The thread, does however, grow through to the cortex which is stimulated to produce new cells that will become part of the housing for the bacterium. As the bacteria multiply and the colony grows, the nodule will swell. It is in the crook of root hairs that the nitrogen fixing takes place.

STEMS

EXTERNAL FORM OF A WOODY TWIG

A woody twig, or stem, is an axis with leaves attached. The leaves are arranged in various ways around and on the axis. You may hear them described as alternate, or alternately arranged, opposite or oppositely arranged, or if they are found in groups of three or more they may be referred to as whorled. The region, just a general area in this case, where the leaves attach to the stem are called nodes. The region of stem between two nodes is called the internode. The leaf blade is attached to the stem via a stalk called the petiole. In the angle, or axil, formed between the petiole and the stem you will find the axillary bud. Axillary refers to a structure that forms an armpit, just for trivia's sake. These buds can become new branches or they may have tissues that will form into flowers for the next season. Most buds are protected by bud scales which fall off as bud tissue begins to grow. In general, at the tip of a twig a terminal (or ending) bud is present. It is larger than the axillary buds and produces tissues to extend twig length during the growing season. When the bud scales of a terminal bud fall off they leave scars on the twig. You can calculate the age of a twig by counting up the terminal bud scale scars. There are other scars on twigs that may look like terminal bud scars that are left by paired appendages called stipules which are found at the base of a petiole in the axil.

Trees and shrubs that lose their leaves every year, deciduous plants, have characteristic leaf scars with dormant, or not active, axillary buds directly above them. Sometimes tiny bundle scars can be seen. These scars are found in the leaf scar and mark the location of food and water conducting tissues. The shape and arrangement of the bundle scars can help distinguish deciduous trees in the winter months when the leaf structures are absent.

THE ORIGIN AND DEVELOPMENT OF STEMS

Recall that the apical meristem is responsible for vertical growth, or increase in length of a stem. Prior to the start of the growing season, the cells in the apical meristem are dormant. The apical meristem is protected at the tip of the twig, by the covering bud scales and by the leaf primordial. The leaf primordia are tiny embryonic leaves that will develop into mature leaves after bud scales drop off and growth commences. When a seed germinates or a bud begins to grow, the cells in the apical meristem undergo mitosis.

From these cells three primary meristems will develop:

- The outermost meristem is the protoderm, which gives rise to the epidermis. This layer is usually one cell thick and becomes coated with a waxy cuticle.
- The second layer is the procambium, which is a cylinder of strands. This layer gives rise to the primary xylem and primary phloem cells.
- The innermost meristem is the ground meristem from which arises two tissues composed of parenchyma cells. The tissue in the centre of the stem is the pith. These cells are large and may break down shortly after being formed which leaves a cylindrical hollow area. If they do not break down, they will be compressed by new additions to the plant girth by other meristems. The second parenchyma tissue that arises is called cortex. Cortex may be quite extensive and also crushed or replaced in woody stems. The function of both tissues is food storage. If chloroplasts are present the tissues may function in producing food.

It is important to note that all five of the above mentioned tissues—epidermis, primary xylem, primary phloem, pith and cortex—are produced by the apical meristem and are thus primary tissues as the plant is increasing in length. Xylem and phloem tissue branch off from the main vascular cylinder and enter into the leaf or bud. Each branching of vascular tissue is called a trace. Each trace branch leaves a small thumbnail shaped gap in the cylinder of tissue and are called leaf gaps and bud gaps.

In between the primary xylem and primary phloem a thin band of cells retains its meristematic nature. This band becomes the vascular cambium of one of the two lateral meristems. In woody plants, and some others, a second cambium arises from the cortex or sometimes the epidermis or phloem. The second cambium is called the cork cambium or phellogen and is responsible for producing cork cells. Recall that the cork cells become filled with suberin which waterproofs the cells. The resulting cork tissue constitutes the out bark of woody plants and functions to reduce water loss and to protect the stem against mechanical injury. We will revisit the role of cork later on in discussing biotechnology and propagation. For now, though, understand that cork tissue cuts off food and water supplies to the epidermis which results in a sloughing off. Also understand that cork tissues do not form a solid cylinder around the exterior of a woody stem. This is to allow vital gas exchange with the environment.

Before we go on, it is important to remember the difference between monocots and dicots, the two main divisions of flowering plants. Most of the distinguishing revolves around the seed leaves, which are called cotyledons. Cotyledons function in storing food needed by the young seedling until true leaves grow and are able to take over the food supplying function.

- *Monocotyledon (monocot) Plants:* These plants form from seeds that have one embryonic seed leaf (hence the 'mono' in monocot).
- *Dicotyledon (dicot) Plants:* These plants form from seeds that have two (hence the 'di' in dicot) embryonic seed leaf.

Cone bearing trees, conifers such as pines, have multiple cotyledons, usually eight, in their seed structure.

There are four tissue patterns to be aware of in the study of plants.

- *Steles*—steles are a central cylinder in most younger stems and roots, composed of primary xylem, phloem and the pith, if present. Sometimes referred to as eusteles, which are vascular bundles in higher vascular plants.

- *Herbaceous Dicotyledonous Stems*—Herbaceous refers to non-woody plants. Plants that die after going from seed to maturity are called annuals. In general, most monocots are annuals, but there are annual dicot plants as well. Annual dicots are mostly composed of primary tissues, although there may be some minimal secondary growth. Remember, the plant only lives a year, so extensive secondary growth, or increases in width, really doesn't make sense as far as using the plant resources. A cross-section of a herbaceous dicot stem will show discrete patches of xylem and phloem, vascular bundles, that are arranged in a proper ring separating the cortex and the pith. If secondary xylem and phloem are to emerge, they will arise from between the two primary tissues.
- *Woody Dicotyledonous Stems*—Wood is essentially secondary xylem growth. These stems look similar to herbaceous dicot stems up until the vascular cambium and the cork cambium start functioning. The differences are then quite obvious. While some tropical trees demonstrate year round secondary growth, most trees in temperate climates grow in the spring and summer and cease through the winter. In the springtime, when water and resources are plentiful, the vascular cambium produces large xylem cells. During the summer months when resources and water may be lacking or reduced, the xylem cells are small. Pressed up against the large, light coloured xylem cells, the small xylem cells look like a thin dark ring. One year of xylem growth, called an annual ring, can be measured as the distance between the dark rings—or the distance between summer xylem growth. Summer growth is called summer wood while the large spring cells are

called spring wood. Much can be learned about the local environmental conditions through the years by looking at tree rings. If water is plentiful the rings will be wider than usual. Years with fires and blights will be evident, as well as insect infestations and fungal infections. All this by looking at a cross section of a tree. In conifers, vessels and fibres are absent and thus the wood consists mainly of tracheids. It is important therefore to remember that environmental conditions affect xylem production and the dark rings may not be completely visible, one year's growth is what constitute an annual ring, not just dark circles.

The vascular cambium produces more xylem than phloem. In fact, the phloem will be difficult to locate as the cells are thinner than xylem and more likely to collapse under the pressure of the cambiums. Phloem grows to the outside of the vascular cambium and xylem grows to the inside. The oldest xylem is in the very centre of the stem/trunk. The wood in the centre is called heartwood. It is usually darker as the vessels and tracheids are filled with old resins, gums and tannins. The younger wood where the xylem is still functioning is towards the outside of the stem nearest the cambium and is lighter in colour. This younger wood is called sapwood. The main role of heartwood is structure and support, since it is unable to conduct water and nutrients. The heartwood sometimes rots out of a otherwise living tree. Sapwood develops at roughly the same rate that heartwood is 'retiring' and thus vital conducting functions are not compromised. Recall that conifers do not have vessels or fibres and are primarily tracheids. Conifers have resin canals scattered throughout the xylem tissue. Conifers are primarily considered to be softwoods while the wood of woody dicot trees are considered to be hardwood. Bark is all of the tissues outside of the cambium, including the phloem. Some have gone so far as to distinguish between inner bark—primary and secondary phlolem and outer bark—the periderm, which consists of cork tissue and cork cambium. The cells in these layers only function briefly as they usually become crushed and then slough off. New layers are annually produced by the cambiums. The youngest phloem cells are the ones nearest the vascular cambium and are most active in transporting nutrients, sugars and water. Mature bark may be composed of alternating layers of crushed phloem and cork.

- *Monocotyledonous Stems:* These plants are usually grass or grass-like and do not grow to great size. Monocot stems do not have vascular cambiums or cork cambiums, as growth will not be laterally. The vascular bundles produced by the procambium are scattered throughout the stem, rather than organized in rings as in woody dicot stems. Every bundle is oriented with the xylem towards the centre of the stem and the phloem towards the stem surface. The xylem in the vascular bundle generally consists of two large vessels with some small vessels in between them, while the phloem consists of sieve tubes and companion cells. The entire vascular bundle is wrapped in a sheath of sclerenchyma cells. The background tissue between vascular bundles is not divided into cortex and pith in monocots, but they do have similar function and appearance as the parenchyma cells in cortex and pith. The concentration of bundles and bands of sclerenchyma cells, give the stem the flexibility and strength to withstand the elements—such as a summer rainstorm. In grasses, there is an intercalary meristem at the base o each internode which contributes to growth in length, like apical meristems. During the growing season, the stems of the grasses elongate rapidly. Because there is no vascular cambium that would produce tissues to increase the girth of the plant, the growth is columnar with very little variation in diameter between the top and the bottom of the plant.

Palm trees are special, because they grow to considerable size, however this is primarily due to the subsequent division and growth of their parenchyma cells. All this growth occurs without a true cambium developing. Other monocot stems have adaptations that allow for specialized growth. Monocot fibres, such as manila hemp and sisal, come from stems and leaves and are used for commercial products however, their fibres are not as strong as dicot fibres.

- *Rhizomes*—horizontal stems that grow beneath the ground, but near the surface of the soil. They resemble roots, but are actually modified stems with scale-like leaves and buds at each axillary node. In addition, adventitious roots are produced along the rhizome on the lower surface in order to increase absorption surface area.
- *Runners and Stolons*—Runners are horizontal stems that grow above ground, usually along the surface (compare with rhizomes). Strawberry plants produce runners after the first flowering of the season, they may extend out up to 3 feet or more beyond the parent plant. Along the runner, adventitious buds will develop in order to propagate new plants. Stolons are similar to runners, except that they grow roughly vertically beneath the surface of the soil. Irish potato plants have tubers at the tips of stolons.
- *Tubers*—Tubers develop at the tips of stolons. The plant accumulates food at the stolon and the area swells at the internodes. When the tuber is mature the stolon will die and the 'eyes' of the potato are actually nodes arranged in a spiral around the modified stem. Each eye has an axillary bud in the axil of a tiny leaf, which is not always visible in maturing tubers.

- *Bulbs*—These are actually large buds with a small stem at the lower end that is surrounded with fleshy leaves. Onions, irises and tulips are good examples of bulbs and their main function is food storage.
- *Corms*—On first glance you might think these guys are bulbs, however, the differences lie beneath the thin layer of leaves covering the outside of the corm. Adventitious roots form beneath the fullness of the base. Corms function in storing food. Crocuses and gladioli are good examples of plants with corms.
- *Cladophylls*—These are usually called the prickly part of a cactus. Cladophylls are flattened and somewhat leaf-like in appearance. They centre of each cladophyll usually has a node with small scalelike leaves complete with axillary buds. The scaly look to asparagus are cladophylls. These specialized stems are not only restricted to cacti, but are found in some orchids and greenbriars.
- *Other Specialized Stems*—Cacti usually have modifications in their stem or 'trunk' structure in order to hold extra water. Other stems may be modified into thorns or briars. It is important to remember that not all thorn-like structures are stems! Raspberry and rose prickles are extensions of their epidermis and are neither thorns nor spines. Other stems are modified for climbing, such as tendrils and ramblers.

Stems are vital to the human cause. They provide building materials, paper products, food and much, much more! Stop and think of how many things you encounter in a day that is either made of wood or plant fibre or a derivative product, chances are good the are a stem derivative.

LEAVES

Leaves are highly efficient solar energy converters. They capture light energy and through the process of photosynthesis they are able to trap energy in the form of sugar molecules that are constructed from carbon dioxide and water (both found in the atmosphere). All the energy required by living organisms is ultimately dependent upon photosynthesis. Leaves are able to twist on their petioles, stalks, in order to maximize sun exposure and photosynthetic activity. Leaves are covered with a thin layer of epidermal cells which permit light to the interior of the leaf, yet protect the cells from physical damage. In addition to photosynthesis leaves are involved in other vital plant functions. Respiration is a metabolic process which produces waste products. These products are deposited outside the plant when the leaves are shed. Leaves are also important to the movement of water absorbed by the roots and transported throughout the plant. The water that reaches the leaves mostly evaporates off into the atmosphere via transpiration. Leaves are complex plant organs upon which life depends.

LEAF ARRANGEMENTS AND TYPES

There are over 275,000 different kinds of plants and most of them can be distinguished from each other by their leaves alone. As mentioned in the last tutorial, leaves originate as primordial in the buds regardless of their ultimate size and shape. When all is said and done, leaves usually consist of a stalk, the petiole and a flattened blade, the lamina, which has a network of veins also known as the vascular bundles. Some leaves have a pair of appendages called stipules at the base of their petiole. In some cases, there is no petiole or stalk, and these leaves are called sessile. Deciduous trees generally lose their leaves once a year, after the growing season. Evergreens, or conifers, usually are only functional for two to seven years.

The overall arrangement of leaves with respect to the plant stem is called phyllotaxy. Leaves may be arranged in an alternate, opposite pattern if they are attached at the same node, or a whorled pattern if three or more are attached at a node. The leaf itself may be a simple leaf, which has an undivided blade; or a compound leaf, in which the blade is divided into leaflets in various ways. A pinnately compound leaf has leaflets in pairs along a central stalk—called the rachis. A palmately compound leaf has all its leaflets attached at the same point on the end of the petiole. The leaflets of a pinnatley compound leaf are sometimes subdivided into even smaller leaflets which makes a bipinnately compound leaf. The venation, or arrangement of vascular bundles, in a leaf blade or a leaflet may be either pinnate or palmate. A pinnately veined leaf has a main vein called the midrib with secondary veins branching out from it. However, in a palmately veined leaf, several veins branch out from the base of the blade—rather than from a central midrib. Monocot plants generally have leaves with parallel venation as compared with dicots, which have branching and diverging veins. The Ginkgo tree is special in that it has no midrib or other large veins. The veins fork evenly and progressively from the base of the blade out to the opposite margin of the leaf. This arrangement is called dichotomous (branching) venation.

In cross section there are three major regions to see in the inside of a leaf: epidermis, mesophyll and veins—or vascular bundles. The epidermal layer is one cell thick and covers the entire surface of the leaf. On the lower surface of the leaf blade, the epidermis is interrupted by stomata. The guard cells in the lower epidermal layer contain chloroplasts, but otherwise the epidermal cells do not have any chloroplasts and function as primary protection for the cells beneath. Most leaves have a thin covering of waxy cuticle.

Stomata

Stomata distinguish the lower epidermis from the upper epidermis. The upper epidermis is generally uninterrupted, but the lower epidermis is perforated by numerous tiny pores called stomata. The stomata (stoma singular) are very numerous and facilitate gas exchange between the interior of the leaf and the environment. Each stoma is regulated by a pair of sausage-shaped guard cells. They, as mentioned earlier, are the only cells in the epidermis with chloroplasts for photosynthesis. The photosynthetic products in the guard cells provide the energy for the functioning of the cells. The walls of the guard cells are thickened, except for the side adjacent to the pore. The cells will expand or contract with changes in the amount of water in the cells, hence the need for energy as the water is moved into and out of the guard cells. When the guard cells are full of water the stoma pore is open and when the water is evacuated the pore is closed.

Mesophyll and Veins

The majority of photosynthesis takes place in the mesophyll between the upper and lower epidermis layers. Usually the two layers of mesophyll can be distinguished from each other. The upper region is made of cells that look like short posts in two rows. These cells are parenchyma cells and make up the palisade mesophyll tissue. It is this tissue that contains more than 80% of the chloroplasts in the leaf. The lower layer of mesophyll, the spongy mesophyll tissue, is composed of loosely arranged parenchyma cells with abundant air space. The lower layer also contains many chloroplasts and its loose structure allows for movement of air in from the stomata. For future reference, parenchyma tissue containing numerous chloroplasts is called chlorenchyma tissue. It is also found in the outer parts of cortex in the stems of herbaceous plants. However, in the leaf, the surfaces of the mesophyll that come into contact with the air are moist. The stomata will close if the internal moisture drops below a certain level in order to reduce drying inside the leaf.

The skeleton of a leaf are the veins, or vascular bundles. They are of various sizes and as described in the leaf arrangement section, are scattered throughout the leaf and are organized distinctly in different types of leaves. The veins are surrounded by a jacket of fibres called the bundle sheath. The sugars produced in the mesophyll are transported via the veins throughout the plant—specifically in solution in the phloem. In dicots, the veins run in all directions. In monocots, the veins are parallel and are not scattered. In addition, monocots do not have mesophyll differentiated into two layers. Instead, some will have large thin-walled buliform cells surrounding the main vein. The thin-walled cells are sensitive to water conditions and will collapse in dry conditions which causes the leaf blade to fold or roll which reduces transpiration (water loss).

Depending on the conditions where a particular plant lives, it may or may not require some specialized adaptations in order to accommodate various environmental factors: humidity, temperature, light, water, and soil conditions for example. We will look briefly at ten types of specialized leaves.

- *Shade Leaves:* In some plants, leaves with barely noticeable or unnoticeable modifications will occur right alongside those that are unmodified. Leaves in the shade tens to be thinner and have fewer hairs than those on the same tree exposed to direct light. In addition, they are generally larger and have less defined mesophyll layers and reduced numbers of chloroplasts than their better lit counterparts.
- *Leaves of Arid Regions:* In growing environments with extremely arid conditions, the plants will generally have thicker more leathery leaves. Their stomata are usually reduced in number and are sunken into the leaf surface in special depressions. Some may have succulent leaves or no leaves at all—where the stem takes over photosynthetic responsibilities—or they may have dense hairy coverings. In areas where the soil freezes and water resources are limited, pine trees may have modifications similar to desert plants. Including sunken stomata, thicker cuticle and a hypodermis (thick walled cells) beneath the epidermis. The compass plant is a unique example of growth set up directionally—East and West—in order to reduce moisture loss.
- *Tendrils:* Many plants have modified leaf structures called tendrils that aid in climbing or supporting the plant's weight. Tendrils are very sensitive to contact and can be readily redirected based on touch and solid contact. Tendrils become coiled like springs and when contact with a support structure is made, the tip not only coils around it but the tip direction reverses. It needs to be noted that not all tendrils are modified leaves, tendrils of the grapevine, for example, are modified extensions of the stem tissue.

- *Spines, Thorns and Prickles:* Desert plants have leaves modified as spines. Water loss is correlated to surface area, so the decrease in leaf surface area consequently decreases water loss to the outside. In plants with spines, photosynthesis is generally conducted by the stem tissue. The tissue is made of sclerenchyma cells and replaces any 'normal' leaf tissues. The modifications arising in the axils of leaves are stem modifications not leaf spines, but thorns. Recall, that the prickles of roses and raspberries are not leaves or stems, but outgrowths of the epidermal or cortex just beneath the prickle.
- *Storage Leaves:* Succulent leaves are leaves modified to retain and store water. Water storage is permitted because of the thin-walled, non-chloroplast parenchyma cells just beneath the epidermis and to the interior of the chlorenchyma tissue. The vacuoles in the non-photosynthetic cells store the extra water resources. There are plants with succulent leaves that have a special photosynthetic process. We will look at these in a later tutorial. The fleshy leaves of onions and lily bulbs store large amounts of carbohydrates which are utilized by the plant in the next growing season.
- *Flower Pot Leaves:* The leaves of some plants, such as the Dischidia plant from tropical Australasia, develop odd pouches that become the symbiotic homes of ant colonies. The colonies carry in soil particles and add nitrogenous wastes, which the leaves collect moisture through the condensation of water vapour via the stomata. The area is a rich medium for the adventitious roots that grow down into the soil contained in the pouch—hence the flower pot function of the modified leaf.
- *Window Leaves:* There are at least three members of the Carpetweed family in the Kalahari desert with unique adaptations to the sandy growing environment. These plants have leaves shaped like

ice cream cones. The leaves are buried in the sand, leaving the transparent dime-sized tip of the leaf exposed at the surface. The transparent surface is covered with a thick epidermis and cuticle and has virtually no stomata. This arrangement allows light nearly direct access to the mesophyll with chloroplasts inside. The plant, for the most part, is buried and away from drying winds and abrasive blowing sands. There are other examples of succulent plants with window leaves.

- *Reproductive Leaves:* Walking fern leaves produce new plants at their tips. Air plants, a succulent, have little notches along their leaf margins where new plant are produced with leaves and roots of their own. The baby plants will produce even if the parent leaf is separated from the rest of the plant.
- *Floral Leaves (Bracts):* Bracts are found at the bases of flowers and are sometimes mistaken as petals. They compensate for small flowers or absent petals. The poinsettia 'flower' is really composed of bracts. The centre cluster of tiny flowers is the main event, while the bracts do all the attracting.
- *Insect-Trapping Leaves:* These plants are always attention grabbers and have intrigued folks for centuries. Plants that trap insects usually occur in swampy areas and bogs of tropical and temperate regions. Generally, the soil is lacking some vital ingredient for life and the plants utilize trapped insects and small organisms to fill the gap. The captured prizes are dissolved and absorbed by the plant. However, if insects are not available (*i.e.* a laboratory situation) the plants will develop if nutrients are given instead. The following four plants represent the four main mechanisms of capture.

AUTUMN CHANGES IN LEAF COLOUR

As leaf cells break down after the growing season is over, the leaves tend to turn some shade of brown or tan due to a reaction between leaf proteins and tannins stored in the cell vacuoles. Prior to going completely tan or brown, the leaves usually demonstrate a wide variety of colours as they go through various stages of degeneration. In the chloroplasts of mature leaves are several groups of pigments such as green chlorophylls and carotenoids including yellow carotenes and pale yellox xanthophylls. These pigments play various roles in photosynthesis. The green chlorophylls are usually found in higher concentrations and during the season of active growth they are able to mask the other pigments. As the chlorophylls break down during the fall, the other colours become apparent. The breakdown of chlorophyll is not completely understood, however, it appears to be tied to the gradual reduction in day length. Anthocyanin, a common red pigment and betacyanin a second red colour may also accumulate in the cell vacuoles as fall progresses. Anthocyanins are red if the cell sap is slightly acidic and blue if the sap is more alkali (basic). Betacyanins are restricted to several plant families, including cacti and beets. While some trees demonstrate brilliant fall displays of chlorophyll breakdown, others such as birch trees have a single shade of colour in their fall leaves.

Abscission

Deciduous trees and plants, the ones who lose their leaves once a year have different cycles depending on where they are at in the world. In temperate climates, the leaves generally drop in the fall in preparation for winter and new growth comes in the spring. In tropical regions, the cycle follows the cycles of wet and dry seasons. Evergreen trees do shed their leaves, however not all at once or even annually. Abscission is the process in which leaves shed; whether deciduous or evergreen.

At the base of the petiole, stalk, of each leaf there is an abscission zone. Changes that take place in this region ultimately result in the drop of leaves. Hormonal changes take place as the leaf ages and two layers of cells become differentiated. (In young leaves hormones prevent these cells from differentiating.) The cell layer closest to the stem becomes the protective layer which is usually several cells deep and suberized, or coated with a fatty suberin substance. The other layer, the separation layer, forms on the leaf side of things. The cells swell and become like jelly. The pectins in the middle lamella of the cells in the separation layer are broken down by enzymes until an external event causes the leaf to fall: this could include the force of gravity overcoming the strength of the strands of xylem holding the leaf to the petiole, thus breaking it off at the gelatinous zone, wind, rain, animals etc. The pectin breakdown begins in response to environmental conditions such as dropping temperature, lack of adequate water, decreasing day lengths, changing light intensities, or damage to the leaf.

Importance to Humans

Leaves are vital to humans. Not just for food but many medicines come from plant leaves. Tobacco products come from leaves, as do some hemp products and other textile fibres. Cocaine and aspirin are from leaves as are some insecticides. Aloe vera for the relief of burns—even x-ray burns will respond to aloe vera. Leaves are also used in floral arrangements and other products of aesthetic value. Bottom line: leaves, like stems are of great value to humans.

SOILS

Where a plant grows and what resources are available to it is of vital importance to the life of a plant. The soil type and quality can be the difference between survival and termination for a plant. Soil is a very dynamic and complex portion of the earth's crust. In some places the soil is only a few centimeters thick, while in others it is hundreds of feet deep. In the grand scheme of things, soil is vital not only to us as humans, but also to the existence of nearly all living organisms. Soil contributes to the plants that grow in it, just as the growing plants give back to the soil. It is a point of dynamic exchange between the living and non-living components of the earth.

The soil as what it is today, is a result of many factors coming together: climate, parent material, local topography, vegetation, living organisms and, of course, time. All of the factors can be involved in various degrees, which is why there are many thousands of soil types. The solid bulk of soil consists of minerals and organic matter. In between the solid particles are pore spaces, which are filled with varying amounts of air and water. The pore sizes and how they are connected within the soil bulk, determine the quality of soil aeration. Aeration refers to how water and air are held within a soil sample.

In looking closer at soils, it is important to understand that there are general regions or horizons of soil development that are usually obvious in an undisturbed area. For example, if we found an undisturbed area, and dug down 3 to 6 feet (1 or 2 meters), we would likely find a soil profile (cross section of the horizons) of three integrated horizons. The composition and stage of development will obviously vary widely depending on where the soil profile is taken. The top horizon is called the A horizon or topsoil. This horizon is usually 4 to 8 inches on average, again depending on where your sample is from.

The A horizon is further subdivided into a darker upper portion, called the A1 horizon and a lighter lower portion A2 horizon. The A1 horizon contains the majority of the organic material out of the three integrated horizons. The next horizon is the B horizon, or the subsoil. This is usually 1 or 2 feet deep on average.

SOIL PARENT MATERIAL

As a quick review, soil development is first predicated on the formation of parent material. Parent material accumulates via the weathering of igneous, sedimentary and metamorphic rocks. Igneous rocks are ones from volcanic activity, sedimentary rocks are formed from glacial deposits, water or wind action, and metamorphic rocks are ones formed from the other two types after undergoing extreme pressures and heat deep within the earth. These three types of rocks would require separate tutorials of their own for complete understanding. However, for now, just realize that these three rock types are the basis for the development of soil.

Climate

The climate is a globally varying feature and weighs heavily upon the weathering of rocks for soil parent material. For example, in desert or arid regions, there is little rain weathering and the soils are poorly developed. In contrast, areas of high liquid precipitation result in well developed soils. In areas where the temperature ranges widely, rocks may split and crack and cause rock breakdown. It is important to understand that the climate plays a direct role not only in the ensuring water resources to plants, but also the soil resources to plants.

Organic Composition and Living Organisms

In addition to nematode activity, the bacteria and fungi present in the soil decompose all sorts of organic material, such as leaves, dead roots, and animal carcasses. Living organisms and their organs, such as roots, produce carbon dioxide, which combines with water and forms an acid. The acidic nature results in a higher dissolving rate for the minerals present in the soil. Bacteria, fungi, nematodes, birds, ants and other burrowing insects all serve as composters for topsoil. As these organisms alter the soil through their activities, they add to it with their wastes and the decomposition of their bodies when they die. The organic composition of soil depends on external factors, such as location and water resources. If an area is constantly wet, and oxygen is limited or lacking in the soil, the microorganism activity may be quite low and the organic content may be as high as 90%. Thus the organic content in that soil will be quite high. On average, topsoil might be composed of 25% air, 25% water, 48% minerals and 2% organic material. Furthermore, with the exception of legumes and a few other plants, almost all of the nitrogen needed by growing plants, and most of the phosphorus and sulphur come from the decomposition of organic matter. As the decomposition progresses, the acid content increases which in turn increases the breakdown of minerals which will be carried into solution into growing plants.

Local Area Topography

Topography refers to the surface features of an area. For example, if an area is steep soil that is weathered from parent material may quickly wash away or erode through the actions of wind, ice and water. On the other hand, if an area is flat and poorly drained, water may pool in slight depressions after it rains. This lack of drainage could result in interrupting the activities of microorganisms in the soil. Thus soil development is stopped. An ideal set of surface features would be ones that allow for soil drainage without erosion.

Mineral Composition and Soil Texture

The size of the individual soil particles is called soil texture. The three general designations are sand, silt and clay. Generally, sands and gravels are composed of many small particles bound together chemically or by a matrix of cementing material. Silt is composed of finer particles that are usually too small to see without a hand lens or microscope. Clay particles are even smaller yet. They are visible individually with a electron microscope as even a powerful light microscope will not render them visible. Clay particles are individually called micelles. These particles are negatively charged, sheet-like and held together by chemical bonds. Because of their negative nature, they attract, trade or capture positively charged ions. The water that adheres tightly to the particle surface acts as a binding agent and a lubricant. This lends to the plastic nature of clay. Clay is also a colloid, meaning it is a suspension of particles that are larger than molecules, yet do not settle out of a fluid medium. The fluid medium is generally water. These three particles in various balances comprise the bulk of soil.

Soils are sometimes referred to as heavy and light. Light soils have a low clay content and a high sand content; while heavy soils have a high clay content and a low sand content. Clay soils have a high water content as they do not allow water to pass through between the particles, recall that water is a binding agent in clay. Sandy, or coarse-textured, soils do not retain much water. Organic matter and clay store more plant nutrients in the form of ions than sand and silt. The smaller clay and organic particles have a greater total surface area for the attachment of ions compared to an equal volume of sand and silt particles.

SOIL STRUCTURE

Soil structure refers to aggregates. Aggregates are formed as a result of the arrangement and grouping of soil particles. Sand and gravel aggregates do not demonstrate cohesion very well. In most good agricultural soils, aggregates that stick together form readily. The structure of soil, aggregates, forms when colloidal particles clump together. The clumping is usually a result of the activities of soil organisms and temperature changes resulting in freezing and thawing. Without a coating of organic matter, the individual granules will continue to clump until they are clods.

Good agricultural soils are granular with many pore spaces, occupying between 40% and 60% of the total soil volume. Recall how important pore spaces are to aeration and drainage. Air and water are trapped within these pores and if the pores are numerous, but small and poorly connected, as in clay soils, the restricted movement does not allow for good drainage or aeration. Furthermore, when the pores are full of water and air is not able to move in, plant roots suffer as there is not enough oxygen for root growth. Sandy soils on the other hand have their problems as well. For one, the large pores allow gravity to drain water out of the soil as soon as the pores are filled. As the water drains, the pores fill with air, which in turns speeds up nitrogen release by microorganisms. Much of the nitrogen released is lost as plants cannot utilize nitrogen that quickly.

Contrary to popular habit, watering can severely damage plants. Mainly, too much water leaches minerals and slows mineralizations processes with anaerobic conditions (due to the reduction or lack of free oxygen). Overwatering can slow the release of nitrogen, which interferes with plant growth and speed up the breakdown of nitrates.

WATER IN THE SOIL

There are three forms of water occurring in soil.

- Hygroscopic water is unavailable to plants, because it is physically bound to soil particles.
- Gravitational water is the water that drains from pore spaces after a rain. Plant grow can be affected if drainage is poor.
- Capillary water is the main source of water for plant needs. This is the water held in soil pore spaces against the force of gravity. Both structure and organic material composition of the soil enable the soil to hold water in this manner. Vegetation density and type and the location of underground water tables are the determinants of how much capillary water is available to the plant.

Following rain or irrigation, gravity drains water away from the soil. The field capacity of the soil is the amount of water remaining after such a draining. This characteristic is mainly determined by the texture of the soil, however, structure and organic material content also play a role. When soil is at or near field capacity plants will readily absorb water. In the process of soil drying, the film of water around each soil particle becomes thinner and more tightly bound to the particle.

As the water film binds to the particle, the likelihood of the water entering the root is lessened. A point of no return is eventually reached, if water is not added to the plant. This point is called the permanent wilting point and refers to the soil moisture. It is at this point that the plant is unable to absorb water at a rate sufficient for its needs. The plant wilts and will die. The permanent wilting point in a clay soil is reached when the water content drops below 15%. In sandy soils this point can be as low as 4%. The soil water between field capacity an the permanent wilting point is called available water.

Earlier we mentioned that the breakdown of minerals lends to the acidity of the soil. It is important to understand that the pH, acidity or alkalinity, of soil affects both the soil and the plant in a variety of ways. Soil that is not balanced, that is either too acidic or too alkaline, may be toxic to roots. However, normally an unbalanced soil pH will affect nutrient availability before they will affect the plant directly. In general, when soil is acidic the nitrogen fixing abilities of plants are affected.

Alkalinity will affect the availability of minerals such as copper, iron and manganese. In areas of high precipitation, soil is usually acidic because alkaline components are leached from the topsoil. Many agricultural operations will counterbalance any soil imbalances by adding lime (compounds of calcium or magnesium) to balance acidic soil, or by adding sulphur to alkaline soils. Bacteria in the soil will convert the sulphur to sulphuric acid, which will lower the overall pH which will make the soil more acidic. Nitrogen based fertilizers may have the same effect on alkaline soils.

It is a fine balance to have, but soil quality directly influences plant quality.

VASCULAR TISSUE

The vascular tissues include xylem, which conducts water and minerals from the roots upward and throughout the plant, and phloem, which transports dissolved foods in all directions within the plant. The main conducting vessels of xylem are the tracheids and the vessels. Tracheids are long, thin tubes found in most vascular plants, while vessels are large tubes found predominantly in angiosperms. The tracheids and vessels form pipelines that have pores and perforated ends, which allow water and minerals to be conducted from one tube to the next and out to the surrounding tissues. Tracheids and vessels also help support the plant body.

The main conducting cells of phloem are sieve cells and sieve tube members. Both cell types have numerous pores through which substances are exchanged with adjacent cells. Sieve tube members occur in angiosperms, while sieve cells are found in other vascular plants. In angiosperms, small cells called *companion cells* assist the sieve tube members in their functions. Vascular tissue is a complex conducting tissue, formed of more than one cell type, found in vascular plants. The primary components of vascular tissue are the xylem and phloem. These two tissues transport fluid and nutrients internally. There are also two meristems associated with vascular tissue: the vascular cambium and the cork cambium. All the vascular tissues within a particular plant together constitute the vascular tissue system of that plant.

The cells in differentiated vascular tissue are typically long and slender. Since the xylem and phloem function in the conduction of water, minerals, and nutrients throughout the plant, it is not surprising that their form should be similar to pipes. The individual cells of phloem are connected end-to-end, just as the sections of a pipe might be. As the plant grows, new vascular tissue differentiates in the growing tips of the plant. The new tissue is aligned with existing vascular tissue, maintaining its connection throughout the plant. The vascular tissue in plants is arranged in long, discrete strands called vascular bundles. These bundles include both xylem and phloem, as well as supporting and protective cells. In stems and roots, the xylem typically lies closer to the interior of the stem with phloem towards the exterior of the stem. In the stems of some Asteriidae dicots, there may be phloem located inwardly from the xylem as well.

Between the xylem and phloem is a meristem called the vascular cambium. This tissue divides off cells that will be become additional xylem and phloem. This growth increases the girth of the plant, rather than its length. As long as the vascular cambium continues to produce new cells, the plant will continue to grow more stout. In trees and other plants that develop wood, the vascular cambium allows the expansion of vascular tissue that produces woody growth. Because this growth ruptures the epidermis of the stem, woody plants also have a cork cambium that develops among the phloem. The cork cambium gives rise to thickened cork cells to protect the surface of the plant and reduce water loss. Both the production of wood and the production of cork are forms of secondary growth.

In leaves, the vascular bundles are located among the spongy mesophyll. The xylem is oriented towards the adaxial surface of the leaf (usually the upper side), and phloem is oriented towards the abaxial surface of the leaf. This is why aphids are typically found on the underside of the leaves rather than on the top, since the phloem transports sugars manufactured by the plant and they are closer to the lower surface.

GROUND TISSUE

The ground tissue of the vascular plant is responsible for storing the carbohydrates produced by the plant. Ground tissue comprises the majority of a young plant and lies between the vascular and dermal tissues. The major cells of the ground tissue are *parenchyma cells,* which function in photosynthesis and nutrient storage. They have thin walls, many chloroplasts, and large vacuoles, and they form the mass of most leaves, stems, and roots.

Another cell of the ground substance is the *sclerenchyma cell*. Sclerenchyma cells are hollow with strong walls, and they help strengthen the ground tissue.

The types of ground tissue found in plants develop from ground tissue meristem and consists of three simple tissues:

- Parenchyma (cells with thin primary walls that retain their protoplasm).
- Collenchyma (cells with thick primary walls that retain their protoplasm).
- Sclerenchyma (cells with lignified secondary walls that have lost their protoplasm at maturity, *i.e.* are 'dead').
- Chlorenchyma (containing chloroplasts).

PARENCHYMA

Parenchyma (Para-beside; chyma-in filling) is the versatile ground tissue. It forms, for example, the cortex and pith of stems, the cortex of roots, the mesophyll of leaves, the pulp of fruits, and the endosperm of seeds. Parenchyma cells are living cells and may remain meristematic at maturity, meaning that they are capable of cell division if given the correct hormone stimulus. They have thin but flexible cellulose cell walls, and are generally polyhedral when close-packed, but approximately spherical when isolated from their neighbours. They have large central vacuoles, which allows the cells to store and regulate ions, waste products and water.

Parenchyma cells have a variety of functions:

- In leaves, they form the mesophyll and are responsible for photosynthesis and the exchange of gases, parenchyma cells in the mesophyll of leaves are a specialized parenchymatous tissue known as chlorenchyma (parenchyma with chloroplasts).
- Storage of starch, protein, fats and oils and water in roots, tubers (*e.g.* potato), seed endosperm (*e.g.* cereals) and cotyledons (*e.g.* pulses and groundnut).
- Secretion (*e.g.* hydathodes, nectaries and cells lining the inside of resin ducts).
- Wound repair and the potential for renewed meristematic activity.
- Other specialized functions such as aeration (aerenchyma) and support.

The form of parenchyma cells varies with their function. The epidermal parenchyma cells of a leaf are barrel shaped in cross section, but have a variety of outline shapes ranging from simple polygons to strongly branched and interlocked shapes resembling the pieces of a jigsaw puzzle, as in the leaves of *Arabidopsis thaliana*. In the epidermis of higher plants, only the guard cells have chloroplasts. This tissue serves as a barrier wall and protects the internal tissues from injury. In the spongy mesophyll of a leaf, parenchyma cells range from near-spherical and loosely arranged with large intercellular spaces to branched or stellate, mutually interconnected with their neighbours at the ends of the arms to form a three-dimensional network, as in the red kidney bean *Phaseolus vulgaris* and other mesophytes. These cells, with the epidermal guard cells of the stoma, form a system of air spaces and chambers that regulate the exchange of gases. They usually contain plastids.

COLLENCHYMA

Collenchyma tissue is composed of elongated cells with unevenly thickened walls. They provide structural support, particularly in growing shoots and leaves. Collenchyma tissue composes, for example, the resilient strands in stalks of celery. Its growth is strongly affected by mechanical stress upon the plant. The walls of collenchyma in shaken plants (to mimic the effects of wind etc.), may be 40%-100% thicker than those not shaken. The wall is made up of cellulose and pectin.

There are three principal types of collenchyma:

- Angular collenchyma (thickened at intercellular contact points).
- Tangential collenchyma (cells arranged into ordered rows and thickened at the tangential face of the cell wall).
- Lacunar collenchyma (have intercellular space and thickening proximal to the intercellular space).

Collenchyma cells are most often found adjacent to outer growing tissues, the vascular cambium and are known for increasing structural support and integrity.

SCLERENCHYMA

Sclerenchyma is a supporting tissue in plants. Two groups of sclerenchyma cells exist: fibres and sclereids. Their walls consist of cellulose, hemicellulose and lignin. Sclerenchyma cells are the principal, supporting cells in plant tissues that have ceased elongation. Sclerenchyma fibres are of great economical importance, since they constitute the source material for many fabrics (flax, hemp, jute, ramie). Unlike the collenchyma, mature sclerenchyma is composed of dead cells with extremely thick cell walls (secondary walls) that make up to 90% of the whole cell volume. It is the hard, thick walls that make sclerenchyma cells important strengthening and supporting elements in plant parts that have ceased elongation. The difference between fibres and sclereids is not always clear. Transitions do exist, sometimes even within one and the same plant.

Fibres

Fibres or bast are generally long, slender, so-called prosenchymatous cells, usually occurring in strands or bundles. Such bundles or the totality of a stem's bundles are colloquially called fibres. Their high load-bearing capacity and the ease with which they can be processed has since antiquity made them the source material for a number of things, like ropes, fabrics or mattresses. The fibres of flax (*Linum usitatissimum*) have been known in Europe and Egypt for more than 3000 years, those of hemp (*Cannabis sativa*) in China for just as long. These fibres, and those of jute (*Corchorus capsularis*) and ramie (*Boehmeria nivea,* a nettle), are extremely soft and elastic and are especially well suited for the processing to textiles. Their principal cell wall material is cellulose.

Contrasting are hard fibres that are mostly found in monocots. Typical examples are the fibres of many Gramineae, Agaves (sisal: *Agave sisalana*), lilies (*Yucca* or *Phormium tenax*), *Musa textilis* and others. Their cell walls contain, besides cellulose, a high proportion of lignin. The load-bearing capacity of *Phormium tenax* is as high as 20–25 kg/mm^2, the same as that of good steel wire (25 kg/ mm^2), but the fibre tears as soon as too great a strain is placed upon it, while the wire distorts and does not tear before a strain of 80 kg/mm^2. The thickening of a cell wall has been studied in *Linum*. Starting at the centre of the fibre are the thickening layers of the secondary wall deposited one after the other. Growth at both tips of the cell leads to simultaneous elongation. During development the layers of secondary material seem like tubes, of which the outer one is always longer and older than the next. After completion of growth the missing parts are supplemented, so that the wall is evenly thickened up to the tips of the fibres.

Fibres usually originate from meristematic tissues. Cambium and procambium are their main centres of production. They are usually associated with the xylem and phloem of the vascular bundles. The fibres of the xylem are always lignified, while those of the phloem are cellulosic. Reliable evidence for the fibre cells' evolutionary origin from tracheids exists. During evolution the strength of the tracheid cell walls was enhanced, the ability to conduct water was lost and the size of the pits reduced. Fibres that do not belong to the xylem are bast (outside the ring of cambium) and such fibres that are arranged in characteristic patterns at different sites of the shoot.

Sclereids

Sclereids are a reduced form of scleremchyma cells with highly thickened, lignified walls. They are small bundles of sclerenchyma tissue in plants that form durable layers, such as the cores of apples and the gritty texture of pears. Sclereids are much elongated and flexible with tapered ends. Sclereids are variable in shape. The cells can be isodiametric, prosenchymatic, forked or elaborately branched. They can be grouped into bundles, can form complete tubes located at the periphery or can occur as single cells or small groups of cells within parenchyma tissues.

But compared with most fibres, sclereids are relatively short. Characteristic examples are brachysclereids or the stone cells (called stone cells because of their hardness) of pears (*Pyrus communis*) and quinces (*Cydonia oblonga*) and those of the shoot of the wax-plant (*Hoya carnosa*). The cell walls fill nearly all the cell's volume. A layering of the walls and the existence of branched pits is clearly visible. Branched pits such as these are called ramiform pits. The shell of many seeds like those of nuts as well as the stones of drupes like cherries or plums are made up from sclereids.

6

Plant Anatomy

Plant anatomy or phytotomy is the general term for the study of the internal structure of plants. While originally it included plant morphology, which is the description of the physical form and external structure of plants, since the mid-20th century the investigations of plant anatomy are considered a separate, distinct field, and plant anatomy refers to *just* the internal plant structures. Plant anatomy is now frequently investigated at the cellular level, and often involves the sectioning of tissues and microscopy.

STRUCTURAL DIVISIONS

Plant anatomy is sometimes divided into the following categories:

> Flower anatomy, Calyx, Corolla, Androecium, Gynoecium, Leaf anatomy, Leaf anatomy, Stem anatomy, Stem structure, Fruit/Seed anatomy, Ovule, Seed structure, Pericarp, Accessory fruit, Wood anatomy, Bark, Cork, Phloem, Vascular cambium, Heartwood and sapwood, Branch collar, Root anatomy and Root structure.

PERMANENT TISSUES (MATURE TISSUES)

The permanent tissues are formed by the differentiated cells, which become specialised to perform specific functions like protection, support, storage and conduction. The permanent tissues always differentiate from the meristematic cells, during the process of growth.

CHARACTERISTIC FEATURES

The cells which form the permanent tissues, exhibit the following characteristic features:

- The cells vary in size and shape considerably. They may be spherical or oval or polygonal or irregular in shape. Sometimes the cells may also be elongated.
- The cells may be either compactly arranged, without any intercellular spaces or loosely arranged with intercellular spaces.
- The cell wall may be either thin or thick. Thin-walled cells contain only cellulose in their cell wall. Thick-walled cells contain other compounds like hemicellulose or pectin, in addition to cellulose. In some cases, a rigid polysaccharide called lignin may be deposited in the cell wall.
- Cytoplasm in these cells in almost always granular. It is usually found surrounding the vacuole. In highly specialised cells, cytoplasm is absent.
- Nucleus may be present or absent at maturity.
- Cell organelles like plastids, Golgi complex etc., when present, are in a highly functional state. In highly specialised cells such cell organelles are absent.
- Every cell has either one or two large and prominent vacuoles. In highly specialised cells, the vacuole is represented by a space in the cell called lumen.
- Ergastic substances are almost always present in the form of secretory products or storage products or excretory products.
- Mitotic divisions occur only in less specialised cells.

TYPES OF PERMANENT TISSUES

The permanent tissues can broadly be distinguished into two types, namely:

- Simple permanent tissues where, the constituent cells are similar in their structure.
- Complex permanent tissues where, the constituent cells are dissimilar in their structure.

PLANT ANATOMY AND THE PRIMARY PLANT BODY

A seed planted in soil will soon germinate, forming a tiny new root and shoot. The cells of this new plant have been produced by the apical meristems near the ends of the root and shoot. There the cells divide, elongate, and differentiate, forming tissues and tissue systems. That part of the plant formed as a result of the activity of the apical meristems is termed the primary plant body. Later in the development of many plants, cells are formed from secondary or lateral meristems located parallel to the long axis of the plant. The cells produced by these meristems add bulk to the plant and cause it to increase in diameter. Thus, a secondary plant body composed of secondary tissues is added to the primary. We will examine the primary tissues and tissue systems present in the root, stem, and leaves of the primary vegetative plant body. Let's start with the root.

Put a shovel in the earth almost anywhere on this planet and you will turn up the roots of some plant. Roots serve to take up water and minerals from the soil and conduct them to the stem. Roots also anchor the plant and may also function in storing foodstuffs that are important in the survival of the plant under certain conditions. Most dicotyledons and gymnosperms have a root system characterised by a large, dominant vertical root, known as a taproot. Grasses and many other monocotyledons, as well as many dicotyledons, have a second type of root system, called a fibrous root system. Here, the primary root is soon replaced by other roots that grow from the stem at or near the soil surface. These are called adventitious roots.

The root system of any given plant is largely an adaptation to the plant's habitat. Apple trees and corn have root systems that both go deeply into the soil and also spread out shallowly just below the surface. This system appears well suited for habitats having moderate rainfall. Many cacti, on the other hand, have extremely shallow but widespread roots, which soak up as much water as possible from the infrequent rain.

An extensive and shallow root system is also found in the coast redwood, which is not a desert dweller, but lives in the damp coastal forests of northern California. Much of the precipitation in these forests is in the form of fog, which condenses against the crowns of the trees and drips to earth, where it is absorbed by the redwood roots lying just under the soil surface.

The growth in length of a root occurs through the division and elongation of cells located in the apical portion of the root. The extreme tip of the root is covered by a mass of cells called the root cap. The cells of the root cap are parenchyma, and frequently have thick, mucilage-containing walls. The root cap protects the root meristem and lubricates the passage of the tip as it is pushed through the soil. The root cap also appears to play a role in the roots' response to gravity. Starch-containing plastids may act as statoliths, or gravity-sensing bodies. The apical meristem of the root is just behind and surrounded on three sides by the root cap. In ferns and other lower vascular plants, there is a conspicuous apical cell in the centre of the meristem. From the various faces of this cell arise files of cells that form the tissues of the root. In the gymnosperms and angiosperms, no single apical cell is present. Instead, there is a collection of cells from which the tissues arise. At the centre of this collection is a relatively inactive group of slowly dividing cells, known as the quiescent centre.

Between the epidermis and the vascular cylinder at the centre of the root is the cortex. The cortex is composed of parenchyma cells which frequently store starch. Other cell types, such as sclerenchyma, may also be present. The parenchyma cells are connected through plasmodesmata, and there are usually conspicuous air spaces between the cells. The innermost layer of the cortex is called the endodermis. This is a cylinder of tightly packed cells without intercellular spaces. The cells of the endodermis have specialised walls that contain a band known as the Casparian strip. Such bands are present in the walls perpendicular to the root surface and are composed of a mixture of compounds containing suberin and lignin. The presence of the Casparian strip makes the walls impervious to water, so that all substances entering the vascular tissue must pass through the cytoplasm of the endodermal cells.

The walls of the epidermis and the cortical cells form a continuous system through which water and dissolved substances can diffuse without entering the cytoplasm; that is, until they reach the endodermis, where the way is blocked by the Casparian strip. Here, any substance entering the vascular tissue must pass through the cytoplasm of the endodermal cells where, presumably, the flow is regulated. In young endodermal cells, only the Casparian strip is suberised, but in older roots, all walls may be suberised and thickened.

Endodermal cells opposite the phloem usually thicken first while those opposite the xylem, known as passage cells, remain thin-walled. They have that name because they are thought to allow passage of water into the xylem. The vascular tissue, or stele, occupies the centre of the root. The stele is composed of xylem and phloem, and is surrounded by the pericycle. The pericycle is the outermost layer of the stele and is directly beneath the endodermis. In young roots the pericycle is composed of thin-walled parenchyma cells, but in older roots the walls may become thickened.

The cells of the pericycle retain their meristematic capacity and are the site of formation of secondary roots. Xylem frequently forms a solid core in the centre of the stele, although in some species the centre may be composed of pith made of parenchyma cells. Xylem forms a series of ridgelike projections, extending outward from the central core to the pericycle. The phloem alternates with the ridges of xylem along the circumference of the stele. The vascular tissue differentiates from the procambium, and the direction of differentiation is from the root tip towards the more mature tissue.

The procambial cells are densely staining meristematic cells that elongate and give rise to the cells of the pericycle, xylem, and phloem. The differentiation and maturation of these tissues can be studied by tracing a file of cells from the mature portion of the root back to the procambium. No. 1 is from a mature portion, and increasing numbers proceed towards the procambium. Near the beginning of the procambium, we can see the differentiation of the protoxylem. This begins from the edges of the procambium and proceeds towards the centre. This type of development is directly opposite that seen in the stem.

Protoxylem differentiates while other cells are still elongating, and as a consequence they may be stretched and crushed. Farther up the root, and therefore later in time, the cells of the metaxylem differentiate. These cells are larger in diameter than the protoxylem and are formed after elongation is completed. They are located inside the protoxylem and may occur in the centre of the root if pith is not present. If pith is present, the metaxylem forms a ring around it. In some cases, as in onion, the first metaxylem vessel that differentiates does so in the exact centre of the root, very near the tip.

The phloem of the root consists of protophloem and metaphloem. The direction of differentiation and maturation of the phloem is the same as the xylem, namely from the younger portions of the root towards the mature and from the edges towards the centre. The phloem differentiates and matures closer to the root apex than does the xylem. The pericycle of the root is usually a single-cell-layer thick in mostangiosperms. It retains its ability to divide long after the other cells of the root have lost this ability. Because of this capacity, it is the site of formation of the secondary roots. It also functions in the thickening of the root during secondary growth, and will be discussed again in the presentation on the secondary plant body.

Before continuing our discussion of apical meristems, we should define a couple of necessary terms concerning planes of division. Divisions that occur at right angles to the surface of the meristem are said to be anticlinal, while those parallel to the surface are called periclinal.

The first sign of secondary root initiation is the periclinal division of a limited number of periderm cells. These are followed by divisions in both periclinal and anticlinal planes. These divisions result in the formation of a group of meristematic cells that soon becomes organised into an apical meristem having the same pattern as the parent root. As this new apical meristem grows, it pushes its way through the cortex and epidermis of the parent root. As the tissues of the new root differentiate and mature, the xylem and phloem develop, so that they become continuous with the xylem and phloem of the parent root.

Roots may be overlooked by the casual observer, but this is not true for the shoot. The shoot of the vascular plant consists of the leaves and stem. We will continue our examination of the primary plant body by first considering the stem and then the leaves. The stem provides the transport system that brings water and minerals from the roots to the leaves. The stem also provides the support to hold the leaves in position to receive sunlight for photosynthesis. In many plants, the stem itself also carries on photosynthesis, and in some, it is the major site of that function, as in the cacti.

Let's begin our examination of the shoot by looking at the extreme tip. Here you see a shoot tip with all of the older leaves removed to reveal a dome of cells flanked by a series of bumps of increasing size as they radiate from the dome. Each of these bumps, called leaf primordia, will develop into a leaf. We can see in this micrograph that the leaf primordia are formed close together, with little space between them. Yet, we know that in most mature plants, the leaves are not closely packed but spread out along the stem. How is this achieved?

The spacing of the leaves is achieved through the growth of the regions of the stem between the leaves. These regions are called internodes, while the places the leaves are attached are termed nodes. The extent of internodal growth has a great impact on the appearance and function of the stem. In the plant to the left, there has been considerable growth of the internodes, while in the rosette succulent to the right, there has been little.

Many gymnosperms and some angiosperms have short branches, known as short shoots or spur shoots, in which the internodes fail to grow. The contrast between the short and long shoots, in which the internodes grow normally, is striking.

Here the long and short shoots of pear tree are the same age yet markedly different in length. The leaves are attached to the stem at the node, and each node may bear one, two, or several leaves. If one leaf is present at each node, the arrangement is called alternate; if two, opposite or decussate; and if several, whorled.

The arrangement of the leaves on the stem is a consequence of the order in which the leaf primordia are formed at the meristem. The arrangement of the leaves on a stem is termed the phyllotaxis, from the Greek words phyllon for 'leaf' and taxis for 'arrangement.' The time between the formation of one leaf primordium and the next is called the plastochron, and is a highly useful measure of time in developmental studies with plants. At the nodes, the leaves join the stem at an angle known as the axil. In the axil is an embryonic shoot, consisting of an apical meristem surrounded by a group of young leaves known as a bud. All leaves have buds in their axils capable of developing into branches, although not all will do so.

A common gardening practice is to pinch off the shoot tips, which stimulates the buds farther down the stem to develop, producing a bushier plant and more flowers. In some species, under certain conditions such as over winter, the bud is covered by a number of overlapping, modified leaves known as scales. Many species lack scales and have so-called naked buds. Buds located in the leaf or stem axil are known as axillary buds or lateral buds. Several buds, called accessory buds, may be located in a single axil. Buds located at the tip of a branch or stem are terminal buds. Floral buds may contain young flowers instead of leaves, or they may contain both young leaves and flowers, making them mixed buds. Sometimes buds arise on the stem at places other than the tip or the leaf axils: these are lateral buds.

Now let's examine the apical meristem in more detail. The apical meristem, which can be defined as the region of the shoot above the youngest leaf primordium, has three basic patterns of organisation. In ferns and the lower vascular plants, there is a large apical cell similar to that which we saw in the roots of these groups. This central cell is a large, tetrahedral cell that divides to give rise to the cells that in turn divide to form the cells of the apex. In the gymnosperms and some angiosperms, the apical meristem shows a type of organisation known as cytohistological zonation. In this type of apical organisation, the apical cell is replaced by a group of cells known as the apical initial group. The zone below these cells, and derived from them, constitutes the central mother cells. These cells usually stain less densely, are more vacuolate, and divide less frequently than the cells surrounding them, which are known as the cells of the peripheral zone.

In most angiosperms, the apex is seen to be divided into two zones: the tunica, which consists of one or more layers of regularly arranged cells covering the surface, and the corpus, which consists of a mass of less regularly organized cells occupying the centre. Cells of the tunica divide predominantly in the anticlinal plane; that is, at right angles to the surface of the shoot. Cells of the corpus divide in all planes.

Leaf primordia in most angiosperms arise through divisions of the tunica and the immediately adjacent corpus. The leaf primordia are formed on the flanks of the apical meristem, in localised regions determined by the phyllotaxis of the plant. In species with opposite, or whorled phyllotaxis, they form simultaneously in more than one site on the apical meristem. Why primordia form where they do on the flanks of the apex has been the subject of much research because their placement is of such importance in determining the ultimate form of the plant. The most widely accepted hypothesis states that the dome of the apex, and the developing primordia, exert a physiological inhibitory field around themselves. Where these fields are not present, a new leaf can be initiated. The cells of the shoot apex divide regularly, with those of the dome dividing more slowly than the ones on the flanks. As these dividing cells begin to enlarge, differences become evident. The surface of the shoot, the tunica in angiosperms, forms the protoderm, that in turn forms the epidermis of the plant.

Other, more deeply located cells that are densely cytoplasmic in nature, differentiate into the procambium, a meristematic tissue that in turn forms the vascular tissue. The ground tissue differentiates from the ground meristem. The procambium gives rise to the xylem, phloem, and the other vascular tissues. The differentiation of these tissues is closely tied to the development of the leaves. This diagram closely tied to the development of the leaves. This diagram shows the course of differentiation of the protophloem and the protoxylem in atypical shoot tip. Note that the three youngest leaves do not have vascular tissue associated with them, and when it does form in the fourth leaf, it is a strand of protophloem that is continuous with that of the older portion of the stem. When the protoxylem forms, it does so in a different manner. It begins differentiation at the base of the leaf primordium and matures both towards the mature portion of the stem and up into the forming leaf. Thus, in the case of the protoxylem, differentiation and maturation occur in two directions, while in the case of the protophloem, it is in one. Metaxylem and metaphloem differentiation always progress from the mature portions of the stem into the leaves.

The protoderm, the procambium, and the ground meristem give rise to the basic tissues of the plant stem, namely the dermal, the fundamental or ground, and the vascular. Let's look at each of these in turn, starting with the dermal. The dermal tissue consists of the epidermis that forms the outer covering of the primary plant body. The epidermis is usually a single layer deep, but a multilayered epidermis is present in some species. Many stems have stomata, particularly if much photosynthesis takes place in the stem. Hairs of various types are commonly found as part of the epidermis of the stem. Some of these are shown here on the stem tip of coleus. These may be either one-celled or multicellular, and either glandular or non-glandular. The fundamental, or ground tissue, may be present as a distinct cortex and pith, as it is in roots. However, the distinction may be far less clear, as in the case of the monocotyledons, where there is no real difference between the two. In this case, the whole tissue is called the ground tissue.

The bulk of the ground tissue is made up of parenchyma cells, although many stems have collenchyma present, either as a complete cylinder or as a ring of bundles. Sclereids may also be present. An endodermis is not usually found in stems, as it is in roots. The vascular tissue system of the stem shows considerable variation in organization. In stems, the xylem and phloem lie on the same radius, with the phloem external to the xylem. There are three main patterns of organization based on the vascular bundle, which is the basic unit of the stem's vascular system. Vascular bundles consist of phloem, xylem, and associated cells, and run from the stem to the leaves and buds. In the first pattern, found in the gymnosperms and some angiosperms, the vascular bundles form a complete cylinder. In this case, there is a clear demarcation between the cortex and pith.

In the second pattern, found in other gymnosperms and dicotyledons, the vascular bundles develop as a cylinder of connecting strands, separated from one another by ground tissue. The ground tissue separating the strands is called interfascicular parenchyma, or pith rays. The third pattern is found in the monocotyledons, where the vascular bundles are scattered throughout the ground tissue and no distinction can be made between the cortex and the pith. Corn and other grasses show this pattern. Most vascular bundles have the xylem on the inside and the phloem to the outside. Frequently, sclerenchyma fibres form a cap over the bundle or completely surround it. Other arrangements, however, are found, particularly in the ferns. In some ferns, the xylem completely surrounds the phloem, while in others, the reverse is true.

In some angiosperms, such as cucumber, phloem is found both outside and inside the xylem. The vascular bundles of the stem are continuous with those of the leaves. In stems where the vascular system forms a complete cylinder, the divergence of a bundle, known as a leaf trace, into a leaf, forms an opening in the cylinder, known as a leaf gap. More than one trace may be diverted into a leaf, and a trace may diverge from the vascular system at one node, and run parallel to the vascular cylinder for one or more nodes before it enters the leaf. The vascular system of the shoot can be compared to a rope, with the vascular bundles forming tough, flexible units that give continuity and strength. The vascular system of the root, on the other hand, is much more like a rod or pipe. At some point, the rope and rod must be joined so that the plant can function as a whole. This place is aptly called the transition region. In the transition region, the distribution of the vascular tissue can often be highly elaborate as the two systems flow into one another. The stem is a highly versatile organ. Through the course of natural selection, a wide variety of modifications have developed in stems. We will briefly examine a few of these. Many vine stems lack internal support tissues needed to grow erect, and have developed slender, modified branches or leaves, called tendrils. These grow around various objects and bind the vine to them for support.

Stolons, or runners, are above-ground horizontal stems of relatively slender form. They grow along the surface of the soil, and at the nodes, aerial shoots and roots arise. Strawberry plants spread through the growth of stolons. Many plants have stems that remain permanently underground, and leaves grow from these to positions above ground. Such stems have a variety of names and forms, but all serve as a way to store food for growth in the next growing season. These include rhizomes, that are perennial underground stems with thickened internodes that store starch. Iris is an example.

A tuber is a greatly swollen rhizome. A good example is the potato. Corms are short, thickened, vertical stems. The 'bulb' of gladiolus is a corm. A true bulb is a short stem surrounded by thickened, fleshy leaves known as bulb scales. The onion is an example of a bulb. Some thorns, as in the common hawthorn, are modified branches. The spines of cacti are modified leaves, not branches. Let's now look at leaves. The function of leaves is photosynthesis, but as in the case of stems, there are many variations in structure and function. Some leaves, as we just saw, are storage organs, while others may be modified into spines or traps for insects. The leaves of gymnosperms are usually needle or scale-like in shape. Only a few, such as ginkgo, have flattened leaves, as found in the angiosperms. The two great subclasses of angiosperms have markedly different types of leaves. The leaves of the dicotyledons are usually composed of three parts: the blade, which is thin and expanded; the petiole, which is a slender stemlike structure; and the leaf base, which may be extended to leaf-like stipules. Moreover, the veins in the leaf of the dicotyledons are usually characterised by a netlike arrangement. The typical monocotyledon, in contrast, has a long narrow leaf, without a petiole and with parallel veins.

Let's look at the leaves of the dicots in more detail, as the shape of the leaf is highly characteristic of the species. Leaves vary in their overall shape, the shape of the apex of the leaf, the nature of the edge or margin of the leaf, and the base of the leaf blade. The pattern of the veins in the blade may be either pinnate, with a single mid vein from which the branches diverge, like that of a pinna or feather; or palmate, with several principal veins, each with smaller branches, radiating from the bases of the blade, much as the fingers spread out from the palm of the hand.

Leaves are either simple or compound. In a simple leaf, the blade is all in one piece while in the compound leaf, the blade consists of separate, leaf-like parts, called leaflets. The arrangement of the leaflets is either pinnate or palmate. The petiole also shows various modifications. They may vary in shape and in their attachment to the leaves. In most cases, the petiole is attached to the base of the leaf, but in the case of peltate leaves, as in nasturtiums, it is attached to the lower side of the leaf. When the petiole is completely lacking, the leaf is termed sessile.

Finally, the leaf bases and stipules show a range of variation. The base may extend around the stem or be much reduced in size. The stipules may be large and leaf like or so small as to be difficult to see. Leaves of the monocotyledons show somewhat less variation, but there is still a great range in size and shape. The grass leaf, however, is typical of the leaf of many monocot species. It is divided into two parts: the blade is the expanded part of the leaf, and the sheath is the part of the leaf below the blade that curves around the stem. The sheath is usually green and may be as long as the blade. It completely encircles the stem and may extend from one node to the next. Many tropical monocotyledons diverge strikingly from this pattern. Blades maybe broad and may not show parallel venation. In the banana, a tropical monocot, the huge leaves have large, overlapping leaf bases, which actually form the trunk of the banana tree. The stem itself is short and inconspicuous. Internally, leaves consist of three tissue systems: epidermis, mesophyll, and veins, or vascular tissue. The leaf has an upper and lower epidermis, often with a variety of hairs, both simple and complex, and with stomata and guard cells. Some species have stomata only on the lower surface; others have them on both surfaces. Many monocotyledons and conifers have them arranged in rows.

The mesophyll lies between the upper and lower epidermis. In grasses, the mesophyll cells are usually the same throughout, but in dicots the mesophyll has two layers: the palisade parenchyma, composed of elongate cells, and the spongy parenchyma, composed of irregularly shaped cells. There is considerable space between all of the mesophyll cells, and it is important for the gas exchange necessary for photosynthesis.

Palisade parenchyma have more chloroplasts than spongy cells do, and the palisade may be several times thicker than the spongy. The entire mesophyll is penetrated by veins of xylem and phloem, so that virtually every mesophyll cell is only a few cells away from a vein. In a vein, the xylem is arranged on the top towards the upper epidermis, while the phloem is on the bottom. In many monocots and some dicots, the vein is surrounded by a special layer of parenchyma cells known as the bundle sheath.

The bundle sheath cells often completely surround the veins and veinlets to the very end, thus separating the vein from the mesophyll. The presence of the bundle sheath has been related to the type of photosynthetic pathway found in the plants. Collenchyma and sclerenchyma cells may also be found in the leaf associated with the vein. Such tissue adds strength to the vein and the leaf. We have covered the primary plant body, those parts that are formed as a result of the activities of the apical meristems. Many plants have extensive growth that is the product of the lateral or secondary meristems. This growth is of great importance in many woody plants and is treated in our next presentation, 'The Secondary Plant Body.'

PLANT ANATOMY AND THE SECONDARY PLANT BODY

The early growth of a seedling results from cell divisions and cell elongation in the apical meristems of the shoot and root. The young seedling is composed of primary tissue and was the subject of our presentation on the primary plant body. As growth continues, additional layers of cells may differentiate along the older portions of the stem and root. These secondary cell layers increase the diameter of the stem and root and are the products of the lateral meristems of the plant. There are two lateral meristems: the vascular cambium that gives rise to the secondary xylem and phloem, and the cork cambium that gives rise to the new outer covering of the plant. The activity of the semeristems forms the secondary plant body.

From the viewpoint of both the plant and humans, secondary growth is of great importance. Without it, we'd not have wood for our homes or cork for our bottles. Without it, plants would be confined to heights of only a few meters, and the whole course of terrestrial evolution of both plants and animals would have been altered. Let's start our examination of secondary growth by considering the vascular cambium. First, let's re-examine the apical meristem and follow the differentiation of the provascular strands. As differentiation progresses, phloem forms towards the outside while xylem forms towards the inside. In many species, a layer of cells in the centre of the strand remains meristematic. This layer is the vascular cambium. The cells of the vascular cambium can divide either parallel to the surface of the stem or parallel to the radius. If the division is radial, two cambial cells result.

If, however, the division is parallel to the surface, one of the cells produced differentiates into either a xylem or a phloem cell, while the other retains the properties of the cambium. Whether one of the daughter cells differentiates into a potential xylem or phloem cell depends on the position of the cell with regard to the centre of the vascular bundle. If the cell is towards the inside, it will eventually be xylem; if outside, phloem. We say eventually because the newly formed phloem and xylem cells frequently undergo additional divisions producing more phloem or xylem cells. The cambium and its immature derivatives are known as the cambial zone.

The immature derivatives are capable of both radial and periclinal divisions, and most of the xylem and phloem produced are the result of periclinal divisions of the derivatives of the cambial initials. There may, for example, be ten derivatives for each cambial initial. The cambium that develops within the vascular bundles is called the fascicular cambium. In most dicotyledons, the vascular bundles of the stem are separated by regions of parenchyma cells, known as the interfascicular regions.

If a continuous cambium is to develop around the circumference of the stem, cambium must differentiate in this region also. The interfascicular cambium differentiates from the parenchyma cells between the vascular bundles. The cambial cells that give rise to the vascular elements of the stem are longer than they are wide and are known as fusiform initials. They and their derivatives are the source of the vertical or axial system of the vascular cylinder, composed of the tracheids, vessels, and fibres of the xylem and the sieve tubes, companion cells, and fibres of the phloem.

But, there is a second system in which the cells form at right angles to the long axis of the stem. This is the radial system, consisting of the rays seen here in a cross section of the stem. The rays are files of parenchyma cells which extend through the vascular cylinder. The rays probably function to transport materials across the vascular cylinder. They are also frequently the site of starch storage. The parenchyma cells of the rays are elongate, but their long axis is at right angles to the axis of the stem. They are not the products of the fusiform initials, but are formed by the ray initials.

Now, let's look at the products of the vascular cambium. First, in most species there is much more xylem produced than phloem. Second, the cells that differentiate from the cambial derivatives reflect in complexity the structure of the xylem and phloem of the species. For example, in the case of the conifers, the products in the xylem are tracheids and parenchyma, while in the woody angiosperms they may be vessels, tracheids, fibres, and parenchyma cells. Third, the cambium demonstrates a periodicity of functioning that is most apparent in trees.

This periodicity of cell division and differentiation in the cambium results in the formation of growth rings. These rings are clearly seen in most woods and are a result of the re-initiation of growth by the cambium after a period of inactivity. In most temperate trees, this is in the spring when water becomes available and the temperature increases. Active growth continues into summer. The result is a growth ring, characterized by relatively large cells with thin walls produced as early or spring wood, and small cells with thick walls, produced as late or summer wood. In many temperate trees under normal environmental conditions, one ring is produced each year. Growth rings can be used to date the age of the tree. The large, thin-walled tracheids of the spring wood are weaker and wear easier than the thicker walled, small-diameter summer wood.

As the growth in height of a tree is always initiated at the apical meristem, the upper part of a tree is younger than the lower portions. Consequently, there are fewer growth rings towards the top of the tree. Under conditions of environmental stress, as during drought or unusual temperature changes or insect attack that causes defoliation, growth rings may not be produced or the amount of growth in the ring may be greatly reduced. In tropical and subtropical climates, there may be little periodicity in cambial activity, making age determinations difficult. However, in many temperate climates, not only can trees be dated by growth rings, but past climatic conditions can be deduced from their width and the size of their cells. Also, past events, such as fires, are recorded as scars. These differences in growth rings can also be used to date archaeological ruins. In the case of this pueblo dwelling, the growth rings in the roof beam can be matched with those of trees that are still alive in the same area. The rings are counted back from the present to determine the time the tree used in the beam was cut down.

Different types of cells may be differentiated in the secondary xylem at specific times during the growth of the ring. In the gymnosperms, such differences are not striking, with tracheids and parenchyma being produced throughout the growth period, although the diameter of the tracheids varies at different times. Such wood is called non-porous. In angiosperms, however, the pattern is quite different. The large vessels of the secondary xylem may be uniformly distributed throughout the growth ring. Such wood is termed diffuse porous, and is found in such trees as maple and the tulip tree. In other angiosperms, such as some oaks and ash, the largest vessels are produced in the early wood and appear as a ring of pores. This type of wood is known as ring porous.

One of the many remarkable features of vascular cambia is that they are capable of reactivation of division year after year, three thousand to four thousand years in the case of the giant sequoia and the bristle cone pine. The activity of the cambium and the accumulation of xylem and phloem results in an increase in the diameter of the stem. As this occurs, the initials must undergo radial divisions, so that the cambium remains intact. The expansion of the xylem crushes the older phloem. This means that, while massive amounts of xylem accumulate in woody plants, there is little more than a year or two of functional phloem present.

As a woody stem continues to grow in diameter, the vessels and tracheids towards the centre cease to be active in transport. Tannins and crystals may be deposited in these non-functional cells, and their colour may gradually change to a darker, often more reddish hue. This wood is known as heartwood, in contrast to the active, functional sapwood close to the cambium. So far, we have been describing the formation of the vascular cambium and secondary growth in stems. Now, let's look at what happens in roots. In some ways the initiation of the vascular cambium in roots is similar to that in shoots:

cells that remain undifferentiated between the primary phloem and primary xylem form the vascular cambium that gives rise to the secondary phloem and secondary xylem. In the root, however, the protoxylem comes into direct contact with the pericycle at the poles. Here, divisions of the pericycle initiate the formation of the cambium. Thus, we have the cambium differentiating from the provascular tissue between the phloem and xylem and from the pericycle over the protoxylem poles.

Once the cambium is complete around the circumference of the whole root, the formation of secondary phloem and secondary xylem pushes the primary phloem out from between the protoxylem poles and rounds out the tissue pattern. Ray initials may be formed from the pericycle opposite the protoxylem poles in some species or in different parts of the vascular cambium in others.

As the stem, or root, grows in diameter due to the activity of the vascular cambium, the phloem, cortex, and epidermal cells are pushed out away from the centre of the organ. In the process, they tend to be crushed, split, and sloughed off. This leaves the plant without an outer covering for protection. The development of a second cambium, the cork cambium, or phellogen, fills this need by providing the plant with a protective outer covering. Cork cambium usually differentiates from a layer of the cortex, rarely from the epidermis.

In long-lived organs, the cork cambium originates in the secondary phloem. In all cases, the cambial cells divide tangentially, producing a layer of cork cells to the outside. Usually, the cork cambium is not continuous around the stem; rather, it forms in overlapping arcs. Not only is cork produced towards the outside, but cork parenchyma or phelloderm, consisting of parenchyma-like cells, is produced towards the inside. Cork cambium, cork, and cork parenchyma are collectively called the periderm.

The walls of cork cells become impregnated with waterproof suberin and some die. It was these dead cells that Robert Hooke observed and named as cells in 1665. Any living cells outside the cork cells no longer receive nutrients from the inside and die. Some cork cambia, initiated when the plant was young, persist throughout the life of the plant, with the number of cambial cells increasing as the plant increases in diameter. Trees like beech, birch, and some cherries have such cambia. In many trees, however, especially in the temperate zones, the first cork cambium ceases to divide after a few years, and successive layers of cork cambia are formed deeper within the stem, particularly in the secondary phloem.

Cork occurs not only on stems and roots, but also is present in some fruits, as some green apples, and various storage organs, such as the potato. Early in the development of the potato, a thin cork layer, the skin of the potato, is formed over the whole surface. When the potato is newly picked, this skin is thin, but as it is kept in storage, the cork becomes thicker and more highly suberised, becoming the potato peel. The cork layer makes potato storage possible.

Cork and bark are related but should not be confused. Bark usually refers to the region from the vascular cambium to the outside of the stem, and it includes more than the cork in most species. Bark can be divided into two layers: the outer layer, which usually includes the cork and cork cambium and is known as the rhytidome; and the inner layer, which consists of the tissue between the outer layer and the vascular cambium, frequently including large amounts of secondary phloem fibres.

The patterns we readily associate with bark are a result of the character of the rhytidome. In some rhytidomes, parenchyma and cork not highly suberised predominate, while in others, a large amount of phloem fibres may be present. Fibrous barks form a network pattern when they split, as in ash and basswood, while those lacking fibres break up into individual, scalelike units, as in pines and maple. Scale barks found in the pines also owe their appearance to the manner of origin of the successive layers of periderm. If the later periderms are formed as overlapping layers, the outer tissue breaks up into scale units clearly seen in the outer bark.

In other plants, such as redwoods and oaks, the periderm cells show considerable cohesion to one another, and the bark then becomes thick and only gradually wears away. In still other species, the periderm cells readily become loose and separate into long strips of rhytidome. An extreme example of this is in the eucalyptus. These trees, native to Australia, are widely introduced into North and South America, southern Africa, and southern Europe. Sheets of enlarged cork parenchyma break down, separating long strips of bark from the stem. Bark has many commercial uses. For centuries the bark of oaks and other trees have been used in the tanning of leather because of the high tannic acid content of the cork cells. On islands of the South Pacific, the fibre-rich inner bark of the paper mulberry is beaten in a fabric and used as clothing. Strips of inner bark of a variety of species were used by many North American natives to weave baskets. The most important commercial use of bark involves the rhytidome of the cork oak.

In this plant, the phellogen forms first from the epidermis, and may remain on the plant indefinitely. For commercial use, however, the first periderm is removed from the tree after about twenty years. When this periderm is removed, the exposed cells die, and a new layer of phellogen forms within the cortex. About every ten years, the cork is carefully removed from the trunk, and new phellogen forms within the cortex. Later, phellogen forms in the secondary phloem. In places where living tissue is exposed to air as a result of a wound, phellogen will develop and a layer of cork will be produced. This is wound cork and can be produced on any part of the plant. It functions to reduce water loss and protect the plant against invasion by bacteria and fungi. Wound phellogen develops several layers deep beneath the wound. After cork is formed and suberised, the damaged cells are sloughed off.

In the normal course of development of the periderm, the stem or root is essentially sealed. Little diffusion of gases is possible, but the underlying tissue is alive and requires oxygen to survive. In these conditions, we find that special openings in the periderm, known as lenticels, are formed in stems and roots. Lenticels develop due to local activity of the cork cambium that results in the formation of a mass of parenchyma cells with intercellular spaces. The lenticel phellogen also has intercellular spaces. This porous tissue protrudes through the outer layer of the cork and provides a pathway for the diffusion of oxygen. In roots they are also a pathway for the uptake of water and minerals. Lenticels are visible as raised areas that may be bean-shaped, round, or elongate. They figure prominently in the bark of many trees, such as the cherry. Some fruits, such as pears and apples, also contain lenticels.

The most important product of secondary growth, in human terms, is secondary xylem, or wood. Millions of board feet of lumber are cut and used yearly for everything from houses to furniture to bowling pins to matches. There are dozens of different types of wood used for myriad purposes. The uses of various types of wood reflect the cellular composition of the species that produced them. The wood of gymnosperms, such as pines and fir, are commonly said to be soft, meaning that they are straight-grained, easily penetrated by nails, readily split. In contrast, the wood of angiosperms, such as maple and oak, is called hard because it is more compact, frequently weighs more per unit volume, and is less easy to nail. Because of its more complex grain, angiosperm wood usually splits less readily and is easier to carve and turn into elaborate shapes. Many of these generalizations are true, but there are exceptions. For example, hemlock is a gymnosperm but has harder wood than some angiosperm species. Balsa, one of the lightest of all woods, comes from an angiosperm species. The grain of Philippine mahogany, an angiosperm, is as straight as that of pine, a gymnosperm.

Now, let's look at gymnosperm and then angiosperm wood in greater detail. Gymnosperm wood is composed of tracheids and parenchyma cells. The tracheids that make up the bulk of the wood are arranged in overlapping files parallel to the long axis of the tree. They compose the vertical system of the plant. The parenchyma cells are mainly in rays, one cell wide and three or four cells tall, oriented at right angles to the long axis of the trunk. They are the radial system of the tree. Rays may be more than one cell wide when they contain resin ducts. Resin ducts are lined with thin-walled parenchyma cells that secrete resin into the duct. Resin ducts may run either parallel or perpendicular to the long axis of the tree. Resin aids in protecting the tree against insect and fungal attack because it is toxic to these organisms. Amber is fossil resin secreted by both gymnosperms and angiosperms. Rich deposits of amber are found around the Baltic Sea in northern Europe. They are forty to sixty million years old and may contain insects in remarkable states of preservation.

To gain a better appreciation of the structure of gymnosperm wood, let's look at it in three planes: the transverse, which is at right angles to the long axis of the stem; the radial, which is along the radius of the stem; and the tangential, which is longitudinal to the long axis and at right angles to the radius of the stem. In the transverse plane, the cross sections of the tracheids are seen, and the rays are seen in longitudinal view. In the radial plane, the tracheids are viewed in longitudinal section, as are the files of ray parenchyma. The tangential plane shows the ray parenchyma in cross section and the tracheids in longitudinal section. Each plane gives a different view; only by studying all three can we analyse the structure of the wood.

From the study of sections, we can construct three-dimensional diagrams, such as the one shown, in their proper relationships. Such diagrams are an excellent means of understanding the characteristics of the wood. It is interesting to note that the cellular composition of the wood creates the character of the lumber derived from gymnosperm trees. Boards from straight-grained gymnosperm wood can be visually uninteresting for use in furniture; although where knots are plentiful, the wood makes attractive wall panelling. However, because of the uniformity of the grain, it is readily sawed, planed, and nailed, making it particularly useful in construction. In addition, conifers are the major source of plywood. In making plywood, logs are placed on huge lathes that peel thin sheets of wood from the log. The sheets are then glued together so that the grain in the various sheets runs at right angles. By this method, wide, thin boards with great strength are obtained. Plywood is extremely important in construction, serving as wall and floor covering and moulds for concrete.

One of the most valued of conifer woods comes from Sequoia sempervirens, the coast redwood. It is sought for its uniform grain, fine red colour, and resistance to insect and fungal attack. The colour and resistance are related, as the lumber is cut from the heartwood, in which the tracheids are filled with a variety of phenolic compounds toxic to many fungi and insects. The huge size of the tree means that there is an abundance of clear, knot-free lumber available per tree.

Knots in lumber are the remains of branches formed when the trunk was smaller in diameter. Two kinds of knots can be seen: tight knots, from the portion of the trunk where the growth rings of the branch are continuous with those of the trunk; and loose knots, where the trunk surrounds the branch but is not continuous with it. As the tree ages, the buried branch is located farther and farther from the surface of the trunk. Consequently, in a tree that reaches the age of a redwood, there is a vast amount of wood unmarred by knots. Now let's look at angiosperm wood. In cellular terms, the secondary xylem of angiosperms is considerably more complex than that of gymnosperms. The cells of angiosperm wood include vessel members, tracheids, several types of fibres, axial parenchyma, as well as ray parenchyma. If we view oak wood in the same way we did the conifer wood earlier, we can gain an appreciation of the complex nature of angiosperm wood.

We can see differences in the cellular composition, specifically the presence of vessels and fibres in addition to the tracheids and parenchyma found in gymnosperm wood. We can also see the massive, multicellular rays and the seasonal distribution of the vessels that makes oak a ring-porous wood. We can also compare oak with diffuse porous wood, such as this maple. Here, the more even distribution of the vessels gives the wood a different appearance in all three planes. Here, too, the rays are less massive and more uniform than in oak. The complex nature of the secondary xylem in angiosperms strongly affects the physical properties of the wood.

Visually, angiosperm woods, such as oak and maple, have grains that exhibit interesting patterns when sawed into lumber. Stains and oils can be used to bring out the differences in the texture of the wood that results from the various mixtures of the wide-diameter vessels, the narrower tracheids, the almost solid fibres, and the thin-walled parenchyma cells. Logs can be cut in a number of ways to enhance either the aesthetic or the practical value of the lumber. Here we have diagrammed the way in which logs are cut to produce plain-sawed and quarter-sawed lumber.

Tangential cuts result in plain-sawed lumber. Plain-sawed lumber is characterised by patterns of strips; concentric, irregular parabolas; or ellipses caused by the differences in colour and structure of the early and late wood. Any wood with pronounced differences in the nature of the early and late wood will show marked patterns when cut this way. As the diameter of the growth ring gradually decreases from one end of a log to the other, a straight cut across them will yield cones of irregular shape and a range of interesting shapes. In quarter-sawed wood, the cut runs approximately parallel to the vascular rays along the radial plane. The rays appear as stripes or ribbons running across the surface. When oak is quarter sawed, the large rays add a great deal to the texture of the wood. Quarter-sawed yellow pine or Douglas fir are used for flooring, because the wearing quality of these soft woods is increased by having the harder area of the late wood exposed vertically to wear. When North America was first settled, extensive forests covered the eastern half of the continent. The composition of these forests differed in various parts of the country, and the type of dwelling built by the early settlers reflected both the species that were common and the characteristics of the available wood.

Log cabins were built where conifers were abundant, because the straight trunks and highly linear character of the xylem facilitated squaring and notching the logs with an axe. Where large angiosperm trees, particularly oaks, were numerous, massive beams were fashioned by axe and saw. Such beams formed the skeleton of the building, with the areas between the beams filled with mud and wattle or bricks. Wooden pegs were used to hold the oak frame together because the dense wood resisted penetration by the handmade nails available at the time. Later, settlements reached the prairies, and lumber of any kind became scarce. The extensive conifer forests of the north were utilised for a different type of construction. In place of massive beams or whole logs, a frame was made of pine or fir boards, two inches by four inches, on which was nailed flat siding, also of pine. This is a major type of construction still in use today.

Finally, let's consider secondary growth in monocotyledons. Most monocotyledons have no secondary growth from a vascular cambium, as do dicotyledons, but some do show secondary growth by other means. This is true for the larger monocotyledons, such as palms and yucca. To understand secondary growth in monocotyledons, it is necessary to consider the shoot tip.

The monocotyledons possess, in addition to the apical meristem, a wide region of cells known as the primary thickening meristem. The distribution of this meristem can be seen here. Meristematic cells that function as a cambium are continuous with the primary thickening meristem. However, these meristematic cells are not located between the xylem and phloem, as in the dicotyledons, but are independent of the established bundles. Moreover, the cambium produces parenchyma towards the inside and usually only a small amount of parenchyma towards the outside.

In palms, secondary growth is known as diffuse secondary growth because it is not restricted to a limited area and occurs far from the apical meristem. We have introduced the concept of secondary growth in plants. Secondary growth allows plants to live longer and grow taller. Secondary growth occurs in both the vascular tissue and in the outer layers of the root and shoot. The vascular cambium produces new layers of xylem, phloem, and rays. The cork cambium produces the cork and cork parenchyma. Lenticels develop in the cork for gas exchange. In trees, the massive accumulation of xylem forms wood, which is exploited as lumber by humans. Our lives would indeed be different without secondary growth in plants.

PLANT CELLS AND PLANT TISSUES

The cell is the basic unit of life. All organisms are composed of cells. In single-celled organisms, the cell and the organism are the same thing. All the functions of an organism are carried out within a single cell. In many-celled organisms, however, there is a division of labour among the various cells. Cells differentiate in both structure and function as they assume different roles within a multicellular plant. For example, in a mature oak tree composed of millions of cells there are many different cell types. Some are modified to transport water and dissolved minerals through the plant. Other cells are specialised to carry carbohydrates and other foodstuffs from the leaves to the roots. Still other cells function to support the various parts of the tree.

Leaves are composed of cells containing chloroplasts for photosynthesis, cells that regulate the flow of gases out of the leaf and other cells. In studying the diversity of cell types found in multicellular plants, such as our oak tree, we say that an aggregation of similar cells is a tissue. A simple tissue contains only one cell type, while a complex tissue contains two or more cell types. In the vascular plant, tissues are organised into tissue systems: the dermal, the vascular, and the fundamental or ground. The dermal tissue is the outer covering of the plant and acts to protect it, the vascular tissue system is involved in the movement of materials throughout the plant, and the ground tissue occupies the region enclosed by the dermal tissue system that is not occupied by the vascular tissue. These tissue systems are, in turn, organised into the three major vegetative organs of the land vascular plant: the root that absorbs and transports water and minerals from the soil and anchors the plant; the stem that transports water upward and food downward and supports the leaves; and the leaves that are the major sites of photosynthesis in the plant.

Before beginning our survey of the various cells and tissues present in the vascular plant, let's review a few of the distinctive features of the plant cell. Almost all plant cells are surrounded by a wall. This wall is usually multi-layered, consisting of a primary wall formed when the cell is young and still actively growing, and a secondary wall laid down after the cell has finished its growth. Cells are held together by means of the middle lamella, a layer common to two adjacent cells.

Primary walls are frequently, but not always, thin and composed of pectins, hemicellulose, and cellulose. Secondary walls contain the same compounds, plus lignin. When secondary walls are formed, the primary wall may become lignified. The middle lamella is composed of various pectic substances that contain calcium. The nature and composition of the wall is important in the characterisation and function of the cells.

Passing through the wall from one cell to the next are protoplasmic connections called plasmodesmata. These often occur in clusters in the wall and are known as primary pit fields. When secondary walls are formed by the cell, they are not laid down over the primary pit fields. This results in a depression in the wall called a pit. Such pits usually occur in pairs on adjacent cells and have in common the middle lamella and the primary walls, collectively termed the pit membrane. The depression is termed the pit cavity. Pits are of particular importance in the cells of the xylem, and we will consider them again when we take up that tissue.

Vacuoles are another prominent feature of plant cells. In some cells there maybe many small vacuoles, but in most, the centre of the cell is occupied by a single large vacuole. The presence of a vacuole is important because it permits large cells to be formed with a minimum amount of cytoplasm. The expansion of the vacuole, as a result of water moving into it, results in pressure on the wall that is important in plant cell growth and the maintenance of form in the plant. When a plant wilts, enough water is not available to keep the vacuoles pressed against the cell walls, and the plant becomes limp.

Characteristically, plant cells undergo a series of changes in size and character during development. Following the division that forms them, the cells enlarge in diameter and then in length. During elongation the vacuoles become large and provide the force necessary for the cells to increase in size. During elongation the cells are surrounded by a thin primary wall that has enough plasticity to allow the cell to increase in size. As elongation ceases, more rigid secondary walls may be formed. Differences between the cells become increasingly pronounced as the secondary walls are formed and other changes take place in the cells. During final maturation of the cells, further changes occur, which, in the case of several cell types, result in the breakdown of the protoplasm of the cell, leaving only the wall at the time the cell is functionally mature.

Now let's look at the various types of cells and tissues found in the vascular plant, starting with the meristematic cell. All of the various cell types and tissues are the product of cell divisions followed by cell differentiation. Such cell division is localized in regions known as meristems. There are two types of meristems: those at the tips of roots and stems, known as apical or primary meristems, and those found along the length of the root or stem, known as the lateralor secondary meristems.

There are two kinds of lateral meristems: the vascular cambium that produces additional vascular tissue, and the cork cambium that gives rise to new protective layers on the outside of the plant. Growth at the apical meristems results in the stem or root increasing in length and in the production of leaves, branches, and flowers. Growth of the lateral meristems results in an increase in breadth of the plant. All vascular plants have apical meristems, but not all have lateral meristems, which are particularly important in longer living plants such as shrubs and trees that have thicker, woody stems. The cells of apical meristems are usually small and relatively the same in all their dimensions; that is, they are isodiametric. They have thin walls and lack large vacuoles. While containing large numbers of ribosomes, they have few mitochondria, plastids, and other cell organelles. Their most conspicuous feature is the nucleus that occupies a greater volume of the cell than in other cell types.

The cells of the lateral meristems are frequently long, narrow cells with conspicuous vacuoles. They have thin walls and relatively few cell organelles. Because they tend to be much larger cells than those of the apical meristems, the proportion of the cell volume occupied by the nucleus is usually less. When meristematic cells divide, both cells resulting from the division do not normally undergo differentiation into cells specialized for some other function. One of the cells retains the ability to divide again. The next cell type we will consider is the parenchyma cell, which comprise the parenchyma tissue. Parenchyma cells are the most common cells found in the vascular plant. Although many are roughly isodiametric, others are several times as long as they are wide. The walls are usually thin and usually do not contain lignin. Parenchyma cells are alive when functionally mature, and the centre of the cell is often occupied by a large vacuole that presses the cytoplasm and nucleus against the wall. Most cell organelles are present. Many parenchyma cells contain numerous chloroplasts and are called chlorenchyma. Such cells occur not only in leaves, but also in stems and even some roots, such as orchids, where the roots grow appressed to the trunks of the trees that support them.

Parenchyma cells may also be filled with amyloplasts, that is, plastids containing starch. When you eat a potato, you are eating starch-filled parenchyma. Such cells often contain so much starch that the vacuoles and nuclei are compressed and almost invisible in the light microscope. Parenchyma cells can develop into a number of other cell types, even when they are mature. They have the capacity, under the proper conditions, to develop into whole new plants. In laboratory experiments, isolated single parenchyma cells have grown into mature plants.

Collenchyma is essentially parenchyma with thickened walls. These long cells with their thickened primary walls help to support the plant. The walls are not uniformly thickened; instead, the corners of the cells have more material than the centre. The walls are rich in pectic substances, hemicellulose, and cellulose. No lignin is present in young cells, but it may occur in older collenchyma cells. Collenchyma cells are alive at maturity. They are present particularly in young, rapidly growing parts of the plant. Here they are found in bundles arranged in circles near the outer edge of the organ. Such bundles are strong yet flexible, and their location furthers their function of adding strength to the plant. The stalks of celery are particularly rich in collenchyma, which can be seen by its pearly white appearance in fresh sections under a microscope.

Sclerenchyma comprise two kinds of cells: fibres and sclereids. Fibre cells are long, narrow, uniformly thick-walled. Sclereids, by contrast, vary in size and shape, ranging from isodiametric through H-shaped to cells with many long arms. Sclereids, like fibres, are thick-walled and highly lignified at maturity. Both sclereids and fibres function to provide mechanical support. Although they occasionally form layers, as in seed coats and nutshells, sclereids usually occur as individual cells or small clusters of cells in many parts of the plant. Sclereids are hard, as their name from the Greek skleros, meaning 'hard,' indicates. The gritty texture of pears comes from groups of sclereids scattered throughout the fruit. Fibres are quite unlike sclereids in shape but similar in their other features. They have thick, lignified secondary walls and are usually quite long. Some of the fibres we use for cloth are sclerenchyma fibres. Linen, for example, is woven from fibres obtained from the flax plant, Linumusitatissimum. In this case, the fibres are from 9 to 70 millimetres long and provide a durable yet pleasant-feeling material. Not all fibres we use for weaving are sclerenchyma fibres. Cotton fibres, for example, are epidermal hairs.

The vascular system of the plant that conducts various solutions through the plant consists of the xylem and the phloem. Water and dissolved minerals are carried in the xylem, while dissolved organic materials are carried in the phloem. Both the xylem and phloem are complex tissues consisting of several cell types.

Let's examine some of the most important of these, starting with the xylem. There are two types of cells through which water is conducted in the plant: the tracheids and the vessels. Tracheids are long, thick-walled cells, while vessels are composed of files of individual cells called vessel members, arranged end to end. Vessels are larger in diameter than tracheids and thinner walled.

Tracheids are relatively long, narrow cells with walls that are about half cellulose and half lignin. They have well-developed secondary walls, frequently with characteristic patterns. The oblique end walls are covered by a thin wall. The cells overlap so that these thin areas are lined up in relation to one another, thus facilitating the flow of water. The water in the tracheids is under great tension, and the thick walls prevent the collapse of the cells. The nucleus and cytoplasm of a tracheid degenerate when the cell reaches functional maturity, and only the cell wall remains at the time the tracheids are conducting water. Vessel members are shorter and larger in diameter than tracheids. The composition of the wall is similar to tracheids, and at maturity the cells no longer contain cytoplasm or nuclei.

One of the last stages in the maturation of a vessel member is the dissolution of major portions of the end walls. End walls of vessel members don't always disappear completely. Often, a perforation plate remains. This may have one large hole, a parallel series of openings, a network of openings, or a group of circular holes. A vessel consists of a number of vessel members, each of which is an individual cell. The vessel members are lined up and connected by perforation plates or simple openings, where the end walls had been. Sometimes, the vessels may reach 1 to 15 metres in length, and vessels extending the height of an entire tree have been reported.

Water conduction is not the sole function of the xylem. The cell walls of the tissue help support the various parts of the plant and give the plant resilience. In the lower vascular plants and the gymnosperms, tracheids form the water-carrying system in the xylem; vessels are rare and found in only a few groups. Vessels occur in most, but not all, angiosperms. In species with vessels, fibres are also found in the xylem. These lend mechanical strength to the tissue. Fibres are usually longer than tracheids; have thick, lignified secondary walls; and are dead when functionally mature. Tracheids are also present in many angiosperms. In addition to the conducting cells and fibres, parenchyma cells also occur in the xylem. These are usually arranged in either vertical or horizontal files. Like all parenchyma cells, they are alive at maturity and remain alive for a long period in the xylem. They function in food and water storage and short-distance transport.

Pits are particularly conspicuous in the walls of cells of the xylem. Two types are present: simple pits and bordered pits. In bordered pits, the secondary wall arches over the pit cavity, while in simple pits it does not. In the conifers, such as pines and firs, the centre of the pit membrane is thickened into a round, convex structure called a torus.

Around the torus, the pit membrane remains thin and flexible. If pressure is built up on one side of the pit, the torus is forced against the border. In this position it prevents the passage of gas bubbles that would break the water columns in the tracheids and block water movement. The phloem transports solutions of organic compounds, primarily sugars, throughout the plant. The actual conducting is done in the sieve elements of the phloem.

There are two types of sieve elements: the sieve cells and the sieve tubes, which are analogous to tracheids and vessels in the xylem. Sieve cells are relatively long, narrow cells, while sieve tubes consist of files of sieve-tube members aligned end to end. As in the case of xylem, phloem is a complex tissue and may contain, in addition to sieve cells and sieve tubes, companion cells, fibres, and parenchyma cells. Sieve tubes are found only in the angiosperms, while sieve cells are present in the lower vascular plants and the gymnosperms. In most angiosperms, the sieve tubes are associated with companion cells.

Sieve-tube members and companion cells originate from the unequal division of a mother cell. The larger daughter cell will form the sieve-tube member, while the smaller one develops into the companion cell. The sieve-tube members and the companion cells appear closely linked, and the death of one means the death of the other. The name sieve element is derived from clusters of pores through which pass plasmodesmata, connecting the end adjacent cells. Under the microscope, these pore areas look like tiny sieves, and the names of the cells derive from this appearance. In sieve-tube members, the pores are larger than in sieve cells and form sieve plates at the ends of the cell. In sieve cells, the pores are smaller, and the sieve areas are more uniform on all walls.

In older sieve elements, the pores may be ringed or blocked with callose, a carbohydrate polymer frequently found in wounded or aged plant cells. Sieve elements at maturity are the only cells in the plant that lack nuclei yet contain living protoplasm. Moreover, in many sieve elements the distinction is lost between the vacuole and the cytoplasm of the cell. Ribosomes, Golgi bodies, and microtubules are lacking from these cells at maturity, but some plastids, mitochondria, and endoplasmic reticulum are found near the side walls of the cells. In some sieve elements there are accumulations of a protein known as P-protein, or slime, adjacent to the wall. When the plant is wounded, this protein accumulates at the sieve plate, where it is not normally found, and blocks the pores. This is considered a defence mechanism in the event of injury to the plant.

Now let's look at the epidermis, a layer of parenchyma cells that covers the exterior surface of the plant. Typically, epidermal cells have relatively thin walls, but the wall surface facing outward is thicker than the other surfaces. In most plants, the epidermis is a single cell layer thick, but in some, as in Ficus elastica, the common rubber plant, the epidermis may be several cell layers thick. Such multiple epidermis is found most often in leaves. Typically, too, this outer wall is covered by a protective layer, the cuticle, composed of fatty substances called cutin and secreted by the epidermal cells.

In many species the cuticle in turn is covered with a deposit of wax, which in some cases is harvested for commercial use. Carnauba wax used in furniture waxes and polishes, candles, and lipstick is obtained from the fronds of a tropical South American palm tree. The structure of the epidermis and the cuticle serves to protect the plant from insects and fungal parasites. The cuticle limits evaporation of water from the plant's interior. Epidermal cells are alive when mature, and they contain nuclei capable of division. In flax and begonia, a single epidermal cell can give rise to a complete plant. The vacuoles are usually large and may contain pigments and tannins. Most of the epidermis covering the above-ground parts of the plant contains microscopic openings called stomates.

It is through the stomates that carbon dioxide and water vapour pass into and out of the leaf, making photosynthesis possible. A square inch of lower leaf surface of a black oak has 375,000 stomates; the same tissue from a corn plant has 64,000. Each stomate is in fact a gap between two specialised cells known as guard cells. The guard cells change shape and thus change the size of the stomatal opening, in response to changes in turgidity.

As with epidermal cells, the wall of a guard cell is uneven in thickness, thicker towards the stomate than towards the surrounding cells. The thickness of the wall bordering the stomate makes it less elastic than the rest of the wall. When the guard cell is turgid and under osmotic pressure, the thin wall stretches more than the thick wall, bending the guard cell into a kidney shape and opening the stomate. If the guard cell loses turgidity, the cell wall springs back and the stomate closes.

The opening and closing of the stomates controls CO_2 exchange and water loss from the leaf. Guard cells arise from an epidermal cell, which divides unequally. The smaller of two daughter cells, called the guard mother cell, divides equally into two guard cells. In addition, cells surrounding the guard mother cell may divide to produce a number of subsidiary cells surrounding the guard cells. Surface projections known as trichomes, found in the epidermis, may be simple; that is, single cells, or elaborate, multicellular structures.

Root hairs, as one example of trichomes, are extensions of the epidermal cells of the root. Sometimes, root hairs may reach two millimetres in length, and they are found in most plants in a one-centimetre zone of the root near the tip. Root hairs live ordinarily for days or weeks and only in a few species persist for as long as a whole season. Root hairs arise from unequal division of an epidermal cell. The small cell becomes the hair, and its development begins with the modification of a portion of the cell wall. Only one face of the cell grows. The hair extends by tip growth, new wall is formed only at the tip of the hair. Root hairs greatly increase the area of the plant in contact with the soil and thus its surface for absorbing water and minerals.

A study of a single rye plant showed that the plant had 13,800,000 roots with a surface area of 2,500 square feet. These roots had 14 billion root hairs with a total surface area of 4,300 square feet. The combined surface area of roots and root hairs was 6,800 square feet, all packed into less than two cubic feet of soil. Some trichomes found on stems, leaves, flowers, and fruit are simple hairs. A familiar example is the cotton fibre, which is actually an epidermal hair formed on the surface of the cotton seed. These cells have much thicker walls than root hairs, and the walls have extremely high cellulose content. Cotton fibres grow from 6 to 60 millimetres in length, depending on the variety of cotton. Other trichomes present on the above-ground parts of the plant are more elaborate. These are many-celled and have a wide variety of forms. Some are simple in shape; others are tufts of cells; many take the form of a plate of cells, often on a stalk; still others are glandular, secreting a variety of substances.

One of the most unusual trichomes is the stinging hair found in the nettle. The hair resembles a fine capillary tube, with calcium in the wall at the lower end and silica at the upper end. At the base, a bulblike structure is embedded in epidermal cells. The upper end of the tube bears a spherical tip that breaks off when the hair comes in contact with an object. The break leaves a sharp edge that readily penetrates the skin, and the cell contents are forced into the wound. This material is highly irritating, and is an effective defence mechanism against animals.

Some epidermal trichomes can secrete substances such as nectar and oils. These glandular trichomes are common and numerous in vascular plants. For example, the hairs of marijuana plants, Cannabis sativa, secrete a resin that contains several complex alcohols, including the tetrahydrocannabinols, which are the active ingredients of marijuana's drug effect. The hairs occur only on pistillate, or female plants; staminate, or male plants, have no hairs and no tetrahydrocannabinols. Insectivorous plants, like the Venus' flytrap and the sundew, have several types of secretory trichomes, each releasing a specific substance that plays a role in capturing and digesting insects. These substances include a nectar to attract insects to the plant, mucilage to trap them, and digestive enzymesto dissolve them into a chemical form the plant can use.

Collections of cells that produce nectar, called nectaries, are usually part of the flower in many species, but they may also occur on stems and leaves. On the left is an immature nectary, and on the right, a mature nectary covered by a drop of nectar. Not all secretory cells in the plant occur on the surface, nor do they secrete substances outside the plant. Some are within the plant, and their secretions collect in internal cavities.

An example is the resin ducts of conifers and other plants, which are cavities lined with living cells. The lining, or epithelium, comprises cells rich in plastids and ER [endoplasmic reticulum]. The epithelial cells secrete resin into the cavity of the ducts, which can form complex systems in the plant. Myrrh and frankincense, important in the ancient Middle East as aromatic substances and among the gifts of the Magi, are products of such internal secretory systems. Waterproofing and maintaining wooden ships required resin and resin products, like pitch, turpentine, and rosin, which were known collectively as naval stores. Resin for naval stores was obtained by tapping pine trees, chipping through the bark and outer wood, and collecting the material that dripped out. Imperial England's power was based on its fleet, which consumed huge quantities of naval stores. The extensive pine forests of North America made the colonies strategically important to England and were one reason it opposed independence for the colonies. Another plant product obtained by tapping trees is rubber. The material drained from the tree is latex, which besides rubber, contains carbohydrates, organic acids, alkaloids, terpenes, oils, resins, and various enzymes. Latex is found in many plants, not only the rubber tree, Heva brasiliensis, but its composition varies greatly with source. Latex forms within the plant in laticifers, which are truly unique secretory cells. Many laticifers comprise files of cells in which the end walls have broken down, so that the cells form a continuous channel. This is the type of laticifer found in the rubber tree and in the opium poppy, Papaver somniferum, which produces the opium refined into morphine and other drugs.

We have reviewed the major types of cells and tissues present in the vascular plant body. We have also seen how these are organised into tissue systems: the dermal, the vascular, and the fundamental, or ground. It is important to understand that there is an almost infinite variety of ways in which the cells and tissues of the plant can be arranged in the different organs of the plant and in different species. It is this flexibility that makes the vascular plant so adaptable to life on land and of so much interest for botanists to study.

7

Plant Cell Structure and Function

The digestibility of plants (*i.e.* how easy they are to digest) affects the efficiency of animals' digestive processes, and is related to the structure of plant cells and tissues.

DIGESTIBILITY OF PLANTS

Animals can easily digest the contents of plant cells, but not their cell walls. All plant cells have an outer cell wall composed of cellulose or lignin.. This reduces the amount of energy animals can extract from plants, because most animals lack the specific enzymes that would allow them to digest cellulose.

Fibre is the amount of cellulose and lignin present in the plant. In general, older and woodier plants have higher levels of cellulose and lignin.

Lignin cannot be digested no matter how long it remains in the digestive system. In addition, lignin interferes with gut microbes that do have the necessary enzymes to digest cellulose, because it both acts as a physical barrier to digestion, and contains chemical bonds that cannot be broken down by normal stomach microbial flora. 'Digestibility' describes how readily the plant can be digested and its energy released for use by an animal.

The digestible part of a plant includes the cell contents and the small amount of fibre that can be broken down. The amount of energy available to an animal eating a plant is determined by the proportion of fibre to cell contents in that plant.

DIGESTIBILITY OF PLANT STRUCTURES

Grasses normally have higher fibre content than legumes such as clover. The amount of fibre in leaves of grass is twice that of legume leaves, and grass leaves are harder to digest than those of legumes. The leaves of grasses typically have a midrib made of lignin to provide support for the leaf, which adds to the higher fibre levels and lower digestibility of the leaves.

The stems of most plant species have greater fibre levels compared to the leaves, and grass stems usually contain more fibre than legumes. Digestibility not only declines down the stem, but also declines more rapidly than leaf digestibility with increasing plant age.

DIGESTIVE EFFICIENCY OF RUMINANTS

Ruminants are better than nonruminants at digesting high-fibre diets. Leaves have a shorter rumen retention time than stems due to both faster rates of fibre digestion and higher rates of passage of undigested material. Ruminants can digest 40-50% of legume fibre and 60-70% of grass fibre.

Small particles of food are digested faster than large particles because they have more surface area exposed relative to the total food volume. This is why ruminants regurgitate and re-chew (ruminate) their food after eating, to reduce the size of the food particles.

Because high fibre plants are harder to break down, ruminants spend more time regurgitating and chewing grasses than legumes and more time chewing mature than immature plants.

Digestive Efficiency of Hindgut Fermenters

Hindgut fermenters such as horses do not re-chew their food. They rely on eating more food to extract enough nutrients. This means that at certain times of the year, nonruminants must eat lower quality feed in order to sustain their energy requirements. So when food becomes limited, animals such as horses and pandas must eat whatever is available, while cattle may pick and choose. In both ruminants and nonruminants efficiency of digestion drops off as dietary fibre reaches certain levels. Above 60% fibre, the efficiency of digestion in both cattle and horses drops to the point whereby not enough energy can be extracted from the food to make it worth eating. This is about the same level of fibre as the wood of many trees.

Environmental Effects of Low Digestibility

Due to the comparatively low digestibility of grass and other vegetative matter, ruminants and hindgut fermenters must consume proportionally more food than carnivores or omnivores. The high food intake and low nutrient extraction of ruminants and hindgut fermenters means that they concentrate and excrete large quantities of plant nutrients such as phosphorus and nitrogen. This leads to problems such as pollution and eutrophication of lakes and rivers when large numbers of cattle are concentrated on a comparatively small amount of farmland. Phosphorus and nitrogen from cattle effluent is washed in to lakes and waterways and causes blooms of algae that reduces water quality.

CELLULOSE AND LIGNIN

The plant cell wall surrounds the cell membrane. It is made up of multiple layers of cellulose which are arranged into primary and secondary walls. Cellulose is the most common organic compound on Earth. About 33% of all plant matter is cellulose-the cellulose content of cotton is 90% and wood is 50% cellulose.

The cell walls of all vascular plants also contain a polymer called lignin. Lignin is water-resistant. It reinforces cell walls, keeping them from collapsing. This is particularly important in the xylem, because the column of water in the hollow xylem cells is under tension (negative pressure) and without the lignin reinforcement the cells would collapse.

Cellulose

Cellulose is a polymer made of repeating glucose molecules attached end to end (Thus cellulose is an example of a polysaccharide.). A cellulose molecule may be from several hundred to over 10,000 glucose units long. Cellulose from wood pulp has typical chain lengths between 300 and 1700 units; cotton and other plant fibres have chain lengths ranging from 800 to 10,000 units.

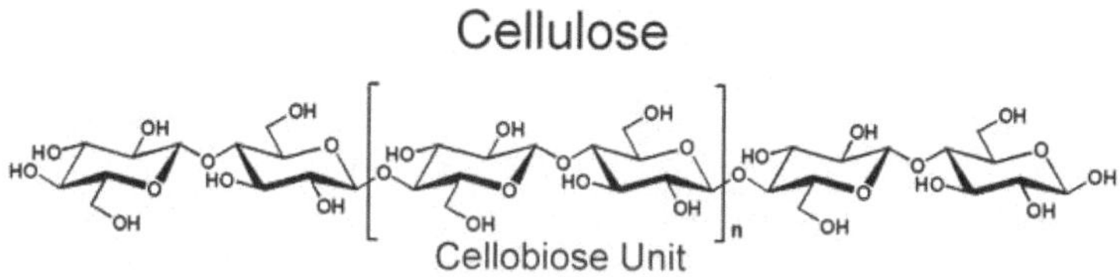

Figure 7.1

Cellulose is similar in form to complex carbohydrates like starch and glycogen. These polysaccharides are also made from multiple subunits of glucose. The difference between cellulose and other complex carbohydrate molecules is how the glucose molecules are linked together. In addition, cellulose is a straight chain polymer, and each cellulose molecule is long and rod-like. This differs from starch, which is a coiled molecule. A result of these differences in structure is that, compared to starch and other carbohydrates, cellulose can not be broken down into its glucose subunits by any enzymes produced by animals.

Lignin

Lignin provides the mechanical support for stems and leaves and supplies the strength and rigidity of plant walls. Lignin provides the structural strength needed by large trees to reach heights in excess of 100 m. Without lignin these trees would collapse on themselves. Also, lignin along with other cell wall constituents provides resistance to diseases, insects, cold temperatures, and other stresses. Lignin plays a crucial part in conducting water in plant stems. The structure of lignin has not been properly determined as it usually fragments upon extraction and there appears to be no consistent structure to it. The polysaccharide components of plant cell walls are highly hydrophilic and thus permeable to water, whereas lignin is more hydrophobic. The crosslinking of polysaccharides by lignin is an obstacle for water absorption to the cell wall. Thus, lignin makes it possible for the plant's vascular tissue to conduct water efficiently. Lignin is present in all vascular plants, but not in bryophytes, supporting the idea that the original function of lignin was restricted to water transport.

Plant Cells and Tissues

Cells are the smallest functional units of life. A living organism may comprise a single cell *e.g.* an alga; or it may be a multicellular organism made up of billions of cells *e.g.* a kauri tree. An individual plant contains many different cell types, each adapted to perform a particular function. However, each living plant cell is made up of the same basic components: a cell wall, plasma membrane, nucleus, and mitochondria and other organelles.

Plant Cell Structure

Each plant cell is self-contained and at least partially self-sufficient. This is because plant cells have a number of organelles that perform functions such as storing food, processing waste, fixing and releasing chemical energy, and copying their genetic material. The nucleus, the mitochondrion, the plastids, the Golgi apparatus, and the endoplasmic reticulum are all examples of organelles. Some organelles, such as mitochondria and chloroplasts, have their own genetic material separate from that found in the nucleus of the cell. Such organelles are thought to have originated through the process of endosymbiosis. Other structures such as the cell wall and the cell membrane serve to protect the cell and maintain the shape, structure, and functioning of the cell.

The Plant Cell Wall

Unlike animal cells plant cells have an outer cell wall composed of polysaccharides, in particular cellulose. Cell walls provide rigidity and mechanical support, maintain cell shape and the direction of cell growth. The cell wall also prevents expansion when water enters the cell.

Cell Wall Structure

The cell wall of a plant cell is made up of primary and secondary cell walls. When one cell divides into two, a primary cell wall forms around each two new cells. The primary cell wall is laid down just outside the cell membrane, and is flexible, allowing the new cells to grow. This new cell wall is mostly made of cellulose molecules, arranged into thin hair-like strands called microfibrils. The microfibrils are arranged in a meshwork pattern along with other components such as hemicellulose, glycans and pectins, which link them together and help strengthen the cell wall.

The secondary cell wall is constructed between the plasma membrane and the primary cell wall after the cell has finished growing. It is made by laying down successive layers of cellulose microfibrils and lignins. Mature xylem cells are heavily lignified-they make up the 'wood' of woody plants.

Cell Plasma Membrane

Every living cell is bounded by an outer membrane called the cell plasma membrane, or plasmalemma. The cell membrane separates the cell's contents from the surrounding environment and controls the movement of materials into and out of the cell. The cell membrane is made up of two phospholipid layers (a bi-layer)which spontaneously arrange so that the hydrophobic 'tail' regions are protected from the surrounding water, causing the more hydrophilic 'head' regions to be pointed towards either the cytoplasm or the exterior of the cell. Substances such as amino acids, nucleic acids, carbohydrates, proteins, and many ions are unable to diffuse across the membrane but must enter or leave the cell through active transport, under the control of the cell membrane.

This involves some of the many different proteins and lipids embedded in the plasma membrane. Other proteins are involved in other cellular processes such as cell linkage, ion channel flow and cell communication. The plasma membrane also serves as the attachment point for both the intracellular cytoskeleton (found in all eukaryote cells) and the cell wall.

Cytoplasm

The cytoplasm is the gooey, semi-transparent fluid in which the other organelles are suspended. Processes such as breaking down food molecules into smaller molecules happens in the cytoplasm. The cytoplasm consists mostly of water, dissolved ions, small molecules, and large water-soluble molecules such as proteins. It also has a high concentration of potassium ions and a low concentration of sodium ions, which help in controlling the amount of water in the cell. If you make a wet mount of a leaf from the pondweed *Elodea*, you may be able to see the cell's organelles, especially the chloroplasts, moving as the cytoplasm flows through the cell.

Nucleus

In eukaryote cells the nucleus is surrounded by a double membrane called the nuclear envelope. This separates the genetic material from the rest of the cell. The nuclear envelope has a large number of holes or 'pores' that allow the cell to move molecules across the nuclear envelope and in and out of the nucleus. These molecules include RNA and ribosomes moving from nucleus to the cytoplasm, and proteins, carbohydrates, and lipids moving into the nucleus. You could say that these molecules provide a means of communication between the cytoplasm and the nucleus. The nucleus performs two important functions: it controls the activity of the cell by determining what proteins are produced and when they are produced by the cell; and it also stores the genetic information of the cell which is then passed on to daughter cells during cell division.

Vacuole

The vacuoles of most plant cells are large, filling much of the space inside the cell wall and pushing the cytoplasm out to the periphery of the cell. A single, large vacuole is found in the cytoplasm of most mature plant cells. (Animal cells have much smaller, multiple vacuoles.) The vacuole is bounded by a membrane that keeps the vacuole's contents separate from the cytoplasm. Young plant cells typically contain a number of small independent vacuoles. These merge together to form one large vacuole as the cell matures, so that in a fully mature cell the vacuole may occupy more than 90% of the cell volume.

Vacuoles typically contain salts, sugars, and sometimes proteins, and have a variety of secretory, excretory, and storage functions. They are usually slightly acidic. Some of them, like those in grapefruit and lemons are very acidic–which is where the sour taste of these fruit comes from. The vacuole may also be involved in the breakdown of old organelles or macromolecules and then recycling the products back to the rest of the cell. For example, an entire mitochondrion may be engulfed by the vacuole, so that it is surrounded by a 'bubble' of the vacuole membrane. This 'bubble' is then pinched off, forming a vesicle suspended in the vacuole. After the mitochondrion has been digested the vesicle disappears.

Endoplasmic Reticulum

The endoplasmic reticulum (often abbreviated to ER) is an extensive network of membranous sack-like folds, tubes and vesicles, held together by the cytoskeleton. This network is continuous with the nuclear membrane. Plant cells contain both rough and smooth ER. The relative proportions of rough and smooth endoplasmic reticulum in a cell can change quickly, depending on the cell's metabolic needs. The endoplasmic reticulum provides a site for the synthesis of lipids and proteins and for the storage and transport of those molecules.

Rough Endoplasmic Eeticulum

The surface of the rough endoplasmic reticulum is studded with ribosomes, giving it a 'rough' appearance. This means that the rough ER is a site of protein synthesis. Once produced, the proteins are packaged into vesicles and transported to the Golgi apparatus, where they are modified and packaged for export from the cell or transport to where they will be used.

Smooth Endoplasmic Reticulum

Smooth endoplasmic reticulum is also made up of tubules and vesicles that branch forming a network attached to the nuclear membrane. The smooth endoplasmic reticulum provides an increased surface area for the action or storage of key enzymes and the products of these enzymes. The smooth endoplasmic reticulum also produces lipids, such as the phospholipids that make up the cell membrane-in fact, it is the source of new cell membrane material. It also metabolises carbohydrates breaking them down into glucose providing energy for the cell.

The smooth ER is also involved in the breakdown and detoxification of drugs and chemicals *e.g.* in human liver cells smooth ER is involved in the metabolism of ethanol. Long-term use of alcohol leads to a increased amount of smooth ER in the cells, which increases the rate of alcohol metabolism. This explains why people who regularly drink large amounts of alcohol often have a high tolerance for alcohol.

Golgi Apparatus

The Golgi apparatus is a collective term for Golgi bodies: flattened, membrane-enclosed compartments arranged into a stack of five or six pancake-like structures, often with globs or cisternae at the ends. The Golgi bodies are processing and sorting centres for cellular materials such as proteins, enzymes and lipids. Cellular materials are transported from production areas such as the endoplasmic reticulum to the Golgi bodies and, after sorting, to cisternae at the ends of the Golgi bodies. At the cisternae the molecules are enclosed in a phospholipid membrane. This membrane is then pinched off to form a vesicle, which transports the molecules to their destination and fuses with a membrane there to release its contents. In plants, cellulose sub-units are packaged into vesicles by the Golgi bodies, which then travel to and fuse with the plasma membrane. The vesicles discharge their contents to the outside of the cell and the cellulose is incorporated in the cell wall·

Mitochondria

Mitochondria-the cell's 'power plants'-generate most of the cell's supply of the energy-carrying molecule adenosine triphosphate (ATP). MItochondria are also involved in a range of other processes: signalling, cellular differentiation, cell death, control of the cell cycle, and cell growth. They evolved as the result of endosymbiosis from ancient bacteria, which were engulfed by the ancestors of eukaryote cells more than a billion years ago.

Mitochondria are much smaller than plastids-around 0.5μm in diameter *i.e.* too small to observe with a light microscope. The number of mitochondria in a cell varies widely: from one to several thousand, depending on organism and tissue type. Mitochondria replicate (by binary fission) mainly in response to the energy needs of the cell. In other words, their growth and division is not linked to the cell cycle. When the energy needs of a cell are high, mitochondria grow and divide. When energy use is low, mitochondria are destroyed or become inactive.

Mitochondria Structure

A mitochondrion is composed of inner and outer membranes separated by a region called the intermembrane space. The inner membrane is highly folded, forming projections called cristae. The membrane folds greatly increase the surface area of the inner membrane, which is studded with the enzymes involved in making ATP. The area inside the inner membrane is called the matrix. The matrix contains enzymes that produce molecules used in the production of ATP on the inner membrane. The mitochondrial matrix also contains the mitochondrion's DNA and ribosomes.

Mitochondria and Aerobic Respiration

The primary role of the mitochondrion is the production of ATP, used to power cellular processes. Glycolysis in the cytoplasm produces pyruvate and NADH. Once in the mitochonrion, pyruvate is oxidised in the Krebs cycle to produce CO_2, a small amount of ATP, and hydrogen ions (H^+). These then enter the Electron Transport Chain, which generates a large amount of ATP, and water (through the combination of the H^+ ions with oxygen). In other words, if oxygen is not available other less efficient anaerobic processes, such as fermentation, must be used to generate ATP.

Aerobic respiration has a much higher yield of ATP than anaerobic respiration. For example, one molecule of glucose will produce between 32 to 36 molecules of ATP under aerobic conditions; compared to 2 molecules of ATP under anaerobic conditions.

Plastids

Like vacuoles and cell walls, plastids are characteristic of plant cells. Plastids are responsible for photosynthesis, storage of products like starch and for the synthesis of many classes of molecules, such as fatty acids and terpenes, which are needed as cellular building blocks and for normal functions of the plant. Like mitochondria, plastids originated through endosymbiosis. In plants, plastids may differentiate into several forms, depending upon which function they need to play in the cell.

Chloroplasts

Chloroplasts are give plants their characteristic green colour and are the site of photosynthesis. Like a mitochondrion, a chloroplast has an outer and inner membrane, with an intermembrane space between them. Within the inner membrane lies the stroma, which contains the thylakoid membranes-the site of photosynthesis. The thylakoid membranes form a series of flattened, fluid-filled, interconnected tubules that are often stacked on top of each other to form a structure called a granum. The photosynthetic pigments, such as chlorophyll, are located in the thylakoid membranes.

Chromoplasts

Chromoplasts-'coloured bodies'-synthesise and store pigments. They are found in coloured organs of plants such as fruit and flower petals, giving them their distinctive colours.

When fruit such as tomatoes ripen, the green chloroplasts to are converted to chromoplasts that mostly contain red carotenoids.

Amyloplasts

During the day, when plants are photosynthesising, amyloplasts store glucose and convert it into a form of starch for storage. They can also convert the starch back into sugar, when the plant needs energy.

Statoliths

Statoliths are a specialised form of amyloplast used by plants in detecting and responding to gravity. Statoliths are denser than the cytoplasm and tend to move towards the bottom of the cell, indicating which direction is 'down'. They are found mainly in root tissues.

EPIDERMAL CELLS

Epidermis

The epidermal tissue functions in prevention of water loss and acts as a barrier to fungi and other invaders. Thus, epidermal cells are closely packed, with little intercellular space. To further cut down on water loss, many plants have a waxy cuticle layer deposited on top of the epidermal cells.

Guard Cells

To facilitate gas exchange between the inner parts of leaves, stems, and fruits, plants have a series of openings known as stomata (singular stoma). Obviously these openings would allow gas exchange, but at a cost of water loss. Guard cells are bean-shaped cells covering the stomata opening. They regulate exchange of water vapour, oxygen and carbon dioxide through the stoma.

PLANT CELL STRUCTURE

Plants are unique among the eukaryotes, organisms whose cells have membrane-enclosed nuclei and organelles, because they can manufacture their own food. Chlorophyll, which gives plants their green colour, enables them to use sunlight to convert water and carbon dioxide into sugars and carbohydrates, chemicals the cell uses for fuel.

Like the fungi, another kingdom of eukaryotes, plant cells have retained the protective cell wall structure of their prokaryotic ancestors. The basic plant cell shares a similar construction motif with the typical eukaryote cell, but does not have centrioles, lysosomes, intermediate filaments, cilia, or flagella, as does the animal cell. Plant cells do, however, have a number of other specialized structures, including a rigid cell wall, central vacuole, plasmodesmata, and chloroplasts. Although plants (and their typical cells) are non-motile, some species produce gametes that do exhibit flagella and are, therefore, able to move about.

Plants can be broadly categorized into two basic types: vascular and nonvascular. Vascular plants are considered to be more advanced than nonvascular plants because they have evolved specialized tissues, namely xylem, which is involved in structural support and water conduction, and phloem, which functions in food conduction. Consequently, they also possess roots, stems, and leaves, representing a higher form of organization that is characteristically absent in plants lacking vascular tissues. The nonvascular plants, members of the division Bryophyta, are usually no more than an inch or two in height because they do not have adequate support, which is provided by vascular tissues to other plants, to grow bigger. They also are more dependent on the environment that surrounds them to maintain appropriate amounts of moisture and, therefore, tend to inhabit damp, shady areas.

It is estimated that there are at least 260,000 species of plants in the world today. They range in size and complexity from small, nonvascular mosses to giant sequoia trees, the largest living organisms, growing as tall as 330 feet (100 meters). Only a tiny percentage of those species are directly used by people for food, shelter, fibre, and medicine. Nonetheless, plants are the basis for the Earth's ecosystem and food web, and without them complex animal life forms (such as humans) could never have evolved. Indeed, all living organisms are dependent either directly or indirectly on the energy produced by photosynthesis, and the byproduct of this process, oxygen, is essential to animals. Plants also reduce the amount of carbon dioxide present in the atmosphere, hinder soil erosion, and influence water levels and quality.

Plants exhibit life cycles that involve alternating generations of diploid forms, which contain paired chromosome sets in their cell nuclei, and haploid forms, which only possess a single set. Generally these two forms of a plant are very dissimilar in appearance. In higher plants, the diploid generation, the members of which are known as sporophytes due to their ability to produce spores, is usually dominant and more recognizable than the haploid gametophyte generation. In Bryophytes, however, the gametophyte form is dominant and physiologically necessary to the sporophyte form.

Animals are required to consume protein in order to obtain nitrogen, but plants are able to utilize inorganic forms of the element and, therefore, do not need an outside source of protein. Plants do, however, usually require significant amounts of water, which is needed for the photosynthetic process, to maintain cell structure and facilitate growth, and as a means of bringing nutrients to plant cells. The amount of nutrients needed by plant species varies significantly, but nine elements are generally considered to be necessary in relatively large amounts. Termed macroelements, these nutrients include calcium, carbon, hydrogen, magnesium, nitrogen, oxygen, phosphorus, potassium, and sulfur. Seven microelements, which are required by plants in smaller quantities, have also been identified: boron, chlorine, copper, iron, manganese, molybdenum, and zinc.

Thought to have evolved from the green algae, plants have been around since the early Paleozoic era, more than 500 million years ago. The earliest fossil evidence of land plants dates to the Ordovician Period (505 to 438 million years ago). By the Carboniferous Period, about 355 million years ago, most of the Earth was covered by forests of primitive vascular plants, such as lycopods (scale trees) and gymnosperms (pine trees, ginkgos). Angiosperms, the flowering plants, didn't develop until the end of the Cretaceous Period, about 65 million years ago—just as the dinosaurs became extinct.

- *Cell Wall:* Like their prokaryotic ancestors, plant cells have a rigid wall surrounding the plasma membrane. It is a far more complex structure, however, and serves a variety of functions, from protecting the cell to regulating the life cycle of the plant organism.
- *Chloroplasts:* The most important characteristic of plants is their ability to photosynthesize, in effect, to make their own food by converting light energy into chemical energy. This process is carried out in specialized organelles called chloroplasts.
- *Endoplasmic Reticulum :* The endoplasmic reticulum is a network of sacs that manufactures, processes, and transports chemical compounds for use inside and outside of the cell. It is connected to the double-layered nuclear envelope, providing a pipeline between the nucleus and the cytoplasm. In plants, the endoplasmic reticulum also connects between cells via the plasmodesmata.
- *Golgi Apparatus:* The Golgi apparatus is the distribution and shipping department for the cell's chemical products. It modifies proteins and fats built in the endoplasmic reticulum and prepares them for export as outside of the cell.
- *Microfilaments:* Microfilaments are solid rods made of globular proteins called actin. These filaments are primarily structural in function and are an important component of the cytoskeleton.
- *Microtubules :* These straight, hollow cylinders are found throughout the cytoplasm of all eukaryotic cells (prokaryotes don't have them) and carry out a variety of functions, ranging from transport to structural support.
- *Mitochondria:* Mitochondria are oblong shaped organelles found in the cytoplasm of all eukaryotic cells. In plant cells, they break down carbohydrate

and sugar molecules to provide energy, particularly when light isn't available for the chloroplasts to produce energy.

- *Nucleus* : The nucleus is a highly specialized organelle that serves as the information processing and administrative centre of the cell. This organelle has two major functions: it stores the cell's hereditary material, or DNA, and it coordinates the cell's activities, which include growth, intermediary metabolism, protein synthesis, and reproduction (cell division).
- *Peroxisomes:* Microbodies are a diverse group of organelles that are found in the cytoplasm, roughly spherical and bound by a single membrane. There are several types of microbodies but peroxisomes are the most common.
- *Plasmodesmata* : Plasmodesmata are small tubes that connect plant cells to each other, providing living bridges between cells.
- *Plasma Membrane* : All living cells have a plasma membrane that encloses their contents. In prokaryotes and plants, the membrane is the inner layer of protection surrounded by a rigid cell wall. These membranes also regulate the passage of molecules in and out of the cells.
- *Ribosomes* : All living cells contain ribosomes, tiny organelles composed of approximately 60 percent RNA and 40 percent protein. In eukaryotes, ribosomes are made of four strands of RNA. In prokaryotes, they consist of three strands of RNA.
- *Vacuole* : Each plant cell has a large, single vacuole that stores compounds, helps in plant growth, and plays an important structural role for the plant.
- *Leaf Tissue Organization* : The plant body is divided into several organs: roots, stems, and leaves. The leaves are the primary photosynthetic organs of plants, serving as key sites where energy from light is converted into chemical energy. Similar to the

other organs of a plant, a leaf is comprised of three basic tissue systems, including the dermal, vascular, and ground tissue systems. These three motifs are continuous throughout an entire plant, but their properties vary significantly based upon the organ type in which they are located.

PLANT TISSUES

In plants, the processes of differentiation and specialisation allow groups of cells that are structurally or functionally distinct to form tissues that have specific functions. Tissues composed of only one type of cell are called simple tissues, while those made up of two or more types of cells are called complex tissues. Parenchyma and collenchyma are simple tissues; xylem, phloem, and epidermis are complex tissues. Tissues can also be grouped into tissue systems, and in plants these are (1) ground tissue, (2) vascular tissue, and (3) dermal tissue. Gground tissue is made up of parenchyma, collenchyma and sclerenchyma. Vascular tissue system consists of the two conducting tissues–xylem and phloem. Dermal tissue comprises the epidermis: pavement cells, guard cells, and trichomes.

Ground Tissue

Most of a plant's body is made up of ground tissue, which has a variety of functions, including photosynthesis, storage of carbohydrates and mechanical support of the plant. Ground tissue can be divided into three tissue types; parenchyma, collenchyma and sclerenchyma.

Parenchyma

Parenchyma is the most common and versatile ground tissue: it forms the cortex and pith of stems, the cortex of roots, the mesophyll of leaves, the pulp of fruits, and the endosperm of seeds. Parenchyma cells are living cells, and may still be able to divide when they are mature. Because of this, parenchyma cells are important for regeneration and wound healing. They have thin but flexible cell walls because the secondary cell wall is usually absent. Photosynthesis usually occurs in parenchyma cells (the mesophyll), and they function in the storage of carbohydrates. They are generally polygonal when packed close together, but are nearly spherical when separated from their neighbours. They have large central vacuoles, which allow the cells to store and regulate ions, waste products and water.

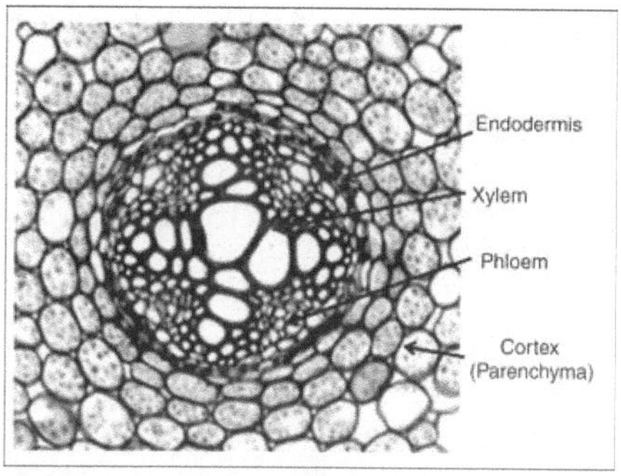

Figure 7.2: Cross-section of a Dicot Root.

Collenchyma

Collenchyma cells are elongated and have unevenly thickened walls. Like parenchyma cells, they are still alive when mature. Collenchyma provides structural support, particularly in growing shoots and leaves. The stringy pieces in the stalks of celery, for example, are composed of collenchyma.

Sclerenchyma

Mature sclerenchyma is composed of dead cells with extremely thick secondary walls cell walls composed of cellulose and lignin: these walls make up to 90% of the whole cell volume. Sclerenchyma tissue is a supporting tissue. There are two types of sclerenchyma cells, fibres and sclereids. Fibres are generally long, slender cells, which commonly occur in strands or bundles. Fibres are of great economical importance, since they make up the source material for many fabrics such as flax, hemp and jute. Sclereids are variable in shape and usually shorter than fibre cells. They make up the seed coats of seeds, the shells of nuts and the stone of stone fruits.

Vascular Tissue

Vascular tissue is a complex tissue and characteristic of vascular plants. The two main components of vascular tissue are the xylem and phloem. The vascular tissue in plants is arranged in long, discrete strands called vascular bundles. These bundles include xylem and phloem, as well as supporting and protective cells. The arrangement of vascular tissue differs in monocot and dicot plants, as you can see by comparing the two previous images with the two that follow below.

Xylem

The xylem forms a continuous system that transports water and dissolved mineral nutrients throughout the plant from the roots. There are two types of conducting cells in the xylem: tracheids and vessel elements. (Xylem also contains parenchyma and sclerenchyma cells.) Both tracheids and vessel elements are dead when mature and have thick, lignified cell walls. Tracheids are long, tapering cells with pits in their walls, through which the water passes as it moves up the plant. Vessels have a larger diameter than tracheids and their end walls have disappeared. They are stacked end-on-end to form a continuous series of tubes up the stem, allowing for more efficient water movement than in tracheids.

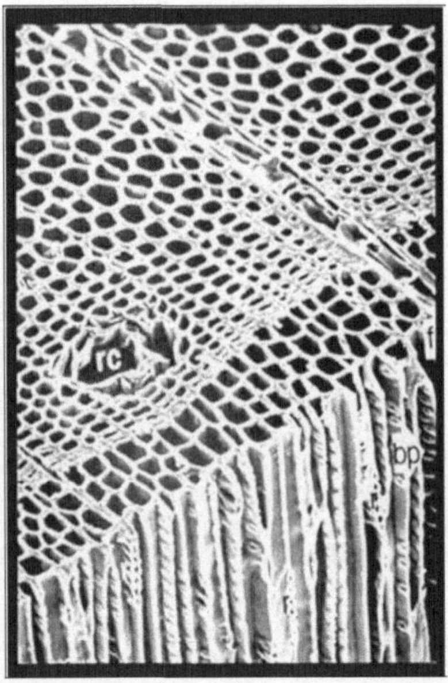

Figure 7.3

Phloem

Phloem transports sugars, proteins and minerals around the plant. Unlike the xylem where flow is only one way, from the roots up, phloem can move sugars both up and down the stem. In flowe-ring plants, phloem is contains four cell types: sieve tube members, companion cells, fibres and parenchyma. Sieve tube members are very highly specialised. The ends of the cell wall are perforated by sieve plates, and sap passes through the sieve plates from one sieve tube member to another. Mature sieve tube members are not dead, but they do lose their nuclei and most of their cytoplasm in order to accommodate the flow of phloem sap once they mature. For this reason, mature sieve tube members have accompanying companion cells which supply the RNA and proteins that keep the sieve tube member cell alive.

Companion cells are also involved in the off-loading and on-loading of sugars from the phloem sap. As with the xylem tissue the fibre cells provide structural support to the tissue and parenchyma cells provide storage for various substances.

Dermal Tissue

The dermal tissue is the boundary between the plant and the outside world. It functions in protection against water loss, regulation of gas exchange, secretion, and (especially in roots) absorption of water and mineral nutrients. There are two main types of dermal tissue: epidermis and periderm. The epidermis is usually transparent (epidermal cells lack chloroplasts) and coated on its outer surface with a waxy cuticle that prevents water loss. Epidermal tissue includes several differentiated cell types, including pavement cells, guard cells, and trichomes (epidermal hairs). The other dermal tissue type is the periderm, or bark. It replaces the epidermis of stems and roots once a plant has developed secondary thickening.

Epidermis

Pavement cells are the most numerous epidermal cells, irregularly shaped and the least specialised. They do not contain chlorophlasts. Because they are transparent, light can penetrate into the interior of stems and leaves, where photosynthesis occurs. Pavement cells are tightly packed together to prevent water loss. The epiderms if leaves and stems is covered by a waxy cuticle, which also helps prevent water loss.

However, the epidermis is also perforated by openings called stomata, which permit gas exchange. Specialised cells called guard cells control the opening and closing of these stomata, regulating the exchange of gases and water vapour between the outside air and the interior of the leaf. A stoma is open when the guard cells surrounding it are swollen (turgid) with water, and closed when the guard cells lose water and become flaccid.

Trichomes are minute hairs on the epidermis. On leaves these hairs can interfere with the feeding of some herbivores, prevent frost forming on and damaging the leaf, reduce evaporation due to wind, and reflect light. And in locations where plants get most of their water from cloud drip, leaf hairs maximise this process by acting as points of condensation. Hairs on the roots increase the surface area available to the plant for uptake of water and minerals.

TISSUE TYPES

The major classes of cells differentiate from undifferentiated meristematic cells (analogous to the stem cells of animals) to form the tissue structures of roots, stems, leaves, flowers, and reproductive structures. Xylem cells are elongated cells with lignified secondary thickening of the cell walls. Xylem cells are specialised for conduction of water, and first appeared in plants during their transition to land in the Silurian period more than 425 million years ago. The possession of xylem defines the vascular plants or Tracheophytes.

Xylem tracheids are pointed, elongated xylem cells, the simplest of which have continuous primary cell walls and lignified secondary wall thickenings in the form of rings, hoops, or reticulate networks. More complex tracheids with valve-like perforations called bordered pits characterise the gymnosperms. The ferns and other pteridophytes and the gymnosperms have only xylem tracheids, while the angiosperms also have xylem vessels. Vessel members are hollow xylem cells aligned end-to-end, without end walls that are assembled into long continuous tubes. The bryophytes lack true xylem cells, but their sporophytes have a water-conducting tissue known as the hydrome that is composed of elongated cells of simpler construction. Phloem is a specialised tissue for food conduction in higher plants.

The conduction of food is a complex process that is carried in the plant with the help of special cell called phloem cells. These cells conduct inter-and intra-cellular fluid (food–proteins and other essential elements required by the plant for its metabolism) through the process of osmosis. This phenomenon is called ascent of sap in plants. Phloem consists of two cell types, the sieve tubes and the intimately-associated companion cells.

The sieve tube elements lack nuclei and ribosomes, and their metabolism and functions are regulated by the adjacent nucleate companion cells. Sieve tubes are joined end-to-end with perforate end-plates between known as *sieve plates,* which allow transport of photosynthate between the sieve elements. The companion cells, connected to the sieve tubes via plasmodesmata, are responsible for loading the phloem with sugars. The bryophytes lack phloem, but moss sporophytes have a simpler tissue with analogous function known as the leptome.

Plant epidermal cells are specialised parenchyma cells covering the external surfaces of leaves, stems and roots. The epidermal cells of aerial organs arise from the superficial layer of cells known as the *tunica* (L1 and L2 layers) that covers the plant shoot apex, whereas the cortex and vascular tissues arise from innermost layer of the shoot apex known as the *corpus* (L3 layer). The epidermis of roots originates from the layer of cells immediately beneath the root cap.

The epidermis of all aerial organs, but not roots, is covered with a cuticle made of the polyester cutin with a superficial layer of waxes. The epidermal cells of the primary shoot are thought to be the only plant cells with the biochemical capacity to synthesize cutin. Several cell types may be present in the epidermis. Notable among these are the stomatal guard cells, glandular and clothing hairs or trichomes, and the root hairs of primary roots. In the shoot epidermis of most plants, only the guard cells have chloroplasts.

PLANTS AND THEIR STRUCTURE

GENERAL PLANT ORGANIZATION

A plant has two organ systems: 1) the shoot system, and 2) the root system. The shoot system is above ground and includes the organs such as leaves, buds, stems, flowers (if the plant has any), and fruits (if the plant has any). The root system includes those parts of the plant below ground, such as the roots, tubers, and rhizomes.

Plant cells are formed at meristems, and then develop into cell types which are grouped into tissues. Plants have only three tissue types:

(1) Dermal; (2) Ground; and (3) Vascular.

Dermal tissue covers the outer surface of herbaceous plants. Dermal tissue is composed of epidermal cells, closely packed cells that secrete a waxy cuticle that aids in the prevention of water loss.

The ground tissue comprises the bulk of the primary plant body. Parenchyma, collenchyma, and sclerenchyma cells are common in the ground tissue. Vascular tissue transports food, water, hormones and minerals within the plant. Vascular tissue includes xylem, phloem, parenchyma, and cambium cells.

Plant cell types rise by mitosis from a meristem. A meristem may be defined as a region of localized mitosis. Meristems may be at the tip of the shoot or root (a type known as the apical meristem) or lateral, occurring in cylinders extending nearly the length of the plant. A cambium is a lateral meristem that produces (usually) secondary growth. Secondary growth produces both wood and cork (although from separate secondary meristems).

Parenchyma

A generalized plant cell type, parenchyma cells are alive at maturity. They function in storage, photosynthesis, and as the bulk of ground and vascular tissues. Palisade parenchyma cells are elogated cells located in many leaves just below the epidermal tissue. Spongy mesophyll cells occur below the one or two layers of palisade cells. Ray parenchyma cells occur in wood rays, the structures that transport materials laterally within a woody stem. Parenchyma cells also occur within the xylem and phloem of vascular bundles. The largest parenchyma cells occur in the pith region, often, as in corn (*Zea*) stems, being larger than the vascular bundles. In many prepared slides they stain green.

Collenchyma

Collenchyma cells support the plant. These cells are characterised by thickenings of the wall, the are alive at maturity. They tend to occur as part of vascular bundles or on the corners of angular stems. In many prepared slides they stain red.

Sclerenchyma

Sclerenchyma cells support the plant. They often occur as bundle cap fibres. Sclerenchyma cells are characterized by thickenings in their secondary walls. They are dead at maturity. They, like collenchyma, stain red in many commonly used prepared slides. A common type of schlerenchyma cell is the fibre.

Some sclerenchyma cells occur in the fruits of Pear. These cells (sclereids or stone cells) give pears their gritty texture.

Xylem

Xylem is a term applied to woody (lignin-impregnated) walls of certain cells of plants. Xylem cells tend to conduct water and minerals from roots to leaves. While parenchyma cells do occur within what is commonly termed the 'xylem' the more identifiable cells, tracheids and vessel elements, tend to stain red with Safranin-O. Tracheids are the more primitive of the two cell types, occurring in the earliest vascular plants. Tracheids are long and tapered, with angled end-plates that connect cell to cell. Vessel elements are shorter, much wider, and lack end plates. They occur only in angiosperms, the most recently evolved large group of plants.

Tracheids, longer, and narrower than most vessels, appear first in the fossil record. Vessels occur later. Tracheids have obliquely-angled endwalls cut across by bars. The evolutionary trend in vessels is for shorter cells, with no bars on the endwalls.

Phloem

Phloem cells conduct food from leaves to rest of the plant. They are alive at maturity and tend to stain green (with the stain fast green). Phloem cells are usually located outside the xylem. The two most common cells in the phloem are the companion cells and sieve cells. Companion cells retain their nucleus and control the adjacent sieve cells. Dissolved food, as sucrose, flows through the sieve cells.

A GENERAL PANT STRUCTURE

The plants we discuss will be vascular plants that have systems of tubes (xylem and phloem) for the transport of nutrients and water. Remember that there is a wide variety of plants on Earth and even a whole group that doesn't have vascular systems. Mosses and liverworts may still have photosynthesis, but they do not have that 'classic' plant structure. Then you will find species such as cacti that don't have leaves. They conduct photosynthesis in their stems. Anyway, just remember that there are many other possibilities in the plant kingdom. We just told you about the many exceptions to the basic plant structure, so let's look at some similarities. An easy similarity is on a cellular level. Plants conduct photosynthesis. This process of converting the Sun's energy into molecular energy happens in chloroplasts with the help of chlorophyll molecules and a variety of enzymes. Vascular plants share a similar set of structures called roots, stems, and leaves. Many plants have specialized versions, but the basics are there. One specialization might be the petals of a flower. Those flower petals are specialized leaves that surround the reproductive structures of the plant.

THE ROOTS BELOW GROUND

We'll start at the bottom with the roots. These structures are designed to pull water and minerals from whatever material the plant sits on. For water plants, the roots may be in the water. For traditional trees, the roots go deep into the soil. There are even plants called epiphytes that live in trees and their root system clings to branches. Humans often capitalize on the roots of plants for food. Carrots are just one big orange root. Root systems also provide support for plants in the form of an anchor in the soil. If the wind blows hard, those roots keep the plant from falling over. Some plant species have roots above ground that provide support for the entire plant. Roots are further broken down into the primary root and lateral roots that each has apical meristem at their tips. Root hairs are also a common structure on roots. They make the roots look fuzzy and help in the absorption of water and nutrients.

SHOOTS ABOVE GROUND

Sure we said that there are some roots above the surface, but the majority of the plant you see is made up of stems and leaves. Think about a tree. The stems are the trunks and branches. Leaves are self-explanatory. Stems are all about transporting food and water and acting as support structures. Leaves are all about photosynthesis, creating food molecules and absorbing carbon dioxide for the plant. These parts are connected by the vascular system of xylem and phloem that spreads through the entire plant.

The tip (terminal bud) of the main stem has a specialized structure that is the source of new growth for plants. You will find the apical meristem that develops into young leaves (primodium). There are other points of growth at each node where leaves and branches develop on the stems. Those branching points are home to axillary buds that can also develop into new branches.

GENERALIZED PLANT CELL

Four features set apart plant cells from those of other organisms:

1. A cellulose cell wall; many protists, some fungi, and most bacteria also have rigid walls, but made of different materials, *e.g.* Chitin strengthens fungal cell walls and peptidoglycan those of bacteria.
2. Plasmodesmata, strands of cytoplasm that protrude through pores in the cell walls and connect the protoplasts of adjacent cells; these are avenues of material transport in plants.
3. Plastids, organelles thought to have an endosymbiotic origin; they have an intricate internal structure of folded membranes that greatly increases the internal surface area on which chemical reactions occur; chloroplasts contain chlorophyll, and their thylakoid membranes are the sites of photosynthesis.
4. Vacuoles are fluid filled sacs present in plants, animals, and some protists; those of plants differ from others in size and function, *i.e.* a typical plant cell has a single, centrally located vacuole whose water-filled interior pushes the cytoplasm outward against the cell wall giving rigidity or turgidity to the cell.

Not all functional cells in plants are alive. Many cells live for only a short time then die, but their cell walls remain in place giving strength and rigidity to the plant body. The dead cells of xylem tissue form effective conduits for water between the roots and the above ground tissues.

Plant cells vary greatly in shape and function, but in general each has a cell wall surrounding a protoplast, which is differentiated into a nucleus and cytoplasm. Suspended within the watery cytoplasm are the membranes, organelles, and particles in which the biochemical processes of life occur. The nucleus contains most of the cellular DNA and is thus the centre from which these cellular activities are directed. Cytoplasm is in more or less constant motion in living cells and the movement is termed cyclosis or cytoplasmic streaming.

The *cell wall* is produced by the cytoplasm and deposited outside of the plasma membrane—the outer boundary of the protoplast. The wall and plasma membrane regulate the kinds of materials that enter and leave the cell thus making it possible for the cell to maintain an identity different from its surroundings. The wall is not simply an inert substance providing strength and giving structure to plant cells as once was thought, but is active in several metabolic processes including absorption and secretion of substances, the detection of bacterial and fungal pathogens, and even regulation of growth and development.

Cellulose, the most common material of plant cell walls, is a polysaccharide composed of long chains of glucose molecules that assume crystalline properties in the cell wall. During wall formation, adjacent cellulose molecules link together forming bundles called microfibrils. The microfibrils, in turn, twist together rope-like, producing strong cords called macrofibrils. Hemicelluloses and pectins are deposited among the fibril network and chemically bind the whole together. The result is a primary wall. The whole process of synthesis and assembly is coordinated by the plasma membrane.

Lignin, the second most common material of plant cell walls, adds additional strength to cells, such as in wood cells. Other substances are deposited in walls of tissues serving particular functions. Walls of cells in the outer layer of leaves often contain cutin or waxes, both of which effectively reduce the loss of water from the leaves. Walls of cork cells in the bark of trees contain suberin, another type of protective material.

Membranes:

- Are the sites of many of the biochemical processes of life.
- Are in constant flux, changing both their physical and chemical structure and composition as long as the cell is alive.

- Partition the cell into compartments in which metabolic reactions take place independently of processes occurring in nearby compartments, thus permitting a variety of reactions to occur simultaneously within a single cell.

The basic structure of all biological membranes is the same: a double layer of lipids in which proteins are embedded. The ratio of proteins to lipids is 3:2. Some of the proteins extend through the lipid layer, each end of a molecule projecting out opposite sides. Others remain on or partially embedded in one or the other surface.

Most membranes are selectively (differentially) permeable, permitting or preventing materials from leaving or entering the cell. When toxic substances destroy the selective permeability and the membrane becomes freely permeable, materials leak unchecked in and out, resulting in death of the cell.

Although it is difficult to study the plasma membrane separately from the rest of the protoplast, it is known that the plasma membrane deciphers the biochemical signals that control cell growth and differentiation and that it organizes the formation of the cell wall.

Table 7.1 Cell Structures, their Composition, and Principal Functions.

Table 7.1: Cell Structure and Functions.

Structure	Function
Cell wall	Outer layer of plant cells; produced by the cytoplasm; gives shape and rigidity to the cell; cellulose the basic constituent
Middle lamella	Intercellular layer (mostly pectin) between primary walls of adjacent cells; binds them together
Primary wall	First wall deposited by actively growing and dividing cells
Secondary	Deposited inside primary wall after cell has stopped wall growing; cellulose, lignin, other materials deposited in layers give strength to plant; pits present—areas where no secondary wall is deposited and through which plasmodesmata extend
Plasmodesmata	Strands of cytoplasm that connect adjacent cells; are pathways for material movement
Protoplast	All of the material contained within the cell wall

Contd...

Structure	Function
Nucleus	Structure that contains the genetic information (DNA) in eukaryotic cells; controls cellular activities
Nuclear envelope	Pair of fused membranes around the nucleus; connected to the endoplasmic reticulum; contains pores through which the nucleoplasm and cytoplasm connect
Nucleoplasm	The fluid portion of the nucleus; also called the nuclear matrix
Chromatin	In non-dividing cells, threads of deoxyribonucleic acid (DNA) plus associated proteins (histones) that are attached to sites on the nuclear envelope; condenses into a compact mass when cells divide, forming chromosomes that carry the genes
Nucleolus	Plural: nucleoli; one or more spherical structures that are the site(s) of ribosomal ribonucleic acid (rrna) assembly from rrna genes; subunits of ribosomes also produced here
Cytoplasm	Living cellular material exclusive of the nucleus
Plasma membrane	Outer boundary of the cytoplasm; a lipid bilayer with embedded proteins; differentially permeable and regulates movement of materials into and out of cells; coordinates synthesis of cell wall; recognizes and transmits internal and external chemical signals
Cytosol	Liquid portion of the cytoplasm in which cellular structures are suspended; also called the cytoplasmic matrix
Organelles	General name for cellular structures bounded by membranes and specialized to perform specific functions
Bounded by	Evidence that these organelles once were independent two memb-prokaryotes; they retain many of their former traits within ranes the eukaryote cells.
Plastids	Semiautonomous, contain DNA and ribosomes and reproduce by fission; have an elaborate internal structure; in algae and plants
Chloroplasts	Green (contain chlorophyll) sites of photosynthesis in thylakoid membranes, amino acid and fatty acid synthesis
Chromoplasts	Yellow, orange, red (contain carotenoid pigments); attract pollinators to flowers and dispersers to coloured seeds and fruits
Leucoplasts	Colorless site with no pigments; amyloplasts synthesize starch; others synthesize oils and probably proteins
Mitochondria	Singular: mitochondrion; sites of aerobic respiration and release of adenosine triphosphate (ATP); similar tolike plastids in being semiautonomous and containing DNA and ribosomes; also reproduce by fission; inner membrane with many folds or cristae
Bounded by one membrane	Phospholipid bilayer that regulates material
Peroxisomes	Also called microbodies; no internal membranes, DNA, or ribosomes, but are self-replicating; some important in

Contd...

Structure	Function
	photorespiration; glyoxisomes contain enzymes that convert fats to sucrose during seed germination; others associated with mitochondria
Vacuoles	Sac of liquid, the cell sap, surrounded by a membrane, the tonoplast; in mature cells may occupy 90 percent of the cell; gives turgor (rigidity) to the cell; serves as temporary storage site for Calcium and other materials; anthocyanin pigments in cell sap give colour (reds and, blues) to leaves and flowers; some small vacuoles (like animal lysosomes) are sites of digestion; others store wastes
Endomembrane	Phospholipid bilayer that regulates material; collective system name for all the cell membranes except those of mitochondria, plastids, and peroxisomes; membranes originate in the ER
Endoplasmic	An extensive membranous system of flattened sacs (reticulum (ER) cisternae) that extends throughout the cytoplasm as a communication and transport system; rough ER is covered with ribosomes and delivers proteins; smooth ER lacks ribosomes, synthesizes lipids; rough ER is cisternal, smooth ER is tubular
Golgi complex	Collection of Golgi bodies (dictyosomes) that are stacks of flattened cisternae associated with secretion; some synthesize and export polysaccharides; others handle glycoproteins
Vesicles	Small sacs of secretory material pinched off from the cisternae; move from the Golgi complex to the plasma membrane (with the assistance of actin filaments) and liberate their contents outside of the cell; process is called exocytosis—secretion of materials carried in vesicles from the cell
Cytoskeleton	Matrix of protein fibres that gives support and on which organelles, enzymes, macromolecules are attached; composed of two kinds of protein filaments with similar functions
Microtubules	Long hollow tubes composed of the protein tubulin; in constant flux, breaking down and reforming; function in cell division, cellular movement, and movement of materials within the cell
Actin filaments	Long chains of the protein actin; responsible for cytoplasmic streaming, movement of nucleus in cell division, organization of the ER, and other movements of cellular materials
Ribosomes	Sites of protein assembly in the cytoplasm or on the rough ER; are small (17– 23 ϕm) particles assembled from a large and a small subunit produced in the nucleolus; are half ribosomal RNA (rrna) and half proteins in composition; messenger RNA (mrna) brings code from a gene, attaches to

Contd...

Structure	Function
	rrna and initiates protein synthesis; at sites of active synthesis clusters of ribosomes are called polysomes or polyribosomes
Oil bodies	Spherical drops of lipids (especially triglycerides used to synthesize membranes) common in the cytoplasm of cells of seeds and fruits; used as energy and carbon sources for developing seedlings; not bound by a membrane; synthesized in plastids or in the ER
Flagella and	Singular: flagellum and cilium; extensions of cytoplasm cilia enclosed by the plasma membrane that project from the cell wall; made of two microtubules surrounded by nine others (a 9 + 2 structure); cilia same structure but shorter; are used as locomotor structures by algae and protists; the only flagellated cells in plants are the motile sperm of mosses, liverworts, ferns, cycads, and ginkgo

PLANT CELL

Plant cells are eukaryotic cells that differ in several key respects from the cells of other eukaryotic organisms.

Their distinctive features include:

- A large central vacuole, a water-filled volume enclosed by a membrane known as the *tonoplast* maintains the cell's turgor, controls movement of molecules between the cytosol and sap, stores useful material and digests waste proteins and organelles.
- A cell wall composed of cellulose and hemicellulose, pectin and in many cases lignin, is secreted by the protoplast on the outside of the cell membrane. This contrasts with the cell walls of fungi (which are made of chitin), and of bacteria, which are made of peptidoglycan.
- Specialised cell–cell communication pathways known as plasmodesmata, pores in the primary cell wall through which the plasmalemma and endoplasmic reticulum of adjacent cells are continuous.
- Plastids, the most notable being the chloroplasts, which contain chlorophyll a green coloured pigment which is used for absorbing sunlight and is used by a plant to make its own food in the process is known

as photosynthesis. Other types of plastid are the amyloplasts, specialized for starch storage, elaioplasts specialized for fat storage, and chromoplasts specialized for synthesis and storage of pigments. As in mitochondria, which have a genome encoding 37 genes, plastids have their own genomes of about 100–120 unique genes and, it is presumed, arose as prokaryotic endosymbionts living in the cells of an early eukaryotic ancestor of the land plants and algae.

- Cell division by construction of a phragmoplast as a template for building a cell plate late in cytokinesis is characteristic of land plants and a few groups of algae, notably the Charophytes and the Order Trentepohliales
- The sperm of bryophytes and pteridophytes have flagellae similar to those in animals, but higher plants, (including Gymnosperms and flowering plants) lack the flagellae and centrioles that are present in animal cells.

CELL TYPES

Parenchyma cells are living cells that have diverse functions ranging from storage and support to photosynthesis and phloem loading (transfer cells). Apart from the xylem and phloem in their vascular bundles, leaves are composed mainly of parenchyma cells. Some parenchyma cells, as in the epidermis, are specialized for light penetration and focusing or regulation of gas exchange, but others are among the least specialized cells in plant tissue, and may remain totipotent, capable of dividing to produce new populations of undifferentiated cells, throughout their lives. Parenchyma cells have thin, permeable primary walls enabling the transport of small molecules between them, and their cytoplasm is responsible for a wide range of biochemical functions such as nectar secretion, or the manufacture of secondary products that discourage herbivory. Parenchyma cells that contain many chloroplasts and are concerned primarily with photosynthesis are called chlorenchyma cells. Others, such as the majority of the parenchyma cells in potato tubers and the seed cotyledons of legumes, have a storage function.

Collenchyma cells—collenchyma cells are alive at maturity and have only a primary wall. These cells mature from meristem derivatives that initially resemble parenchyma, but differences quickly become apparent. Plastids do not develop, and the secretory apparatus (ER and Golgi) proliferates to secrete additional primary wall. The wall is most commonly thickest at the corners, where three or more cells come in contact, and thinnest where only two cells come in contact, though other arrangements of the wall thickening are possible.

Pectin and hemicellulose are the dominant constituents of collenchyma cell walls of dicotyledon angiosperms, which may contain as little as 20% of cellulose in *Petasites*. Collenchyma cells are typically quite elongated, and may divide transversely to give a septate appearance. The role of this cell type is to support the plant in axes still growing in length, and to confer flexibility and tensile strength on tissues. The primary wall lacks lignin that would make it tough and rigid, so this cell type provides what could be called plastic support–support that can hold a young stem or petiole into the air, but in cells that can be stretched as the cells around them elongate. Stretchable support (without elastic snap-back) is a good way to describe what collenchyma does. Parts of the strings in celery are collenchyma.

Sclerenchyma cells—Sclerenchyma cells (from the Greek skleros, *hard*) are hard and tough cells with a function in mechanical support. They are of two broad types–sclereids or stone cells and fibres. The cells develop an extensive secondary cell wall that is laid down on the inside of the primary cell wall. The secondary wall is impregnated with lignin, making it hard and impermeable to water. Thus, these cells cannot survive for long' as they cannot exchange sufficient material to maintain active metabolism. Sclerenchyma cells are typically dead at functional maturity, and the cytoplasm is missing, leaving an empty central cavity.

Functions for sclereid cells (hard cells that give leaves or fruits a gritty texture) include discouraging herbivory, by damaging digestive passages in small insect larval stages, and physical protection (a solid tissue of hard sclereid cells form the pit wall in a peach and many other fruits). Functions of fibres include provision of load-bearing support and tensile strength to the leaves and stems of herbaceous plants. Sclerenchyma fibres are not involved in conduction, either of water and nutrients (as in the xylem) or of carbon compounds (as in the phloem), but it is likely that they may have evolved as modifications of xylem and phloem initials in early land plants.

8

Plant Physiology

INTRODUCTION

Plant physiology is a subdiscipline of botany concerned with the functioning, or physiology, of plants. Closely related fields include plant morphology (structure of plants), plant ecology (interactions with the environment), phytochemistry (biochemistry of plants), cell biology, and molecular biology. Fundamental processes such as photosynthesis, respiration, plant nutrition, plant hormone functions, tropisms, nastic movements, photoperiodism, photomorphogenesis, circadian rhythms, environmental stress physiology, seed germination, dormancy and stomata function and transpiration, both part of plant water relations, are studied by plant physiologists.

SCOPE

The field of plant physiology includes the study of all the internal activities of plants—those chemical and physical processes associated with life as they occur in plants. This includes study at many levels of scale of size and time. At the smallest scale are molecular interactions of photosynthesis and internal diffusion of water, minerals, and nutrients. At the largest scale are the processes of plant development, seasonality, dormancy, and reproductive control. Major subdisciplines of plant physiology include phytochemistry (the study of the biochemistry of plants) and phytopathology (the study of disease in plants). The scope of plant physiology as a discipline may be divided into several major areas of research.

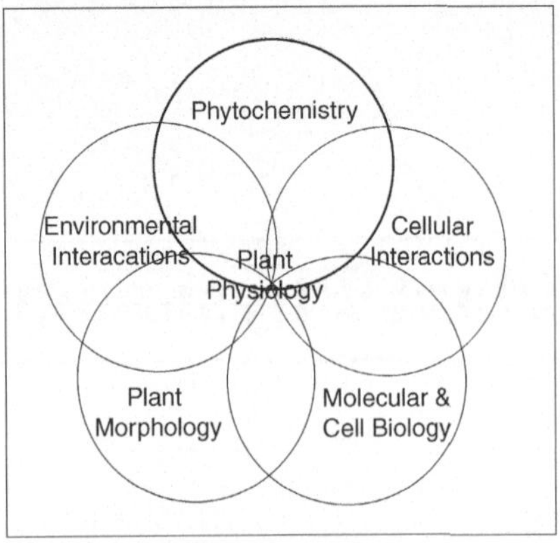

Figure 8.1: Five Key Areas of Study within Plant Physiology

First, the study of phytochemistry (plant chemistry) is included within the domain of plant physiology. To function and survive, plants produce a wide array of chemical compounds not found in other organisms. Photosynthesis requires a large array of pigments, enzymes, and other compounds to function. Because they cannot move, plants must also defend themselves chemically from herbivores, pathogens and competition from other plants. They do this by producing toxins and foul-tasting or smelling chemicals. Other compounds defend plants against disease, permit survival during drought, and prepare plants for dormancy. While other compounds are used to attract pollinators or herbivores to spread ripe seeds.

Secondly, plant physiology includes the study of biological and chemical processes of individual plant cells. Plant cells have a number of features that distinguish them from cells of animals, and which lead to major differences in the way that plant life behaves and responds differently from animal life. For example, plant cells have a cell wall which restricts the shape of plant cells and thereby limits the flexibility and mobility of plants. Plant cells also contain chlorophyll, a chemical compound that interacts with light in a way that enables plants to manufacture their own nutrients rather than consuming other living things as animals do.

Thirdly, plant physiology deals with interactions between cells, tissues, and organs within a plant. Different cells and tissues are physically and chemically specialized to perform different functions. Roots and rhizoids function to anchor the plant and acquire minerals in the soil. Leaves catch light in order to manufacture nutrients. For both of these organs to remain living, minerals that the roots acquire must be transported to the leaves, and the nutrients manufactured in the leaves must be transported to the roots. Plants have developed a number of ways to achieve this transport, such as vascular tissue, and the functioning of the various modes of transport is studied by plant physiologists.

Fourthly, plant physiologists study the ways that plants control or regulate internal functions. Like animals, plants produce chemicals called hormones which are produced in one part of the plant to signal cells in another part of the plant to respond. Many flowering plants bloom at the appropriate time because of light-sensitive compounds that respond to the length of the night, a phenomenon known as photoperiodism. The ripening of fruit and loss of leaves in the winter are controlled in part by the production of the gas ethylene by the plant. Finally, plant physiology includes the study of how plants respond to conditions and variation in the environment, a field known as environmental physiology. Stress from water loss, changes in air chemistry, or crowding by other plants can lead to changes in the way a plant functions. These changes may be affected by genetic, chemical, and physical factors.

BIOCHEMISTRY OF PLANTS

The list of simple elements of which plants are primarily constructed—carbon, oxygen, hydrogen, calcium, phosphorus, etc.—is not different from similar lists for animals, fungi, or even bacteria. The fundamental atomic components of plants are the same as for all life; only the details of the way in which they are assembled differs. Despite this underlying similarity, plants produce a vast array of chemical compounds with unusual properties which they use to cope with their environment. Pigments are used by plants to absorb or detect light, and are extracted by humans for use in dyes. Other plant products may be used for the manufacture of commercially important rubber or biofuel. Perhaps the most celebrated compounds from plants are those with pharmacological activity, such as salicylic acid (aspirin), morphine, and digitalis. Drug companies spend billions of dollars each year researching plant compounds for potential medicinal benefits.

Constituent Elements

Plants require some nutrients, such as carbon and nitrogen, in large quantities to survive. Such nutrients are termed macronutrients, where the prefix *macro*-(large) refers to the quantity needed, not the size of the nutrient particles themselves. Other nutrients, called micronutrients, are required only in trace amounts for plants to remain healthy. Such micronutrients are usually absorbed as ions dissolved in water taken from the soil, though carnivorous plants acquire some of their micronutrients from captured prey.

The following table lists element nutrients essential to plants. Uses within plants are generalized.

Table 8.1

	Element	**Form of uptake Notes**
Macronutrients. (Necessary in large quantities)		
Nitrogen	NO_3^-, NH_4^+	Nucleic acids, proteins, hormones, etc.
Oxygen	O_2 H_2O	Cellulose, starch, other organic compounds
Carbon	CO_2	Cellulose, starch, other organic compounds
Hydrogen	H_2O	Cellulose, starch, other organic compounds
Potassium	K^+	Cofactor in protein synthesis, water balance, etc.
Calcium	Ca^{2+}	Membrane synthesis and stabilization
Magnesium	Mg^{2+}	Element essential for chlorophyll
Phosphorus	$H_2PO_4^-$	Nucleic acids, phospholipids, ATP
Sulfur	SO_4^{2-}	Constituent of proteins and coenzymes
Micronutrients. (Necessary in small quantities)		
Chlorine	Cl^-	Photosystem II and stomata function
Iron	Fe^{2+}, Fe^{3+}	Chorophyll formation

Contd...

Boron	HBO_3	Crosslinking pectin
Manganese	Mn^{2+}	Activity of some enzymes
Zinc	Zn^{2+}	Involved in the synthesis of enzymes and chlorophyll
Copper	Cu^{+}	Enzymes for lignin synthesis
Molybdenum	MoO_4^{2-}	Nitrogen fixation, reduction of nitrates
Nickel	Ni^{2+}	Enzymatic cofactor in the metabolism of nitrogen compounds

Pigments

Among the most important molecules for plant function are the pigments. Plant pigments include a variety of different kinds of molecules, including porphyrins, carotenoids, and anthocyanins. All biological pigments selectively absorb certain wavelengths of light while reflecting others. The light that is absorbed may be used by the plant to power chemical reactions, while the reflected wavelengths of light determine the colour the pigment appears to the eye.

Chlorophyll is the primary pigment in plants; it is a porphyrin that absorbs red and blue wavelengths of light while reflecting green. It is the presence and relative abundance of chlorophyll that gives plants their green colour. All land plants and green algae possess two forms of this pigment: chlorophyll *a* and chlorophyll *b*. Kelps, diatoms, and other photosynthetic heterokonts contain chlorophyll *c* instead of *b*, while red algae possess only chlorophyll *a*. All chlorophylls serve as the primary means plants use to intercept light to fuel photosynthesis. Carotenoids are red, orange, or yellow tetraterpenoids. They function as accessory pigments in plants, helping to fuel photosynthesis by gathering wavelengths of light not readily absorbed by chlorophyll. The most familiar carotenoids are carotene (an orange pigment found in carrots), lutein (a yellow pigment found in fruits and vegetables), and lycopene (the red pigment responsible for the colour of tomatoes). Carotenoids have been shown to act as antioxidants and to promote healthy eyesight in humans.

Anthocyanins (literally 'flower blue') are water-soluble flavonoid pigments that appear red to blue, according to pH. They occur in all tissues of higher plants, providing colour in leaves, stems, roots, flowers, and fruits, though not always in sufficient quantities to be noticeable. Anthocyanins are most visible in the petals of flowers, where they may make up as much as 30% of the dry weight of the tissue. They are also responsible for the purple colour seen on the underside of tropical shade plants such as *Tradescantia zebrina*. In these plants, the anthocyanin catches light that has passed through the leaf and reflects it back towards regions bearing chlorophyll, in order to maximize the use of available light

Betalains are red or yellow pigments. Like anthocyanins they are water-soluble, but unlike anthocyanins they are indole-derived compounds synthesized from tyrosine. This class of pigments is found only in the Caryophyllales (including cactus and amaranth), and never co-occur in plants with anthocyanins. Betalains are responsible for the deep red colour of beets, and are used commercially as food-colouring agents. Plant physiologists are uncertain of the function that betalains have in plants which possess them, but there is some preliminary evidence that they may have fungicidal properties.

Signals and Regulators

Plants produce hormones and other growth regulators which act to signal a physiological response in their tissues. They also produce compounds such as phytochrome that are sensitive to light and which serve to trigger growth or development in response to environmental signals.

Plant Hormones

Plant hormones, known as plant growth regulators (PGRs) or phytohormones, are chemicals that regulate a plant's growth. According to a standard animal definition, hormones are signal molecules produced at specific locations, that occur in very low concentrations, and cause altered processes in target cells at other locations. Unlike animals, plants lack specific hormone-producing tissues or organs. Plant hormones are often not transported to other parts of the plant and production is not limited to specific locations. Plant hormones are chemicals that in small amounts promote and influence the growth, development and differentiation of cells and tissues. Hormones are vital to plant growth; affecting processes in plants from flowering to seed development, dormancy, and germination. They regulate which tissues grow upwards and which grow downwards, leaf formation and stem growth, fruit development and ripening, as well as leaf abscission and even plant death. The most important plant hormones are abscissic acid (ABA), auxins, ethylene, gibberellins, and cytokinins, though there are many other substances that serve to regulate plant physiology.

Photomor Phogenesis

While most people know that light is important for photosynthesis in plants, few realize that plant sensitivity to light plays a role in the control of plant structural development (morphogenesis). The use of light to control structural development is called photomorphogenesis, and is dependent upon the presence of specialized photoreceptors, which are chemical pigments capable of absorbing specific wavelengths of light. Plants use four kinds of photoreceptors: phytochrome, cryptochrome, a UV-B photoreceptor, and protochlorophyllide *a*. The first two of these, phytochrome and cryptochrome, are photoreceptor proteins, complex molecular structures formed by joining a protein with a light-sensitive pigment. Cryptochrome is also known as the UV-A photoreceptor, because it absorbs ultraviolet light in the long wave 'A' region. The UV-B receptor is one or more compounds not yet identified with certainty, though some evidence suggests carotene or riboflavin as candidates. Protochlorophyllide *a*, as its name suggests, is a chemical precursor of chlorophyll.

The most studied of the photoreceptors in plants is phytochrome. It is sensitive to light in the red and far-red region of the visible spectrum. Many flowering plants use it to regulate the time of flowering based on the length of day and night (photoperiodism) and to set circadian rhythms. It also regulates other responses including the germination of seeds, elongation of seedlings, the size, shape and number of leaves, the synthesis of chlorophyll, and the straightening of the epicotyl or hypocotyl hook of dicot seedlings.

Photoperiodism

Many flowering plants use the pigment phytochrome to sense seasonal changes in day length, which they take as signals to flower. This sensitivity to day length is termed photoperiodism. Broadly speaking, flowering plants can be classified as long day plants, short day plants, or day neutral plants, depending on their particular response to changes in day length. Long day plants require a certain minimum length of daylight to initiate flowering, so these plants flower in the spring or summer. Conversely, short day plants flower when the length of daylight falls below a certain critical level. Day neutral plants do not initiate flowering based on photoperiodism, though some may use temperature sensitivity (vernalization) instead.

Although a short day plant cannot flower during the long days of summer, it is not actually the period of light exposure that limits flowering. Rather, a short day plant requires a minimal length of uninterrupted darkness in each 24 hour period (a short daylength) before floral development can begin. It has been determined experimentally that a short day plant (long night) does not flower if a flash of phytochrome activating light is used on the plant during the night. Plants make use of the phytochrome system to sense day length or photoperiod. This fact is utilized by florists and greenhouse gardeners to control and even induce flowering out of season, such as the *Poinsettia*.

ENVIRONMENTAL PHYSIOLOGY

Paradoxically, the subdiscipline of environmental physiology is on the one hand a recent field of study in plant ecology and on the other hand one of the oldest. Environmental physiology is the preferred name of the subdiscipline among plant physiologists, but it goes by a number of other names in the applied sciences. It is roughly synonymous with ecophysiology, crop ecology, horticulture and agronomy. The particular name applied to the subdiscipline is specific to the viewpoint and goals of research. Whatever name is applied, it deals with the ways in which plants respond to their environment and so overlaps with the field of ecology.

Environmental physiologists examine plant response to physical factors such as radiation (including light and ultraviolet radiation), temperature, fire, and wind. Of particular importance are water relations (which can be measured with the Pressure bomb) and the stress of drought or inundation, exchange of gases with the atmosphere, as well as the cycling of nutrients such as nitrogen and carbon. Environmental physiologists also examine plant response to biological factors. This includes not only negative interactions, such as competition, herbivory, disease and parasitism, but also positive interactions, such as mutualism and pollination.

Tropisms and Nastic Movements

Plants may respond both to directional and nondirectional stimuli. A response to a directional stimulus, such as gravity or sunlight, is called a tropism. A response to a nondirectional stimulus, such as temperature or humidity, is a nastic movement.

Tropisms in plants are the result of differential cell growth, in which the cells on one side of the plant elongate more than those on the other side, causing the part to bend towards the side with less growth. Among the common tropisms seen in plants is phototropism, the bending of the plant towards a source of light. Phototropism allows the plant to maximize light exposure in plants which require additional light for photosynthesis, or to minimize it in plants subjected to intense light and heat. Geotropism allows the roots of a plant to determine the direction of gravity and grow downwards. Tropisms generally result from an interaction between the environment and production of one or more plant hormones.

In contrast to tropisms, nastic movements result from changes in turgor pressure within plant tissues, and may occur rapidly. A familiar example is thigmonasty (response to touch) in the Venus fly trap, a carnivorous plant. The traps consist of modified leaf blades which bear sensitive trigger hairs. When the hairs are touched by an insect or other animal, the leaf folds shut. This mechanism allows the plant to trap and digest small insects for additional nutrients. Although the trap is rapidly shut by changes in internal cell pressures, the leaf must grow slowly to reset for a second opportunity to trap insects.

PLANT DISEASE

Economically, one of the most important areas of research in environmental physiology is that of phytopathology, the study of diseases in plants and the manner in which plants resist or cope with infection. Plant are susceptible to the same kinds of disease organisms as animals, including viruses, bacteria, and fungi, as well as physical invasion by insects and roundworms.

Because the biology of plants differs from animals, their symptoms and responses are quite different. In some cases, a plant can simply shed infected leaves or flowers to prevent to spread of disease, in a process called abscission. Most animals do not have this option as a means of controlling disease. Plant diseases organisms themselves also differ from those causing disease in animals because plants cannot usually spread infection through casual physical contact. Plant pathogens tend to spread via spores or are carried by animal vectors. One of the most important advances in the control of plant disease was the discovery of Bordeaux mixture in the nineteenth century. The mixture is the first known fungicide and is a combination of copper sulfate and lime. Application of the mixture served to inhibit the growth of downy mildew that threatened to seriously damage the French wine industry.

ECONOMIC APPLICATIONS

Food Production

In horticulture and agriculture along with food science, plant physiology is an important topic relating to fruits, vegetables, and other consumable parts of plants. Topics studied include: *climatic* requirements, fruit drop, nutrition, ripening, fruit set. The production of food crops also hinges on the study of plant physiology covering such topics as Optimal planting and harvesting times and post harvest storage of plant products for human consumption and the production of secondary products like drugs and cosmetics.

CARBON ASSIMILATION IN C_3 PLANTS

The realization that crop yields are reaching a plateau, while population increases continue at pace, has placed manipulation of photosynthesis in a central position to achieve increases in yield. Increasing flux through the C_3 cycle will be a major focus of this effort. Through application of new technologies together with novel modeling approaches, increased yield through improved photosynthetic carbon fixation should be an attainable goal in the near to mid term.

Improving crop yield to meet the demands of an increasing world population for food and fuel is a central challenge for plant biology. This goal must be achieved in a sustainable manner (*i.e.* with minimal agricultural inputs and environmental impacts) in the face of elevated levels of CO_2 and more extreme conditions of water availability and temperature. Agricultural yields have generally kept pace with demand in the recent past as a result of the gains made through breeding programmes and farming practice, but crops yields are now reaching a plateau. One fundamental component of plant productivity that has not been used to select for increased yield is photosynthesis. There is now the opportunity to exploit our extensive knowledge of this fundamental process for the benefit of humankind.

In the plant kingdom, there are three pathways of photosynthetic, atmospheric CO_2 fixation. However, the vast majority of plant species fix atmospheric CO_2 using the enzyme Rubisco in the Calvin-Benson cycle. The first stable product of this cycle is a three-carbon compound, phosphoglycerate (3-PGA), and for this reason this process is referred to as the C_3 cycle. Plants utilizing this pathway are often referred to as

C_3 species. A major problem with the C_3 cycle is the enzyme Rubisco. This is because Rubisco is not only an inefficient enzyme with a low turnover number, but it also catalyzes two competing reactions: carboxylation and oxygenation. The oxygenation reaction directs the flow of carbon through the photorespiratory pathway, and this can result in losses of between 25% and 30% of the carbon fixed. Environmental variables, such as high temperature and drought, can result in an increase in the oxygenase reaction. Therefore, reducing the Rubisco oxygenase reaction has the potential to increase carbon assimilation significantly and would represent a step change in photosynthesis.

Two metabolic pathways have evolved to overcome this, the C_4 (the first stable compound synthesized is a C_4 acid, oxaloacetate) and crassulacean acid metabolism pathways. Both the C_4 and crassulacean acid metabolism pathways are additional to the C_3 cycle and increase the supply of CO_2 to Rubisco, thereby reducing the oxygenation reaction and flux to the photorespiratory pathway. This review will focus on progress and future prospects to improve the C_3 cycle.

THE C_3 CYCLE

The C_3 cycle is the primary pathway of carbon assimilation in the majority of photosynthetic organisms. It is the single largest flux of organic carbon in the biosphere and assimilates about 100 billion tons of carbon a year (15% of the carbon in the atmosphere). Understanding the responses of the Calvin cycle to altered demands for photosynthate within the plant and to external environmental conditions is essential for attempts to increase yield and to redirect carbon into important products.

The C_3 cycle utilizes the products of the light reactions of photosynthesis, ATP and NADPH, to fix atmospheric CO_2 into carbon skeletons that are used to fuel the rest of plant metabolism. The C_3 cycle is initiated by the enzyme Rubisco that catalyzes the carboxylation of the CO_2 acceptor molecule ribulose-1,5-bisP (RuBP). 3-PGA formed by this reaction is used to form the triose phosphates glyceraldehyde phosphate

(G-3-P) and dihydroxyacetone phosphate via two reactions that consume ATP and NADPH.

The regenerative phase of the cycle involves a series of reactions that convert triose phosphates into the CO_2 acceptor molecule RuBP. Carbon compounds produced in this cycle are essential for growth and development of the plant. While the majority (five-sixths) of the triose phosphate produced in the Calvin cycle remain within the cycle to regenerate RuBP, one-sixth of the carbon exits the cycle for biosynthesis of a range of compounds. Triose and hexose phosphates are used to synthesize Suc and starch, and erythrose-4-P (E-4-P) goes directly to the shikimate pathway for the biosynthesis of amino acids and lignin, G-3-P to the isoprenoid pathway, and Rib-5-P (R-5-P) for nucleotide, thiamine metabolism, and cell wall biosynthesis. Clearly, the Calvin cycle occupies a central position in carbon metabolism. Manipulation of this pathway has the potential to increase yield and production of carbon for the synthesis of products made in secondary metabolic pathways.

LIMITS OF C_3 PHOTOSYNTHESIS

It has been known for some time that a large proportion of the limitation to carbon assimilation in plants using the C_3 cycle is due to the catalytic properties of the enzyme Rubisco. During the 1990s, metabolic control analysis was used to explore the possibility that enzymes other than Rubisco may also have a role in determining rates of carbon flux through the C_3 cycle. To undertake metabolic control analysis of a pathway, it is necessary to be able to reduce specifically the amount of an individual enzyme in that pathway; the effect of this reduction on flux can then be compared to the control. The flux control coefficient can vary from 0, for an enzyme that makes no contribution to control, to 1, for an enzyme that exerts total control.

One fundamental difference between this approach and that based on the kinetics of individual enzymes is that metabolic control analysis allows for all enzymes in a pathway to share control of flux in that pathway. The flux control value for any single enzyme is not a constant and can change depending on the conditions under which the analysis was carried out.

Transgenic plants with reductions in Rubisco protein levels produced using an antisense construct were used to assess the relative contribution that Rubisco imposed on carbon flux. This approach has demonstrated clearly that the limitation imposed by Rubisco on C_3 carbon fixation is greatest in high light and temperature conditions.

In contrast, as expected, this is reduced in plants grown in elevated CO_2. Importantly, these transgenic studies also showed that Rubisco does not limit the C_3 cycle in all conditions and that enzymes of the regenerative phase of the cycle also play a role in determining the rate of photosynthesis.

Regenerative Capacity

Regeneration of the CO_2 acceptor molecule RuBP involves eight enzymes. To identify enzymes that have significant control over carbon flux through the Calvin cycle, antisense plants with reduced levels of individual enzymes were created and analysed. Under many conditions, reductions in the activities of enzymes catalyzing highly regulated, effectively irreversible reactions, glyceraldehyde-3-phosphate dehydrogenase (GAPDH), Fru bisphosphatase (FBPase), and phosphoribulokinase (PRK), had little impact on carbon assimilation.

In contrast, small reductions in the enzyme sedoheptulose-1,7-bisphosphatase (SBPase) resulted in a decrease in CO_2 fixation and growth, identifying this enzyme as a major control point in the C_3 cycle. The relative importance of SBPase in determining flux through this cycle varied with development and environmental conditions, confirming that no one enzyme limits the C_3 cycle under all conditions.

Somewhat surprisingly carbon flux through the C_3 cycle was also reduced in plants with relatively small reductions in the activity of either transketolase (TK) or aldolase, enzymes that are not highly regulated and operate close to equilibrium. This was unexpected, as it was thought that enzymes that were highly regulated would be most important in determining the rate of carbon flow through the cycle. These analyses of the antisense C_3 cycle plants identified enzymes other than Rubisco that can limit CO_2 fixation.

PAST SUCCESSES TO IMPROVE THE C_3 CYCLE

Rubisco-Related Bottlenecks

Three approaches to improve the C_3 cycle have targeted Rubisco-associated bottlenecks. Expression of the cyanobacterial ictB protein in higher plants to reduce the oxygenation reaction of Rubisco resulted in the production of transgenic tobacco (*Nicotiana tabacum*) with higher photosynthetic rates under limiting, but not saturating, CO_2 levels. Similar results were obtained in Arabidopsis (*Arabidopsis thaliana*) plants expressing the *ictB* from *Anabaena* PCC7120; in low humidity conditions, the growth of transgenic Arabidopsis plants was faster and the final dry weight was higher than that of wild-type plants. A second approach introduced the enzymes of the bacterial glycolate pathway into plants, creating a photorespiratory bypass in the chloroplast. In Arabidopsis, this resulted in reduced photorespiration and increased CO_2 assimilation and biomass yield. These two strategies for overcoming the oxygenase reaction of Rubisco offer more immediate alternatives to improve crop photosynthesis in the near future, compared to the more ambitious CO_2-concentrating strategies.

Manipulation of Rubisco Activation

The activation state of Rubisco is dependent on the enzyme Rubisco activase, which at temperatures above 30°C has been shown to be unstable in vitro. This led to the suggestion that Rubisco activase is responsible for the reversible temperature-sensitive reduction in the activation state of Rubisco, leading to inhibition of photosynthesis when plants are subjected to mild heat stress. The introduction of a thermostable version of the Rubisco activase enzyme into an Arabidopsis activase deletion mutant resulted in transgenic lines with higher photosynthetic rates and increased biomass and seed yield when compared with control plants expressing the wild-type activase. All three of these approaches have demonstrated the potential to stimulate photosynthesis and growth in model species, and the next step will be to test this in crop plants in natural environments.

Increasing Regenerative Capacity of the C_3 Cycle

Transgenic antisense work described above identified SBPase, plastid aldolase, and TK as enzymes that might be targets for improving C_3 cycle flux. Indeed, overexpression of either a bifunctional SBPase/FBPase or plant SBPase in tobacco plants resulted in increased photosynthetic CO_2 fixation and growth. Analysis of CO_2 response curves revealed that this increase in photosynthesis could be attributed to an increase in the capacity to regenerate the CO_2 acceptor molecule RuBP. Measurements of ambient photosynthesis over the daily cycle revealed an increase in photosynthetic rates of between 6% and 12%. Of particular interest for crop improvement is that these plants also displayed an increase in leaf area and biomass of up to 30%. Young seedlings (4/5 leaves) with increased SBPase activity were shown to have an increase in leaf area compared to wild-type plants. Chlorophyll fluorescence imaging of these young plants revealed a higher photosynthetic capacity at the whole plant level. These plants also showed an increased growth rate during the early phase of development. This result is of significance in an agricultural context as rapid, early seedling establishment is known to contribute to yield increases at maturity. In contrast to the results with tobacco, increasing SBPase activity in rice (*Oryza sativa*) did not lead to increases in photosynthesis or growth. However, if the plants were subjected to heat or salt stress conditions, photosynthesis rates in the transgenic plants with increased SBPase plant were higher than in wild-type controls. The rice studies highlight the fact that increasing photosynthesis and yield by manipulation of SBPase is likely to be dependent not only on species but also growth conditions.

Plastid TK was also identified as a potential target to increase the regenerative capacity of the C_3 cycle. To explore this possibility, transgenic plants have been produced overexpressing TK, either on its own or together with overexpression of SBPase. Analysis of these transgenic plants has shown that photosynthetic rates were similar to wild type but that the plants have reduced growth and display a chlorotic phenotype. The basis of this phenotype has not been fully resolved, but preliminary analysis would suggest that increasing TK activity has perturbed the balance of export of carbon from the C_3 cycle. This is in keeping with data from antisense studies that revealed a reduction in carbon flow from the C_3 cycle to the shikimate pathway that correlated with reductions in TK activity. This work highlights the need for modelling approaches that not only allow identification of potential targets for improving CO_2 assimilation but that will also allow flux from the C_3 cycle to be determined.

FUTURE PROSPECTS FOR IMPROVING THE C_3 CYCLE

Improving Known Bottlenecks

The oxygenase reaction of Rubisco and subsequent photorespiratory pathway are clear targets for improvement of the C_3 cycle. Over the last 20 years, considerable effort has been focused on reengineering the Rubisco protein, using site-directed mutagenesis to increase the carboxylase relative to the oxygenase reaction. However, this approach has yet to produce an improved Rubisco. Recently, it has been shown that it is possible to form an active Rubisco in vitro using unfolded large subunits with the chaperone proteins GroEL/ES, RbcX, and ATP. This work paves the way for in vitro analysis of mutants and has the potential to allow screening for improvements in the Rubisco catalytic parameters of genetically engineered mutants. A new opportunity has also arisen from interspecies comparison of Rubisco catalytic properties that has revealed variation in the specificity, k_{cat}, and temperature response of Rubisco from natural vegetation in the Mediterranean. The variation in the properties would indicate that transferring Rubisco from these species into crop plants could substantially increase the rate of CO_2 assimilation. The recent demonstration of the successful expression of Rubisco large and small subunits as a single fusion protein in the chloroplast that assembled into an active holoenzyme provides the opportunity to use expression of foreign Rubisco as a strategy to improve the C_3 cycle.

CO_2-concentrating mechanisms (CCMs) have been found in all plant groups, in algal species, and in the cyanobacteria. These adaptations present the possibility to exploit existing solutions that have evolved in these organisms to improve C_3 plants. To realize the potential of these strategies will likely be in the long term; nevertheless, it is essential to begin the research now to determine the feasibility as a realistic option for future improvements. Transferring C_4 photosynthesis to C_3 species is one strategy to reduce photorespiration. But engineering C_3 plants to carry out C_4 metabolism will be a challenge as not only is there a requirement for additional metabolism but there are also changes in anatomy needed. Fundamental research aimed at understanding the molecular basis of the anatomical specialization and the regulatory processes determining the location and the level of expression of the C_4-specific enzymes is under way. Although this has not yet led to any major breakthroughs, the combination of new sequencing and proteomic technologies together with a large international programme give optimism for future success in this area.

The prokaryotic carboxy some provides a micro-compartment in the cell that transports and fixes CO_2, acting as a CCM. Eukaryotic algae (and some primitive land plants) possess a structure, the pyrenoid, that may act to concentrate CO_2 at Rubisco. Both of these CCMs provide components that could be transferred to higher plants to reduce photo-respiration and increase water and nitrogen use efficiency. However, it is likely that engineering the complete CCM from either of these groups of organisms into higher plants will be a complex feat of gene engineering, and given that the components of the pyrenoid remain to be elucidated, these approaches are likely to be successful only in the longer term. However, both the carboxysome and pyrenoid CCMs involve more than just the microcompartmentation of Rubisco. It might be more attainable in the shorter term to exploit the CO_2 transport systems in these organisms to boost CO_2 levels in C_3 plants and thereby have a positive effect on atmosphere CO_2 assimilation by Rubisco.

Identifying Novel Targets

Modelling-Based Strategies

Redistribution of Enzymes of Carbon Fixation. Although antisense studies described above revealed enzymes in the C_3 cycle as targets for manipulation, it would be impossible to analyse every potential manipulation in this way. It is even less attainable to select multiple targets that may impact synergistically to improve the cycle. In order that significant advances can be made in a sensible time frame, it will be essential to have a dynamic kinetic model that is predictive. A model of photosynthetic carbon metabolism has been developed, and its application, in conjunction with an evolutionary algorithm, indicated that the distribution of resources between enzymes of carbon metabolism (that is the amount of each) is not optimal. An overinvestment in enzymes of the photorespiratory pathway, namely Gly decarboxylase, and an under investment in ADP-Glc pyrophosphorylase, SBPase, and plastid aldolase enzymes were identified. This suggests that the rate of light-saturated photosynthesis in existing C_3 plants could be increased significantly by redistribution of the amounts of these enzymes in carbon assimilation, photorespiration, and starch biosynthesis. The hypotheses generated from this modelling can easily be tested using current transgenic technology using a model plant system. Importantly, the results from this work have the potential to provide clear strategies for improvement of photosynthesis in a time frame of 2 to 3 years.

A neglected aspect of the C_3 cycle is the control of flux from the cycle to the output pathways of starch, Suc, isoprenoids, shikimate, and nucleotides. Although detailed analysis of the regulation of Suc, starch, and shikimate biosynthetic pathways have been undertaken, there is no complete model that can simulate the way the relative flux to these pathways changes during development, in response to stress or availability of light. This lack of knowledge places limitations on the ability to exploit the enormous potential for manipulation of the cycle for the synthesis of high value chemicals such as pharmaceuticals, plant protectants, nutraceuticals, and flavour/colour compounds that are products of the shikimate and isoprenoid output pathways of the C_3 cycle.

Design and Introduction of a Synthetic Carbon Fixation Pathway. Although the majority of photosynthetic organisms fix atmospheric CO_2 through the C_3 cycle, in nature there are five other CO_2 fixation pathways that are found in the Archaea (organisms that have structure and metabolism similar to bacteria and transcriptional regulation more closely aligned with the eukaryotes.

Although none of these organisms use either Rubisco or phospho*enol*pyruvate carboxylase as the carboxylation enzyme, they do reveal a diversity of metabolism that has evolved in response to a range of environmental niches. This raises the possibility of employing a combination of modelling together with synthetic biology, to construct completely novel CO_2 fixation pathways that may be more efficient than the C_3 cycle. In addition, this approach may offer a solution to the problem of Rubisco without having to redesign plant development, required for introduction of the C_4 pathway. Using a constraint-based modelling approach that included approximately 5,000 enzymes known to occur naturally, a number of hypothetical alternative carbon fixation pathways were identified.

This study showed that some of these hypothetical pathways may be more efficient than the naturally occurring C_3 cycle. Interestingly, all of the pathways predicted to be 2 to 3 times faster than the C_3 cycle included the enzyme phospho*enol*pyruvate carboxylase, which is the carboxylating enzyme found in C_4 species, and not any of the carboxylating enzymes found in the Archaea. These model-generated, hypothetical pathways also share a core set of reactions and have been termed the malonyl-CoA-oxaloacetate-glyoxylate (MOG) pathways. Although the glyoxylate produced could be converted to G-3-P by introducing enzymes from *Escherichia coli*, there is still a requirement to synthesize hexose phosphates, Fru-6-P, E-4-P, and R-5-P, needed to supply the essential carbon compounds for growth and development of the plant.

If a MOG-type synthetic pathway was to be engineered into it may require coupling to a partial Calvin cycle, creating Rubisco-independent carbon assimilation. To maintain the MOG pathway, it would also be necessary to use some of the G-3-P to regenerate the phospho*enol*pyruvate needed for CO_2 assimilation. The technical challenges to engineer such large changes in the core CO_2 pathway(s) in higher plants using synthetic biology will be significant. But redesigning metabolism based on the modelling strategy of Bar-Even *et al.* (2010) offers a novel and exciting approach that warrants experimental study.

Elucidation of Mechanisms Underlying Natural Variation in Photosynthesis

There is considerable variation in photosynthetic rates per unit leaf area between C_3 species. This is an overlooked and untapped resource yet has huge potential to identify natural mechanisms that have evolved to allow plants to survive in different environments. Systematic analysis of plants from different geographic regions, using high-throughput in vivo photosynthesis tools, has the potential to identify novel targets for manipulation in crop plants.

Development of photosynthetic capacity also differs in the same species when grown under different environmental conditions; this can result in changes in morphology and anatomy and is termed developmental acclimation. In addition, some plant species are able to alter photosynthetic capacity in fully mature leaves, displaying a dynamic acclimatory response. A recent study revealed that developmental and dynamic acclimation are distinct processes and that dynamic acclimation may have a role in increasing the fitness of plants in natural environments. However, most studies focus on plants grown in constant conditions or after a shift to different conditions, *e.g.* low to high light. There have been few studies where plants have been exposed to fluctuating conditions. Elucidation of the mechanisms that are employed by plants during environmental fluctuations can provide novel targets for improving crop yield. This is particularly relevant given that many crop species lack any dynamic range to respond to this variation.

Another aspect we know very little about is the relative importance of regulatory mechanisms in determining carbon flux in the C_3 cycle. It has been known for several decades that a number of enzymes of the C_3 cycle, FBPase, SBPase, PRKase, and GAPDH, are subjected to light activation via the ferredoxin/thioredoxin system. Importantly, there is a lag in this response when plants experience a dark to light shift, resulting in a delay of minutes in photosynthetic rates reaching a steady-state maximum. It has also been shown recently that the enzymes PRK and GAPDH are subject to rapid inactivation/activation in response to changes in light availability, mediated by a small protein, CP12, together with Trxf. These regulatory mechanisms are believed to match the rate of carbon fixation with the availability of energy from the light reactions. However, the relative importance of this regulation in determining photosynthetic capacity is unknown but may be important in the acclamatory response of plants dealing with fluctuating conditions. Furthermore, the extent to which this regulation varies between species is also relatively unexplored.

PERSPECTIVES OF C_3 CYCLE

Manipulation of the C_3 cycle offers an opportunity to increase photosynthesis and yield. A number of clear targets have been shown to have the potential to impact yield in the 3-to 5-year period but to date have been tested only in model species. It is now important that this knowledge is fully exploited in crops. Clearly, the reduction of the Rubisco oxygenase reaction remains a target for future improvement of photosynthesis. However, although the current strategies that might be exploited to achieve this goal are conceptually straightforward, all of these approaches will be technically demanding, requiring fundamental research to identify the genes involved. Improvement of the C_3 cycle is not just about increasing CO_2 fixation but should also aim to increase both nitrogen use efficiency and water use efficiency while maintaining high productivity. Therefore manipulation of the C_3 cycle to improve these parameters is also an important goal. The range of genetic and molecular techniques that are now available, together with the development and application of rapid in vivo techniques to allow in-field analysis of a wider range of species in their natural environments, will facilitate the wider analysis of natural variation in photosynthetic carbon assimilation. This approach has enormous and unexplored potential for future exploitation to improve yield through manipulation of the C_3 cycle.

ESSENTIAL AMINO ACIDS IN CROP PLANTS

The inability of humans and many farm animals to synthesize certain amino acids has long triggered tremendous interest in increasing the levels of these so-called essential amino acids in crop plants. Knowledge obtained from basic genetic and genetic engineering research has also been successfully used to enrich the content of some of these essential amino acids in crop plants. Among the essential amino acids, Lys, Trp, and Met have received the most attention because they are most limiting in cereals (particularly Lys and Trp) and legumes crops (particularly Met), which represent the major sources of human food and animal feed worldwide. Enriching crop plants in essential amino acids has both economical and humanitarian interest. In developed countries, the interest is mostly for the livestock feeding industry because farm animals generally provide sufficient amount of essential amino acids for human diets. In developing countries, where plants directly account for the majority of the food, the interest is both humanitarian and economical.

So far, the success of genetic approaches has been mostly restricted to maize (*Zea mays*) by generating quality protein maize (QPM) cultivars, which are enriched in Lys and to some extent Trp in their seeds. However, genetic approaches have resulted in relatively limited success in other crop species. This is mostly due to limited availability of genetic resources for plant breeding, and the fact that genetic traits for high contents of Lys, Trp, or Met are generally associated with abnormal plant growth because these traits do not operate in a seed-specific manner. In contrast, results from genetic engineering research appear to be more promising, particularly because this approach allows seed-specific expression of specific traits of interest, using seed-specific promoters. In fact, one high-Lys maize cultivar, LY038, developed by genetic engineering, represents the first genetically modified (GM) crop with high nutritional value to be approved for commercial use in a number of countries. The potential to increase the contents of Trp and Met in a seed-specific manner have already been proven successful in basic research studies. Another advantage of genetically engineered traits is that they can be transformed into multiple plant species and genotypes and function synergistically with many other agronomically important traits. These genetic engineering approaches were generally aimed at tailor-made improvements of essential amino acid metabolic pathways and expressing native and genetically engineered proteins enriched in essential amino acid contents. However, improvements of metabolic pathways by genetic engineering also requires a detailed understanding of how these pathways interact with regulatory networks that fine tune plant development. These are now beginning to be elucidated by modern systems biology approaches, including transcriptomics, proteomics, and metabolomics. Due to space limitation, we focus this review only on approaches that have been extensively studied and proven suitable to improve the nutritional quality of food and feed. We also only cover research associated with nutritional improvements for monogastric mammals, namely, human and certain farm animals, particularly poultry and swine. These approaches are not as important for ruminant livestock, such as beef, because these animals require the presence of the essential amino acids in proteins that are resistant to rumen proteolysis.

MAIZE BY GENETIC APPROACHES

Maize is one of the most important cereal crops, providing between 50% and 70% of the dietary protein for humans, depending on geographical distribution. It is also one of the major crops used for feeding farm animals, particularly poultry and swine. Since maize seeds are very low in Lys, a major effort was initiated at the mid 20th century to identify high-Lys corn varieties by genetic approaches. These efforts resulted in the discovery of the high-Lys *opaque2* mutant, which contains low levels of the Lys-poor seed storage proteins (called zeins) and a compensatory increase in Lys-and Trp-rich, non-zein, seed proteins as well as free Lys and Trp, compared to normal maize. The *opaque2* mutant seeds, together with minerals and vitamins, were proven to significantly increase growth in rat feeding trials, and they were found to have 90% the value of milk protein when fed to Guatemalan children. A diet based solely on *opaque2* flour was further shown to cure children who suffered from the protein deficiency disease kwashiorkor. Success with *opaque2* maize stimulated extensive research to identify similar mutants in other cereals, including barley, and sorghum.

Despite the initial optimism, field analyses showed that opaque mutations were associated with inferior agronomic traits that could not be easily overcome. The undesirable traits included reduced yield and protein content as well as a soft endosperm that increased disease and insect susceptibility, kernel breakage, and poor food processing. Commercial utilization of *opaque2* mutants seemed unlikely until 1992, when researchers at the Maize and Wheat Improvement Centre in Mexico and the University of Natal in South Africa generated *opaque2*-derived QPM lines with normal kernel properties and yields comparable to other maize cultivars. The QPM genotypes are generally associated with an increased level of the 27-kD γ-zein storage protein, which somehow compensates for the reduced level of the Lys-poor α-and β-zein storage proteins, but the molecular nature of this compensation is not understood. Progress with developing commercial QPM lines has been slow, particularly because of the complexity and multiple loci of the *opaque2* modifier genes. Research led to the discovery of the molecular basis of *opaque2* and other *opaque* mutant genotypes in maize, and this knowledge has accelerated the development and commercialization of QPM maize varieties. Further details associated with the molecular basis of different opaque mutants in maize can be found in the following references.

Since its discovery, QPM maize has been used worldwide. Based on adaptation of QPM maize in many developing countries, the World Food Prize was awarded to the Maize and Wheat Improvement Centre in Mexico researchers who contributed significantly to their development. The performance and nutritional value of the QPM varieties appears promising as exemplified by analysis of a number of QPM cultivars adapted to conditions in Canada.

The high Lys and Trp contents of *opaque2* and QPM maize genotypes is associated with a major reduction in the Lys-poor α- and β-zein storage proteins. Attempts have also been made to reduce the content of these storage proteins by genetic engineering, using constructs designed to reduce their expression in seeds. Interestingly, specific reduction of zeins by this approach also causes an opaque phenotype, implying that this phenotype is directly associated with the reduction of zein storage proteins. Since many of the natural opaque mutations are associated with regulatory components of maize seed development, it will be interesting to test the agronomical potential of zein reduction traits when combined into QPM genotypes.

GENETIC ENGINEERING

Lys is considered the most important essential amino acid, because it is most limiting in the cereals grains, which are major crops worldwide. Hence, much genetic engineering research was devoted to: (1) understanding the regulation of Lys metabolism and its exploitation for increasing free Lys level in seeds; and (2) using proteins that are enriched in Lys content. Research on increasing free Lys content provides an excellent example of how utilizing model plants can speed up research and later efficiently utilize it to improve crops, particularly maize, which is a staple crop for the livestock feeding industry.

Lys is synthesized by a branch of the Asp family pathway that also leads to the synthesis of two additional essential amino acids, namely, Met and Thr. Flux through the Lys biosynthetic branch is strongly regulated by a feedback inhibition loop in which Lys inhibits the activity of dihydrodipicolinate synthase (DHDPS), the first enzyme specifically committed to Lys biosynthesis. Genetic mutations in the tobacco (*Nicotiana tabacum*) *DHDPS* gene, rendering the enzyme Lys insensitive, or constitutive expression of a bacterial Lys-insensitive DHDPS in transgenic tobacco or Arabidopsis (*Arabidopsis thaliana*) plants caused Lys overproduction in all plant organs, including the seeds. However, high levels of Lys in all plant tissues can cause abnormal vegetative growth and flower development that, in turn, reduce seed yield. Targeting the expression of bacterial Lys-insensitive DHDPS to seeds of tobacco, using a seed-specific promoter, resulted in plants with normal growth characteristics that also accumulate higher amounts of Lys in their seeds, but not yet nutritionally desirable levels.

The increased accumulation of Lys in tobacco seeds was correlated with enhanced activity of a bifunctional LKR/SDH enzyme that controls the first two reactions of the α-amino adipic acid pathway of Lys catabolism. To elucidate the role of Lys catabolism in balancing the Lys level in seeds, a bacterial Lys-insensitive DHDPS was expressed in a seed-specific manner either in wild-type Arabidopsis or in an Arabidopsis *LKR/SDH* knockout mutant.

While seeds of transgenic plants expressing the bacterial DHDPS or the knockout mutant contained approximately 12- or 5-fold higher levels of seed free Lys, respectively, than wild-type plants, the combination of these two traits caused a synergistic approximately 80-fold increase in the seed free Lys level. This showed that Lys catabolism can become very important when Lys overaccumulates.

The excessive Lys accumulated in mature seeds of Arabidopsis plants expressing bacterial DHDPS in the LKR/SDH knockout mutant background also severely reduced seed germination. Since the *LKR/SDH* knockout eliminates Lys catabolism in all tissues, it could not be determined whether the inhibition of seedling growth was due to a negative physiological effect of excess Lys on seed maturation or defective postgermination catabolism of the high Lys level. This question was addressed by coexpressing the bacterial *DHDPS* gene with an RNAi construct of the Arabidopsis *LKR/SDH* gene, both under control of the same seed-specific promoter.

In this genetic background, both enhanced Lys synthesis and its suppressed catabolism are restricted to developing seeds. Coexpression of the two seed-specific constructs significantly boosted seed Lys content, while seed germination was significantly improved.

Following the studies with model plants, the bacterial DHDPS was expressed in a seed-specific manner in the embryos of soybean (*Glycine max*), rapeseed (*Brassica napus*), and maize. Unlike tobacco and Arabidopsis, the transgenic soybean and rapeseed showed a significant elevation of free Lys in the mature seeds, which in some cases nearly doubled total seed Lys content.

The differences in Lys content between plant species may be due to the use of different DHDPS enzymes from different bacterial sources. Lys overproduction in these plants was also associated with increased levels of various Lys catabolites. Interestingly, the bacterial DHDPS caused Lys overproduction only when expressed in the embryo, but not in the endosperm. This is likely because Lys is efficiently catabolized in the endosperm, as it was also shown that endosperm-specific reduction of Lys catabolism by an RNAi approach significantly increased Lys content in maize.

The observation that Lys catabolism is highly active in the maize endosperm provided additional support for this supposition. To overcome Lys catabolism in the endosperm, maize plants were transformed with a single endosperm-specific bifunctional expression/silencing transgene, which encodes a bacterial feedback-insensitive DHDPS with a LKR/SDH RNAi sequence in an intron. This construct resulted in a significant elevation in the seed Lys level, proving that maize endosperm possesses enzymatic activity responsible for both Lys biosynthesis and catabolism.

Substantial increases in free Lys in the embryos of transgenic plants expressing a bacterial feedback-insensitive DHDPS were in some cases associated with abnormal seed germination.

Yet, shifting Lys overproduction into the endosperm enabled free Lys accumulation in maize grains to over 4,000 ppm, compared to less than 100 ppm in control plants, with no detectable negative effect on seed germination. This could be explained by the fact that either Lys is more toxic in the embryo than in the endosperm and/or that the volume of endosperm is much larger than the embryo; hence, Lys can accumulate in the endosperm to higher levels, while maintaining a relatively low cellular concentration of this amino acid.

Most of the free amino acids in sink tissues, such as developing seeds, are incorporated into storage proteins. Thus, another approach to enhance the level of a given amino acid in seeds is to increase the protein sink for this amino acid. This can be done by transforming plants with genes encoding stable proteins that are rich in the desired amino acid(s), and can accumulate these proteins to high levels. Several types of recombinant genes encoding Lys-rich proteins have been tested so far: (1) natural genes encoding Lys-rich proteins derived from different plant or nonplant sources; (2) natural genes that have been mutated to increase the number of Lys codons and make proteins richer in Lys; and (3) synthetic genes encoding Lys-rich proteins.

However, most of these attempts did not prove satisfactory because the proteins were unstable and did not accumulate to sufficiently high levels. Yet, among the different proteins that were tested, some were proven to accumulate to reasonably high steady-state levels. The most significant increases in seed Lys levels were obtained by expressing a genetically engineered gene encoding HORDOTHIONINE12 or the BARLEY HIGH LYSINE8 (BHL8) protein, which contain 28% and 24% Lys, respectively.

These proteins accumulated in transgenic maize seeds to 3% to 6% of total grain protein, and when introduced together with a bacterial DHDPS resulted in an elevation of total Lys to over 0.7% of seed dry weight, compared to around 0.2% in wild-type maize.

BHL8 is a recombinant protein derived from a barley CHYMOTRYPSIN INHIBITOR-2, which was genetically engineered to substantially increase the number of Lys codons and those of other essential amino acids, based on a three-dimensional structure analyses. This protein also serves as a model for elucidating mechanisms of protein folding.

In conclusion, a number of studies in maize have shown that it is possible to increase the Lys content in cereal grains to sufficiently high levels to meet the requirements for animal feeding, with no need for addition of supplemental Lys. These studies demonstrate that a combination of the traits of *DHDPS* expression, *LKR/SDH* suppression, and expression of genetically engineered high-Lys proteins, all in an endosperm-specific manner, shows the greatest potential for producing cereal crops with an optimal dietary Lys level and minimal penalties of growth performance and yield.

Yet, even simpler approaches employing only the expression of a bacterial feedback-insensitive DHDPS in an embryo-specific manner could suffice for commercial use in livestock feed. Indeed, a high-Lys maize line (LY038) expressing a bacterial feedback-insensitive DHDPS in an embryo-specific manner has recently been approved for commercial use in the livestock feeding industry in a number of countries. The maize LY038 line, as well as a maize LY038 × MON 810 hybrid, proved superior in broiler chicken performance, compared to the same lines that lacked the LY038 trait.

Recently, another interesting approach has been adapted to increase the Lys content in cereal seeds, utilizing a recombinant tRNA(lys) species that introduces Lys at alternative codons during protein synthesis. Expression of a recombinant gene encoding this tRNA in transgenic rice (*Oryza sativa*) caused a meaningful enrichment of the Lys content of seed proteins.

Notably, even stable expression of a wild-type Arabidopsis gene encoding a Lys tRNA synthetase in transgenic maize caused translational recoding of Lys into the Lys-deficient zein storage proteins, apparently using non-Lys codons, and resulted in significantly enriching the Lys content in the grain. It will be interesting to test the extent to which such transgenes also introduce Lys at nonnatural locations in other seed proteins and what impact this approach has on the performance of the crop plants and on their safety regulations.

IMPROVING MET CONTENT BY GENETIC ENGINEERING

Met is synthesized by another branch of the Asp-family pathway that also synthesizes Lys. Besides being a building block of proteins, Met, through its catabolic product S-adenosyl-Met (SAM), is a precursor for the hormone ethylene, for polyamines, and it is also the primary methyl-group donor for multiple biological processes, such as DNA replication, cell wall development, and secondary metabolite production. It is likely that under favourable growth conditions, a significant portion of the flux through the Asp-family pathway results in the production of Met and in its further metabolism.

A number of attempts were made to improve the Met level in plants, mostly by manipulation of genes encoding various Asp-family and Cys biosynthetic enzymes, which were described in previous reviews. These experiments generally met with limited success, either because they were associated with severe phenotypes or Met did not accumulate, due to extensive catabolism.

Indeed, reduced catabolism of Met to SAM, due to suppression of SAM synthase, generally caused increased levels of soluble Met. It is also likely that many of the metabolic phenotypes resulting from an increased Met level are indirectly associated with the reduced production of SAM. The major regulatory enzyme of Met biosynthesis is cystathionine γ-synthase (CGS), and this activity in Arabidopsis is also regulated by the level of SAM via a compound post-transcriptional control mechanism involving interactions with a highly regulatory multicomponent domain located in the N terminus of the mature CGS polypeptide.

Interestingly, mutations in this region, or its deletion, result in overproduction of Met, which is likely independent of a reduction of SAM synthesis. Moreover, the combination of expression of a mutated form of CGS with a bacterial feedback-insensitive Asp kinase (the first enzyme of the Asp-family pathway) further increases the accumulation of Met. Utilization of CGS enzymes with either deleted or mutated N-terminal domains currently appears as a potentially promising approach to increase the production of free Met with minimal negative effects. Yet, it is still questionable whether the regulatory characteristics of the Arabidopsis CGS are conserved in other plant species. It also remains to be demonstrated whether utilization of a mutated CGS can improve Met production in seeds.

Another important metabolite regulating Met metabolism in plants is *S*-methyl-Met (SMM), a Met storage and phloem mobile metabolite that can be efficiently transported from leaves to developing seeds. SMM is synthesized from Met by Met *S*-methyltransferase (MMT) and is recycled back to Met by homo-Cys methyltransferase.

However, despite the efficient transport capability of SMM, Arabidopsis and maize *mmt* mutants, which are unable to synthesize SMM, grow and reproduce normally, suggesting a minimal regulatory role for SMM in sulfur transport of at least these two species. Notwithstanding, a recent report showed that a mutant Arabidopsis plant overaccumulating Met in its seeds is due to a mutation eliminating the activity of HMT2, one of the three Arabidopsis HMT isozymes that recycle SMM into Met.

The *HMT2* gene is expressed in vegetative tissues where it apparently shifts the balance from Met to SMM in these source tissues. The accumulated SMM in this mutant apparently transports more efficiently than Met into the sink tissues, where it is converted back to Met by the two other HMT isozymes. Why plants need a delicate balance between Met and SMM is an interesting question, but certainly the increased accumulation of Met in the seeds of the *HMT2* mutant suggests a novel approach to increase the nutritional value of crop plants.

Another approach to increase the Met content in plants involved the expression of sulfur-rich proteins. Although a large array of sulfur-rich proteins have been tested, the most commonly used and most successful approaches in terms of increased Met content included expressing heterologous, natural Met-rich storage proteins, such as the 2S albumin from Brazil nut (*Bertholletia excelsa*) and sunflower (*Helianthus annuus*). Therefore, we will focus in this review on expression of these two proteins in seeds of transgenic plants.

The Brazil nut and sunflower 2S albumins have been transgenically expressed in seeds of a number of plant species, including tobacco, canola (*B. napus*), narbon bean (*Vicia narbonensis*), and soybean. Significant enhancement of total seed Met was observed in some of these plant species, and in some cases was still below the optimal level required for human food and animal feed.

This was largely because production of the proteins came at the expense of endogenous sulfur-rich compounds, such as free Met, Cys, and glutathione, as well as endogenous Met-rich proteins. These results indicate that the available soluble Cys and Met in seeds of these species limits the accumulation of sulfur-rich proteins. Moreover, studies preformed in lupin (*Lupinus angustifolius*) expressing the sunflower 2S albumin demonstrated that the seed Cys and Met content is not only dependent on their transport from the canopy, but also on their de novo synthesis in seeds.

Transgenic lupin seeds expressing the sunflower 2S albumin were tested in various nutritional studies. Rat feeding experiments showed not only an increase of Met availability, but also an increase in general dietary value. Furthermore, the transgenic lupin seeds were superior to control lupin seeds for poultry feeding, requiring lower amounts of supplemental Met. They also increased the efficiency of wool growth in Merino sheep. Unfortunately, despite their nutritional potential, the plant 2S sulfur-rich albumins were found to be allergenic, reducing their usefulness as Met sink proteins, at least for human nutrition. Nevertheless, accumulating data suggest that a combination of specific transgenes that allow increased free Met accumulation and its incorporation into sulfur-rich proteins could considerably enhance Met accumulation in crops, such as the forage alfalfa.

IMPROVING TRP CONTENT BY GENETIC ENGINEERING

Trp is the second most limiting essential amino acids in cereal grains. Trp synthesis in plants is strongly feedback regulated by inhibiting its biosynthetic enzyme, anthranilate synthase. The discovery that a mutation rendering the Arabidopsis α-subunit of anthranilate synthase insensitive to feedback inhibition by Trp enhances Trp accumulation led to a number of studies using this trait to improve the Trp content in crop plants. Expression of a transgene, termed *OASA1D*, encoding an analogous feedback-insensitive α-subunit of the rice anthranilate synthase, under control of the constitutive ubiquitin promoter in transgenic rice, led to a significant increase in free Trp in the seeds. Yet, this caused significant negative effects on a limited number of important agronomical traits, including germination, spikelet fertility, and yield. Expression of the transgene also caused a nearly 2-fold increase in auxin content in the seed, which is produced from Trp. Whether constitutive expression of the transgene caused a similar auxin increase in vegetative tissues, and whether the hormonal imbalance is associated with the deleterious agronomical traits is unknown. It could be interesting to test whether specific expression of this transgene, either in the developing embryo or the developing endosperm of the rice grains, will reduce the deleterious agronomical traits. Embryo-specific and endosperm-specific promoters are currently available, both from rice and other cereals, rendering such experiments highly feasible.

The rice *OASA1D* transgene was also shown to raise the free Trp level when expressed in transgenic potato, adzuki bean, and Arabidopsis plants. In addition, an analogous increase in free Trp was obtained in transgenic soybean plants upon expression of a different transgene encoding a feedback-insensitive tobacco anthranilate synthase driven by the cauliflower mosaic virus 35S promoter. These results, when taken together with those obtained by genetic approaches, support an evolutionarily conserved mechanism for regulation of Trp synthesis in plants by feedback inhibition of anthranilate synthase. It is important to notice that besides being an essential building block of proteins, Trp is a precursor for a variety of secondary metabolites and therefore its overproduction may reduce or stimulate their levels. Since some of the Trp secondary metabolites are harmful either to mammals or to plant pathogens, it is important to elucidate whether increased Trp accumulation alters their production.

FUTURE GOALS AND OPPORTUNITIES

Most if not all of the currently grown commercial GM crops contain traits that are considered to be beneficial for farmers and not consumers, such as the herbicide resistance Roundup Ready trait. GM crops with enhanced nutritional quality, such as the high-Lys LY038 maize, should be beneficial not only to farmers, but also to consumers, an issue that will hopefully increase their public acceptance. It was estimated that doubling the Lys content in maize without changing the grain protein content could increase the gross value of the U.S. maize in the world feed market by additional $360 million. This is important in view of the competition between maize used for ethanol production and maize used for feeding.

The progressively increasing prices of foods and feeds resulting from the massive and growing markets for biofuels are expected to further increase the value of GM crops with enhanced nutritional quality. Such crops will be important in developing countries for uses as food and feed. High Lys QPM maize has already penetrated into developing countries, such as those in Africa, and it is likely that GM crops with enhanced nutritional quality will do the same if freely available to developing countries. Individual traits for enhanced nutritional quality, such as those described in this review, could be combined into a single plant, along with other valuable traits, such as high protein and high oil content, to further improve a crop's value and competitive abilities. Moreover, the technology developed for producing high-Lys corn could be transferred to other crops used as foods and feeds, particularly to important cereals such as wheat, rice, and barley. Since cereals have comparable seed characteristics, namely, relatively large endosperms and small embryos, it is likely that the endosperm-specific approaches that have been proven most successful in maize will also succeed in the other cereals. The success with high-Lys maize also provides an optimistic basis for generating GM crops with enhanced levels of other important essential amino acids. A second GM crop that has already been proven beneficial in feeding trials is the transgenic high-Met lupin. In addition, future production of GM crops with higher levels of two other important amino acids, namely, Trp and Thr, is also expected.

Another important aspect of enhancing the nutritional quality of crops is related to the rapidly growing demand for crops for biofuel production. Ethanol production from maize generates large amounts of nonextractable seed material, called dried distiller grain solubles, the production of which progressively increased in recent years. Historically, most of the DDGS has been fed to cattle, but in the past several years, researchers have been evaluating its nutritional value and feeding recommendations for swine and poultry. Hence, research projects under way could modify the amino acid composition, protein composition, and phosphorous content of DDGS. The feed quality of DDGS can be further improved by expressing recombinant proteins enriched in essential amino acids that will not be lost during ethanol extraction. Nutritional improvement for cattle requires the presence of essential amino acids in proteins that are resistant to rumen proteolysis.

Like all other GM crops, the opportunities for and the impacts of GM crops with enhanced nutritional quality depend on public acceptance. Although recent years have shown gradual increases in the acceptance of these crops and GM foods in some countries, there is still public debate about the safety of GM crops. A detailed study based on a number of categories, including molecular studies and comparative safety assessments, concluded that the high-Lys LY038 maize is as safe as conventional maize. Yet, despite the fact that the high-Lys LY038 maize was approved for commercial use in a number of countries, there remains public debate about its safety, which can be viewed on the Internet. The outcome of this debate is central to the development of additional GM crops with a high content of essential amino acids.

Bibliography

Bisht, B.S.; Uma Melkania: *Climate Change and Agriculture : Emerging Scenarios and Adaptation Strategies*, Biotech Books, Delhi, 2012.

Chahal, S.S.; I.B. Parashar: *Achievements and Prospects in Mycology and Plant Pathology*, International, Delhi, 1997.

Choudhary, Ravinder : *Agriculture Growth in India*, Educational Pub., Delhi, 2011.

Das, Susheela M. : *A Textbook of Plant Physiology : Theory and Objectives*, Wisdom Press, Delhi, 2011.

Diwakar, D.M.: *Agriculture and Industry: Dynamics of Imbalances in India*, Manak, Delhi, 1992.

Hanumantha Rao, C.H. : *Agriculture, Food Security, Poverty and Environment : Essays on Post-reform India*, Oxford University Press, Delhi, 2006.

Hegde, H Parameshwar : *Agriculture and Cash Crops*, Discovery Publishing House, Delhi, 2011.

Jain, Abhilash : *Advanced Plant Physiology*, Campus Books International, Delhi, 2010.

Jain, Vinod Kumar : *Biofertilisers for Sustainable Agriculture*, Oxford Book Company, Delhi, 2009 .

Kannaiyan, S. : *Bioresources Technology for Sustainable Agriculture*, Associated Pub., Delhi, 1999.

Khurana, Mahesh : *Agriculture Development and Capital Relation : A Modern View*, Cyber Tech Pub, Delhi, 2010.

Kishore P. Singh: *Biotechnological Applications in Environment and Agriculture*, Surendra Publications, Delhi, 2011.

Kumar, Arvind : *Concepts of Tropical Agriculture*, Daya, Delhi, 2006.

Mishra, Mridula : *Agriculture and Food Economics*, Serials Pub., Delhi, 2010.

Ram, P.C. and G.S. Chaturvedi: *Abiotic Stresses and Plant Productivity*, Aavishkar Pub, Delhi, 2010.

Rao, B. Sambasiva : *Agriculture in India: Policy and Performance*, Serials Pub., Delhi, 2003.

Sannigrahi, Asoke Kumar : *Agriculture and Waste Management for Sustainable Future*, New India Publishing Agency, Delhi, 2011.

Singh, A.K. : *Conversion to Organic Agriculture*, International Book, Delhi, 2007.

Singh, Gaurav : *Development of Agriculture Biotechnology : Research and Analysis*, A.K. Publications, Delhi, 2011.

Singh, S B and O P Charasia Et. All: *Advances in Agriculture Environment and Health*, Serial Pub., Delhi, 2009.

Singh, S.R.J. : *A Textbook of Agriculture Statistics*, Oxford Book Company, Delhi, 2012.

Srivastava, V.C. : *Achieving Sustainability in Agriculture : Issues, Challenges and Opportunities*, Agrobios, Delhi, 2010.

Index

D